The Immigrant

Kurt Suter

© Copyright 2004 Kurt Suter. All rights reserved.

No part of this publication may be reproduced, stored in a retrieval system, or transmitted, in any form or by any means, electronic, mechanical, photocopying, recording, or otherwise, without the written prior permission of the author.

Printed in Victoria, Canada

A special thank you to Michela, who worked extensively in editing the book for me. Michela is working as a freelancer Editor in Victoria British Columbia.

Note for Librarians: a cataloguing record for this book that includes Dewey Classification and US Library of Congress numbers is available from the National Library of Canada. The complete cataloguing record can be obtained from the National Library's online database at: www.nlc-bnc.ca/amicus/index-e.html

ISBN 1-4120-2005-0

TRAFFORD

This book was published on-demand in cooperation with Trafford Publishing.
On-demand publishing is a unique process and service of making a book available for retail sale to the public taking advantage of on-demand manufacturing and Internet marketing. On-demand publishing includes promotions, retail sales, manufacturing, order fulfilment, accounting and collecting royalties on behalf of the author.

Suite 6E, 2333 Government St., Victoria, B.C. V8T 4P4, CANADA
Phone   250-383-6864   Toll-free 1-888-232-4444 (Canada & US)
Fax   250-383-6804   E-mail   sales@trafford.com
Web site www.trafford.com   TRAFFORD PUBLISHING IS A DIVISION OF TRAFFORD HOLDINGS LTD.
Trafford Catalogue #03-2484   www.trafford.com/robots/03-2484.html

10   9   8   7   6   5   4   3   2   1

Acknowledgments

The author likes to thank all the friends who
encouraged him to write this book.
His wife
Mary for all the time she missed out while I was
sitting in front of the computer writing.

Let there be peace among all People!

Foreword:

Immigrants come from all walks of life, with backgrounds as colorful as a forest on a day in the fall, with the trees beaming in colors so wonderful, it is as if God himself had spent a few days down on Earth and painted them.

To understand immigrants, one must have knowledge of their upbringing and their reasons to immigrate.

Conrad will try to take you on a journey with a story, sometimes hard to believe or even yet, to imagine. Let Conrad take you away on a journey; let him lead you in to a world of adventure, into a world that you may have never thought possible. A world of love, adventure, fate and hardship, luck and intrigues.

Why do people immigrate?
Adventure, hardship, dictatorship, freedom, love or just because!

Note:
Some foul language is present in this book. Times were harsh, people were hardened from the wartime. Although I have fictionalized some events, most of them are true. The idea behind the book is to make people understand that life is not one smooth ride from start to finish, it has lots of bumps in it, and sometimes it seems as though you will never overcome them. However, if there is a will there is a way. Let us follow Conrad from childhood to adulthood and right through to when he emigrates, still believing in the good of *all* people. When you are down and out, someone will pick you up, or you will find a way to get out provided that you want to!
What happens to Conrad once he immigrates to Canada can happen anywhere in the world, I have not written this to make a point against Canada or its people.
I have written this book, because I have been slipping in to a depression, writing this book has helped me to overcome my fear and depression. Furthermore I have written this Book for my Grandchildren, for them to know a little bit about parts of there roots!

The Immigrant

A story written by Kurt Suter

Prepare for the Journey,

Close your eyes for a few minutes lie back in your chair and think about it. How would it feel if suddenly you did not understand the language, you did not understand the new culture, you had grown up in sight of the mountains, and then suddenly you were in the prairies?

People around you act differently from the ones back home, you don't understand, you feel lost, the music you used to listen to is only a faded memory in your head. You feel frightened, but you want to make it in this new world because you chose to, you wanted to and you are determined.

A trip to the market could be a nightmare, even a task as simple as buying a bag of sugar may prove to be difficult, and you may buy a bag of sugar and once you want to use it you discover that you may have bought a bag of icing sugar. Does that make you stupid? No but people around you may think so because they cannot understand how you could possibly goof up with a bag of sugar.

I have worked with people who were assigned to my team as operators, yet they seemed useless for the task of operating a simple machine; stupid? No. As I found out, one of them was actually a professor of mathematics. He had no other choice but to make some sort of a living

The Swiss
Conrad the little Guy

It was a warm summer day, back in 1959. Some of the kids where gazing outside the school windows as they would rather be playing in the farmers' fields, or stealing some cherries from some of the trees which were growing plentiful just behind the church. In those days, popping cherries from a farmer's tree was not really stealing; the farmer knew that the boys, in return, would also help him out in the summer days ahead.
Mocking the old priest also was a favored past time, even though every now and then, when the kids were caught, revenge from the priest could be hurtful to their little behinds. There was so much to do and so little time for these kids. No they did not have TV, what the heck is that anyway? Oh yeah, you mean that box, were you can see people or animals doing funny things? Yup there was one, the pub just below the old school house had one, and every Thursday afternoon when it was raining, they could go and watch "The Black Stallion" for twenty cents and you also got a soda with it.

However, it was their last third grade class just before summer holidays started. The teacher, stern and not very well liked, stood in front of the class, and demanded answers to his geography questions. They were learning about North America, Canada in particular.

"So who can name me the three great lakes in Canada?" The teacher demanded, but only one hand rose, none of the kids except one were much interested in the great lakes far away which they would never see anyway... so, "...What the heck leave me alone with your Great Lakes and let me go play outside" they thought.

Little Conrad however kept his hand in the air; the teacher did not like him, because he and that little boy's father were not best of friends. What better way for the teacher to show revenge, than give this little guy a hard time at school, where he had absolute authority? Hans, Conrad's sidekick on the other hand, had not much sympathy for this grumpy old teacher either, as most kids lived in fear of him. The one who hit him with a bamboo stick whenever he had a chance. However, the kids got him back for that. Twice a week he would ask the boys, manly Conrad and Hans, to wet the sand in the large sandbox.

"When we get back from recess I want the sand nice and wet for geography lesson so we can form mountains and valleys," he demanded. Conrad and Hans were wetting the sand all right, but not, as the teacher thought, with water... oh no they were no angels either; one stood guard at the door and the other one peed in the sandbox. That was their revenge.

Finally, the teacher had no choice but to ask this little boy, and would you listen to him? He had all the answers and then some. Conrad knew everything about the Great Lakes. In his dreams, he was on a canoe, paddling the great rivers and lakes of this country far away… he was fending off some Indians, befriending others. He hunted bears, wolves, caribou in the great north, or moose. He was a welcomed white man in the homes of many native Indians, and in his dreams, he often fought side-by-side and helped them fend off some foes.

Little Conrad read every book from the old priest's library, and whenever he had time he would bury himself somewhere in the woods or up in the attic of the old baker's house his family used to live in. Adventure was his favorite thing! He sailed the Seven Seas with the pirates, or ran through the woods with some tribal peoples over on the other side of the great Atlantic, there were the Indians who once roamed the prairies, wild and free.

Then suddenly, with a big boom, there it was! Summer holidays had started, and the third-graders along with all the other kids in this small farming community of 800, screamed outside the old school house. With a big bang, the large door of the old school house opened, spilling out all the kids like a big dragon spitting out flames. They were free for the next six weeks to roam the mountains or the forest, they could be themselves, play, dream be kids. But not the older ones, as they had to help in the fields to bring in the hay. Help on the farm was much needed in those days, people were rather poor and big machines had not been invented yet, though most kids enjoyed themselves, as they were breaking free whenever they could.

The Second World War was just over by about ten years, but you could still feel the fear in the people, still ten years after the war, they were gathering food and made sure that they had at least four weeks of supplies on the shelf.

Every family used to have their own garden, to grow vegetables and possibly fruit. Large amounts of potatoes, apples and other provisions were stored in the basement, including the odd Moonshine in the far corner… out of Mother's sight of course.

Mary the little Girl!

Ten kilometers to the west of Oberdorf, Conrad's little village, there was Bettlach. A tiny community, much the same as Oberdorf, and as well nestled at the feet of the always-present Mountain of Jura.

Mary, the little girl in grade two, raced out of her school just as Conrad did. A quirky and lively little thing she was. She did not much care about school, all she wanted was to break free, and she wanted to be nothing else but a little girl enjoying herself on a warm, cozy summer day. Maybe climb a tree, bounce some apples off the neighbors' garden and acting like a tomboy. Her parents, in a nearby apartment, were always on high alert when she was on the prowl, never knowing whether she would be coming home all bruised up or with a broken leg. Not that her parents were overly concerned about that little girl's whereabouts. They knew come nightfall she would be home along with her younger sister and the two older brothers.

A badly twisted ankle, a bruised up arm or a broken leg, were almost as certain as the sunrise on the horizon in the morning.

Little Mary had plenty of opportunities to get in harm's way; she was a tomboy at best. A pretty little girl she was, she had all the features to grow into a beautiful young woman. Red, full cheeks, with lots of freckles dotted all over her friendly little face. She ran her chubby little fingers through her long black hair, blinking into the warm bright afternoon sun, just as her older brother, Will, walked by her side, whacking her on the back of her head.

"Let's go, stupid!" He yelled. He always called her stupid if he wanted her to be angry. Slowly she followed her brother, the look on her face not promising much good. Just as she caught up to him, she planted her foot well aimed and powerful right into his rear end. Will, screaming in pain, wanted to grab her to give little Mary a lesson of his own but he was too slow. Mary ran off, down the dusty country road, leaving Will behind. She was not about to wait for her brother to teach her a lesson; she was way smarter than to wait for her brother's revenge.

The future was theirs for the taking, but for most of these postwar kids, education was not in their parents' vocabulary. Like most parents, they were poor with very little money to spare. Mary's parents were no different. Her Dad was a painter by trade, and her mother a homemaker.

Alf and Olga, Conrad's parents, had very little education themselves and it was not easy to make a living. There was a lot of abuse, sexual and mental.

Mary's Dad had other priorities most the time, than to look after his family; he liked to flirt with any woman who crossed his path, and wedlock was no reason for him to hold back. He played the drums in the community band and so there were plenty of opportunities to cross the line of being faithful.

Of course, Elli, his wife knew about it and did not want to be left behind or lose out, and so she had her own little affairs going too. One night for example, she wanted to go dancing; there was a community "Waldfest" in Selzach, one community away. It was a dance party in the bush, a dance floor was set up and a live band was going to play traditional dance music. There was a barbeque and beer, lots of it, and Thomas that bastard, little Mary's Dad, was not home yet. Well if he was not home in time then Elli, his wife, would go by herself; she was sure to find a dance partner, no problem there. Besides, that was more fun than with stupid Thomas who would only get drunk and afterwards would not be able to perform, unlike her other dance partners who were more than willing to show her what a real man can do. Oh yes there was no shortage of willing men to show a good looking woman what can be done if willing, and willing she was.

So it was that Thomas was late, well, to be honest, he did not get home till midnight. Therefore, Elli took the road and went dancing by herself and little Mary and Will got lucky, no beating that night.

Conrad in trouble!

"Where is that little bastard? I am going to ream his rear end with my belt as soon as I can lay a hand on him!" Alf thundered to his wife, Olga. Oh here we go again, loaded with alcohol right to the brim, it was not pretty when he got home.

Little Conrad overheard his parents arguing once again, and so often in those days when big Alf got home from work, there was only one solution: hide out.

Conrad was hiding away under the bridge, damn well aware of the fact that he did not do his task. He should have towed the heavy wooden wagon up the mountain, as he was told the night before by his Dad. The wagon would be up there waiting for him so it could be loaded with wood for the winter. Besides what about his sibling, Wren? Yeah he should have helped him too, but no, he himself was too busy chasing some stray cat down the street.

"So there, it was not all my fault, you are going to get your share too, just you wait," Conrad thought.

Under that bridge, Conrad felt safe from his Dad, especially when Dad got home drunk from his shift, which started at four in the morning and ended at two in the afternoon. Oh yeah he could get drunk the old man, he could drink like a Russian horseman when he felt like it, and he felt like it rather often.

Life had not been too good for Alf, as a farmhand or as cheap laborer. He had been given up by his mother who could not afford to keep him. Then later, when he married Olga, the dream of a faithful wife also got shattered.

In fear for her son, Olga ran out the door wobbling like a duck.

"Conrad, Conrad come home little guy, Daddy is looking for you!"

"Forget it my dear" Conrad said to himself.
"I get it tonight that is just as good as right now. Besides why should I ruin a perfect afternoon?"

Many unusual things happened in those days, little Conrad thought to himself, as he crawled into a cave he had discovered earlier on. The river was low this time of the year, only about 60 centimeters deep at best, but watch out for the spring, when the snow melts on top of the mountain, or if there was a heavy thunderstorm roaring over the village. The water came down screaming with white cold foam, within minutes, so high it sometimes could flood the streets, in spite of the fact that the riverbank was about seven meters, and it could be coming fast, that old wild river, as the villagers used to call it.

    Conrad settled into his favorite space below the bridge where he could be sure no one was to find him, for sure not his drunken Dad. For hours he sat there and watched the rats swimming by or chasing one another, and sometimes, but only on rare occasions, German, his best school buddy would join him down there. It was their best-kept secret and they shared it well. German was in the same rotten position as Conrad was at home. He had so many chores given to him, that sometimes the two joined and helped one another with the workload. However, most the times it only ended in some sort of mischief, so that both parents did not allow the boys to be together too often.

    Oh yeah, he could hear his mother impatiently yelling his name. After all, she was just about 2 meters above him on the bridge, searching for him everywhere but he was nowhere to be found because he did not want to be found. She knew that if she could not bring the boys home, both Conrad and Wren would be in trouble, big trouble. At best, the big guy could yell at them and then take off to the Pub, having just another excuse to wet his throat.

    "Uh, look at Olga over there," the older villager said to his companion, sitting on the bench just across the river. "She must be looking for

Conrad and Wren again. Alf must be loaded; I have seen him coming home from his shift earlier on. Frank, I would like to put my hands on her, just look at the way she wiggles her rear end, the way she walks, man oh man what a feast for an old man's eye" he said.

"Oh shut up Bill," Frank replied. "You would not know what to do with her, stupid. Besides, most of your mouth is empty, and what is left is nothing but a black stump. By the way, she already has a favorite 'knight' down in the big city, so you just stay put and leave her alone. You know that very well...Alf would beat the living crap out of you."

"Hmm only if he caught me" replied Bill with a big grin on his face. The two were among the village elderly and they had special rights, such as being allowed to sit on that bench and do nothing all day. They were also the people's 'newspaper' because everything that went on in the village they knew about and were more than willing to share. The good as well as the bad news, were divulged in their favorite Pub, to whomever was willing to listen to them, and the willing were many.

"Well, let us go for a beer Frank," Bill moaned. "It is going to rain shortly just watch how dark it is getting over there on the mountain peak; we may be able to play some cards with Alf, I am sure he is at the Lion's Pub."

So, up they went, but not without throwing a last hungry, filthy look at Olga, salivating out of their dirty mouths after her. She had just expanded her search for the two boys to the cemetery, also a favorite hang out of the kids.

The room was thick with smoke from cigars and cigarettes, as the two elders entered the Lion's Pub, a sharp smell of beer hang in the air. It was hard to see who was present, the men in the pub were loud and rowdy, and they had some issues with the local authorities.
"… These bastards, what the hell are they thinking to restrict us from cutting up some old trees up on that mountain? We need that shit to keep warm in the winter," someone complained. In addition, of course, there was Alf, that loud mouth, who was never ok with the authorities at any level. Alf hated the authorities, and somehow it was understandable. Ever since he was a little boy, authorities had always messed up his life in one way or another.
At the round table, Alf was the loudest of them all. The round table or the "Stammtisch" always had been the special table at which the locals sat and talked politics. No one who was not a local dared to sit at the table, everybody knew that, and this was respected. The harder you could bang your fist on the tabletop, the better your argument was considered. The argument was considered really good when you called all the politicians stupid boneheads, and every other name in the book. That, most the times, made the men feel a lot better. The better your name-calling was the smarter you appeared, that was the name of the game.

"Alf, want to play a good card game? It is raining, and there is not much to do anymore today anyway," Frank said as he and Bill entered the pub. Alf was quick to change the tables: only politics was acceptable at the Stammtisch, no card games.

Oh yeah rules were important in that little village, everything needed to have its place or things were out of order, and how, I am asking you, can we exist if something has not its place?

A good card game was something you better not interrupted, unless of course, your house was on fire, and even then only if the fire fighters were not involved in a card game themselves, or if something really serious happened, like the beer truck got stuck in the snow.

"Dad, Dad you have to come home right away, we are missing Conrad, and it is raining hard out there!" Wren yelled as he entered the pub, soaking wet from the downpour.

"What the hell do you think you are doing boy, can't you see that we are in the midst of a Jass, 'The Card Game'? He is likely hiding out some place, that little monster, don't worry I'm sure he will be home soon. Go on boy go home, I will finish this game and then come home for supper, and now leave me alone." Alf turned around and hammered a good deck on the table announcing to his companions that he was the winner and they had to pay up. Alf was ok now, a little too much beer inside but no longer grumpy as he won the game.

"I really worry about Conrad," Olga said to Alf later when they had just finished supper and it was getting dark outside.

"Ok, ok" Alf muttered. I will go and look for him.

"Please Alf, do not beat him up when you find him" Olga pleaded with him. "I am sure he is just scared to come home because he did not do his duties as you asked him."

"All right" Alf replied; he now was in a much better mood with a full belly and enough of a mind-fog from the beer. Besides, he himself started to worry now. He was not really that big bad monster; deep down inside he loved his family and would do anything for them. It just was, he had a real hard time showing his feelings. He himself was brought up as a farm hand, not remembering who his mother was; he never had a family of his own as a kid, never experienced a loving mother's hand stroking his hair, never heard a kind word or was shown any tenderness. So how, I ask you, could he ever express his feelings? They were locked down inside his poor little soul.

Unable to support him, his mother gave Alf away when he was six years old. He was only a burden, one more mouth to feed, so off he went to a farmer who needed cheap help, and a cheap help to the farmer he was.

"What the hell do you need a bed for, Boy?" He never had a name, *Boy* was good enough they thought.

"We feed you, we give you clothes," they would say. He was given no shoes in the summer, and the clothes were old and used from their own son.

"Go on, it is warm enough over in the barn. Use some hay, and do not forget tomorrow morning at four o'clock the cows need fresh hay and water. Then they have to be milked and make sure you are done before school starts or you going to miss it again." The farmer would say. It was likely that Alf missed more school than it was good for him. Who needs to know how to properly write a sentence if you work with cows all day long anyway?

The farmers who took Alf were a family who lived by God's word, so up skywards they locked their eyes, during the daily prayer.

"Look Lord how good we are, we take on the duty of raising this little bastard, who comes from a mother not worth having children, and look down on us oh almighty. We feed him, we give him clothes, and we give him a home. What oh Lord, we ask, are we to do with this boy who will not listen to us, is always late in the morning, even though we let him go to bed at ten, why we ask you almighty, does this stupid boy always have red eyes in the morning? Why does he always look like he is crying at night? Why do we deserve such treatment oh Lord? Every Sunday we go to mass, we pray every day, and look what this left-over of a boy is doing to us, oh Lord almighty please enlightens us good people."

Deep inside, Alf was a good, down-to-earth man, working hard to support his family, trustworthy, honest and true to his words. A man one could rely on. When he told you he would beat the crap out of you, you could believe him.

So off he went to look for Conrad, after all Conrad was *his* little boy, and the boy meant the world to Alf.

Nightfall came quick that evening, as dark clouds were overhanging the mountain and Conrad was nowhere to be found. Now even big Alf started to worry for his little boy. He only knew too well of the dangers lurking out there, when the thunder was rolling over the mountain, echoing back and forth times fold from the steep walls.

Little Mary in a mess!

"Maary, Maary, Wiill, Wiill, where are you?" Elli's high-pitched voice echoed through the narrow streets of Bettlach, desperate. "You have to come home kids, don't you see that it is going to rain any minute now? Maary Maary, Wiill where are you damned kids?"

"I am here Mommy," a little voice was chirping from above. "Where? Can't see you, where are you?" Finally, she looked up a tree and sure as hell, there she was, Mary was hanging upside down on a thick, strong branch, her arms dangling freely with an apple in her little hand.

"Oh my god!" Mary's mother lamented. "Look at you, your dress is all ripped, the apron I gave you this morning is dirty, and your underwear is showing, would you come down right this instant you shameless rotten girl! Just wait until your father gets home, I hope he is going to teach you a lesson you will never forget." She always scared the kids with the threat of a good beating by their father; it was her defense against the kids.

"Come down it is going to rain any minute now, and besides that you are all dirty I don't need you wet too!" Her mother kept lamenting away as she started to dart homeward, and in the meantime rain had started to fall, heavy rain, and that was no promise for much good at that time of the year. The hay was getting wet, just before they wanted to bring it inside, now they had to wait another couple of days for the hay to dry off. Besides, lightening and thunder accompanied the rain most often, and in the mountain range that meant heavy, rolling, scary thunder, so heavy that left the kids sleepless all night, and the animals in the barn howling after every thunder roll or lightening bolt. The women in the village got up when the thunder happened to be at night, lit the candles and started to pray to the Lord to spare them. The rain could come down so hard that small rivers could build up down the main street.

Even Mary now started to dash home, she felt a little uneasy because not only was she dirty but also dripping wet.

"Well cannot change that now either," she said to herself, "so I will have to face a little beating, and then go to bed and in the morning, it's all gone…with a little luck Dad is not home yet, or maybe he is in a good mood, after he had beaten his opponents at the card game at the pub. A little luck and I am going to be safe."

On the other hand, maybe Will, her older brother, could get it first, who knew? It was unpredictable when and who was getting the beating. But the beating was as sure as the Amen in the church after mass; a good beating kept them little bastards straight thinking and grateful and appreciative for what they had, and respectful of the elders, so they were told and so they got used to it. God knows why, but they still had great love and respect for their parents.

Conrad in the river!

And down it came; the worst rainstorm was brewing up over the old mountain, pouring straight down as if the Last Day had arrived.

Conrad started to feel the swelling of the river, it was time to leave his cave and face the fancy treatment at home. But just as he wanted to get out of his cave, a big branch washed down by the wild river and tangled his foot. Quickly he grabbed an opening in the wall to prevent being dragged with the branch and be washed down.

Just 6 meters after the tunnel there was a small waterfall, not very high, just about three and half meter.
To the little kids it looked almighty high, besides, there were big boulders at the bottom of the fall. Conrad started to feel a big panic crawling up his neck. The river rose about sixty centimeters and the water was fast and powerful. Hard it was on the little boy to hang on; the branch that caught his leg was pulling and pulling harder and harder on the little man. He got scared so much he started to yell for help, darn well knowing that no one could hear him down there.

He was so scared, his pants were full and he wet himself, as if the water he was in was not enough, but no help arrived. He started to feel the pull in his little arms, he slipped, but he did not want to give up, oh no, he was a fighter!

"Help, help!" He yelled in to the darkness, his small fingers started to get numb, he knew only too well he could not hold on much longer, and then with a big thunder, scaring the living daylights out of him, he let go. In an instant, the river grabbed hold of him and washed him away.

Suddenly there he was: quiet, peaceful and warm. Conrad had washed down over the waterfall. He hit his head on a big boulder then was thrown over the riverbank like a wet rag-doll by a huge wave that came rushing down. There it was, where he lost consciousness, and there it was where big scared Alf had found him. He loaded the seemingly lifeless little body into his big, strong arms and carried him home like a wet wheat bag, praying, and yes! Praying that his little guy would be ok. Alf never prayed, he was not at ease with the church and everything it represented.

"Oh my god!" Olga screamed when Alf entered the old living room with the boy in his arms. She began stuttering, praying. Olga was a strong believer in prayers whenever she saw it fit. That was where Alf, the big guy, could not follow her in prayer… the farmer with whom he grew up prayed a lot, but never lived by what he prayed. Olga prayed but he never had much in common with her prayers either, so who would judge him for not understanding religion too well?

The boy, now on the wooden floor in the living room, suddenly started to putter like a dying old motor, water pouring out of his open mouth.

"Well that was a close call!" Alf said to his wife Olga. "Good thing I saw him coming out under that bridge, what the hell was he doing there anyway? Look at him now, all banged up, wet and dirty; that was close, now I really need a beer. Put the boy to bed, I am just going to grab a cold one down at the Lion's Pub, be home soon" he muttered, grabbing Olga on her soft, well- rounded rear end. He did not have a big understanding of human relations and he grabbed Olga like that only when he felt "romantic."

Her eyes grew bigger and in excitement, she agreed to wait up for him, as she knew darn well that this was going to be the night she had been so thirsty for. Man oh man what a night that was going to be! When Alf was in a good mood, as he was then, he could be a strong, sensitive and very passionate lover, so full of energy that he would put a high priced stallion to shame. However, nights like that did not happen too often, so good old Olga had her substitutes to help her through the lonely nights.

    Wren, the youngest of them all, was the result of such an adventure. He was the youngest child of five and had blonde curly hair, while all his siblings had black hair. Don't get him wrong though, Alf was not stupid, slow or blind, and he knew darn well that a cow could not give birth to a goat or vice versa, and it was not much different with humans; he had figured that out all right. Nevertheless, he loved her, as she was the first human being in his life who had actually shown affection toward him.

    It was on a cold winter night back in 1928; Alf just came out of the hills from the Swiss Emmental where he had slaved away his child hood, and then finally broke loose from his tyrant farmer family after he served in the Army. Back then, on one snowy morning in the big city, that is where they locked eyes and he never left sight of her ever since. (Or did he?)

    At the time, Alf picked up a job as milkman; he was to deliver fresh milk every morning throughout the city. His shift started at four in the morning, picking up the horse and the wagon, then went to the central milk distributor, picked up his share then did the daily routine, which also brought him to Olga's house, the one where she worked.

He loved his new job. For the first time in his life he was his own master, he could work with his beloved animal, the horse, which he understood much better than people. Best of all he would see Olga every morning when she picked up the daily milk supply for her master's family. The two could squeeze in a couple of minutes when they could touch each other's hand or lock their thirsty eyes, provided nobody was close-by.

Olga, was a maid in the big city, she served a wealthy, well-respected family. She cleaned, cooked and baby-sat their two kids, rotten, spoiled little bastards, but Olga's small income was much needed by her parents. Besides, Olga did like the job somewhat, as they had a very good-looking son about her own age. He was well traveled and his etiquette was superb compared to Olga's. Not that those two ever dreamed of getting married or anything like that, but they had much fun with one another, especially when his bride was out of town. After Alf and Olga got married, Olga quit the job but kept visiting the family frequently; whether for old times' sake, or for the young man's attention, we will never know.

Olga rolled her eyes in excitement as she cleaned up the boy and put him to bed. There he was, sleeping like a little angel. He would be no distraction tonight. Wren, his younger sibling, shared a bed with Conrad. Tess, and Liz, their two older sisters shared the same room, but had a bunk bed and they were not home that night. Alf junior, named after his father, was the eldest of them all and had his own room up in the attic.

When Alf senior got home that night, he was not drunk, he was just in the right mood to please his 'silly little calf' as he called Olga when he was in the mood for romance. When they finally went to sleep, drenched in sweat and satisfied, it was almost time for Alf to get up for his early shift down in the city. After they got married, Alf had worked himself up to a factory worker where he made a better living than as a milkman.

It was the almost perfect summer for little Conrad. Nearly every day he was on his beloved mountain. Plenty of caves they had to discover. He knew most of them, as he used them as hideouts. One in particular, it was located right behind the "Steinbruch." The Steinbruch was a big scarf in the mountain, which you could see from miles away. There big stones were carved out of the mountain, and they blasted big boulders with dynamite.

Every Thursday a horn would sound making the community aware that there was an explosion about to happen. Then the road was closed and all traffic had to stop, as it was dangerous to be within 2 kilometers or so of the site. The boulders could be thrown too far if too much dynamite was used. It was the boy and his friends' ultimate "chicken out" game. They would stay way above the explosion, about 100 meters high, right on the edge, the best spot, as you could feel the mountain vibrate. You had to hold on to a tree and you were safe.

This game always made the boys hungry. They had plenty of potatoes with them, which they could roast on a fire that they made in their cave. Girls were not allowed with the boys, because all they did was to go home and tell the parents, which always ended with some sort of extra duties for the boys the next day.

A single man had occupied this particular cave during the Second World War. He was so scared of a possible German invasion that he had been hiding out on that mountain. An old fireplace, a broken chair and a table were quiet witnesses to the man's earlier presence.

That night, it was late in the summer, Conrad got home just before suppertime. He wanted to race upstairs, but something was holding him back. Something was just not right. A black car was parked right in front of the house. Cars where not seen too often in those days but the curiosity got the better of Conrad. He circled the car a couple of times but could not find evidence to support his suspicions. A villager passing by looked at Conrad with anger, as if he smelled bad or had a disease.

"Why don't you go home boy?" The man said, "Rather than sneaking around the Police car? Go home you little rat, and see what's wrong this time." Conrad could not make any sense out of the old man's behavior or his remarks. He knew that Police cars were something official, and that he had to obey. He could not think of anything he had done that would prompt the Police to visit. All he had done in his spare time was roaming the mountain and the forest, which he loved so very much. This was a day like any other summer days before that, and never before had the Police come. So, what did they want this time?

Wren, his younger brother, was in the schoolyard; he could see him playing there with other kids from the village as he circled the car. Conrad wet himself. He always did that when he felt insecure or when he thought that he was in trouble for one thing or another. Now he had an excuse to go home and see his mother; she would then give him a clean pair of underwear, and after comforting him a little, he would be on his way out again, assured that all was ok.

Conrad, climbing two stairs at a time, hurried up the wooden steps; he wanted to see his Mom, begging for clean clothes and then he would go off to play some more. However, as he entered the old living room, there they were, two very important men were sitting at the table. He knew they were important people because they were dressed just like Alf was on Sunday. They both had black ties, and were dressed in clean suits. Their shoes were also black and very shiny. Their faces were frozen and they seemed to have no emotion in their eyes.

Alf was sitting at the head of the table where he always sat, he was the absolute ruler there in his home, therefore, his place was at the table's head where he could overlook his family.

Alf with his hands on the table and his head hanging, did not even look at Conrad as he entered the living room. A sunbeam coming through the window just behind Alf was shining on his black thinning hair, and Alf looked down on to the floor as if the seven-tailed devil himself was sitting there.

Olga, just about in the same condition as Alf, was sitting on the couch, her hands working uneasily on a handkerchief, her eyes red with tears still rolling down her cheeks. The couch was against the wall, right beside the table. An old wood stove at the end kept them warm in the wintertime. Olga was not about to sit at the table, as it was custom for only a man to sit there when there was important business to discuss. Women in those days did not know about important business, it was their job to give birth, keep the house clean, cook, work the garden and keep the family happy. Everybody had their place and this custom was strictly obeyed.

The one important-looking man sitting closer to Alf finally lifted his head and looked at Conrad. He had a somewhat friendly face, his eyes were promising, reassuring, his voice was dark and sounded a little like the priest in church at a Sunday mass.

"Well, Conrad" the friendly man said after a short pause observing the boy. "Why don't you go outside and look for your little brother, you can stay out a little longer, and when you see us driving away in the car you can come back inside, I am sure it is all right with your mother." He looked at Olga and she nodded lightly with her head.

"Ok "Conrad responded with a chirpy voice. "But I have wet pants sir." He looked at the man as if *he* would punish him for it.

"Don't worry, Mom will fix that for you" he said looking now at Olga, forcing her to get up and get the little guy out of the room. In spite of the fact that it was warm, Conrad shivered a little, and kept wetting himself, expecting a beating; he always wet himself when he was afraid. A small puddle at his naked feet had built up, and one could see the pee making its way down his dusty dirty leg. Olga got up, her eyes still locked on the floor; she took him by his small hands and escorted him out of the living room into his bedroom. There it was, when his mother, for the first time since he entered the house, spoke to him with sadness in her voice.

"Listen to me Conrad," she said, her voice trembling. "Dad may have to go away for a little while, but we are going to make it, ok?" She said, reassuring herself more so than little Conrad. Conrad just nodded not knowing what to make of all this, and with a fresh pair of undies dry and clean he went back outside to look for Wren. Strange things happened in those days.

"Wren, Wren!" Conrad yelled across the schoolyard. "Where the hell are you? I have important news Wren, come on, let's go." Wren was sitting on top of the school's climbing unit in the playground. About twenty feet up, he was sitting on top of the steel structure, overlooking the schoolyard, the church and to the left, he could see the house.

"What kind of news would you be able to give me?" Wren thought. Wren yelled looking down to Conrad.

"Do you think I have not seen the two men with that car going to our house? Do you think I am stupid or something, what did you do now that they are at our home?"

"Oh no, not me!" Conrad replied with pride. "These guys are not here for me you know."

"Oh no?" Wren said with curiosity in his voice. "So what do they want?"

"Well come down you stupid monkey, and I will tell you." Nosy as Wren was, he slowly got on his tummy, wrapped his little legs around the steel beam, and slowly, so as if he would have to think about coming down, he glided towards the sand box, which provided some sort of safety for the kids in case they fell down from the steel structure.

"I want to go home!" Wren demanded as he stood beside Conrad.

"Nope, that is not possible right now." Conrad said with authority; after all, he was a full year older than Wren and that made him responsible for all things that happened to his brother, good or bad.

"Well then, let's go to the graveyard and scare the shit out of some old women, they are always there at nightfall as if they could talk to the ones below them." It was fun for the village kids to hide behind a headstone. Using an old can with the bottom cut out, they could make their voices sound like they were coming from the grave.

One day, a grumpy old woman almost did not get back up after the shock of hearing her beloved one answering from the grave. Oh no, the kids definitely had no use for TV, there was enough entertainment!

So the two boys strolled towards the old graveyard, just behind the church. It was a really old church, with paintings on the windows, lots of old figurines and pictures of Jesus. All the way around the walls where pictures of Jesus, with the cross he was forced to carry by the Roman Soldiers. Before every Easter, each picture would be covered with a purple cloth, every day the old priest would remove one, up until the day of Jesus' Resurrection at Easter Sunday.

It was a close-knitted community this little Oberdorf at the feet of the mountain. On Sundays, you would better go to church or all of the villagers knew about it, and that was not good. Of course Alf never did go, as he hated everything that came close to sound like religion. His two youngest, Wren and Conrad paid for this, as the priest punished the two little guys for Alf's failure to attend Sunday mass.

The church, overlooking the village, was built on top of a hill, a stone throw away from the school. It was several hundred years old, and sure was a beautiful reminder of ancient old architectural achievements. Behind the church, there was a monastery, about fifty or so nuns were looking after the old graveyard, the church, and sometimes they also went out to help the old and sick in the village. The church with its eerie graveyard, the school, the big old house with the bakery below, where Conrad and Wren grew up, beside the butcher's house and the river running under the bridge, that was the boys' daily center of activities.

For the boys to go to the graveyard they had to pass by the priest's home, which was build right next to the church. A steep, long stairway lead them up to the church's courtyard. Between the priest's home and the church, the priest loved to sit on the bench reading a book or made conversation with some villagers.

He was always very fond of the people, especially the older women who liked to bring him homemade jam, a ham or some sausages from the last pig the farmer had killed. Bacon was also a good way to have the reassurance from the priest that they would go to Heaven.

Just as the two boys crossed the courtyard, they heard a thundering voice.

"Where are you going boys? It is almost suppertime and you should be at home by now," the priest said, demanding an answer in his black robe with the long, white beard, as it was custom for a priest to have. He looked like a man with authority, He stood there looking at the two in disgust.

"We... we just wanted to visit our grandma's grave" Conrad stuttered. The two never knew their grandparents, but it made a good excuse right then.

"Oh all right then boys, go on" the priest mumbled. "But if I catch you scaring some old woman or in some kind of trouble, I am going to have you dust the entire library, and that will keep you busy for the next five days or so!"

Oh yeah, the two knew that it was an impressive library the priest had. Conrad himself borrowed some books from it, especially in the wintertime. So the boys, slowly and full of respect, well aware of where they were, backed off and with relief got out of the priest's sight.

"So what happened at home?" Wren demanded to know. "You said you have important news, so spit it out you loud mouth!"

"Hmm…" Conrad said. "Well I know that the two men are from the Police; Mom was crying on the couch and Dad did not say anything, so I think he is in some sort of trouble" Conrad said.

"Oh, I know what happened" Wren said with a look on his face, as if to say, "See? I am just as smart as you!"

"Well you tell me!" Conrad demanded.

"See, the night I had to go and get Dad from the Lion's Pub, the night you went missing, the waitress, Susie, I have seen her sitting on Alf's lap, while Alf was playing cards. I think that somebody did call the Police, she had no business sitting on Alf's lap, don't you think?"

"You're stupid," Conrad said. "They do that all the time, especially Susie, she sits on everybody's lap; I have seen it more than once" Conrad said. In the meantime, Conrad and Wren had reached the graveyard. Not that they were there to visit their grandparents' graves, oh no! Far from it. But they still had the priest's warning in their little minds, so they crossed the graveyard, went all the way to the end where a big stone wall was, about two meters high and fenced off the eerie site. They climbed on top of the wall to sit on it, so they could overlook it all.

"Besides," Conrad picked up their conversation. "I like Margaret from the Cross Inn a lot better, she always is giving me a soda, lets me sit on her lap, then she plays with my curly hair, and she has way bigger boobs than Susie from the Lion's Pub."

They had already forgotten the two Policemen at home. Kids forget easily if it is not an immediate threat to them.

"What are we going to do tomorrow? Wren asked.

"I am going fishing down by the little stream, back by the dump. Maybe I search the dump first for some treasures, then go fishing" Conrad replied. "Just last week I found an old bike, which I am going to fix up for myself."

"Ok I am coming with you," Wren nodded.

Slowly the Sun gave way to a peaceful evening, shadows started to grow longer, and it was time for the two boys to head home. One last time they passed by the old priest, who was still sitting on his bench, this time accompanied by an old woman. She looked at the two boys in disgust, as if they had killed someone in her presence. Politely, the children wished the two on the bench a pleasant evening as they passed by.

"Oh these two boys," Conrad overheard the old woman whisper to the priest. "I just hope they are going to be all right with all that is going on in their home."

The two did not pay attention to this, as they were hungry like wolves after a long winter. As Wren and Conrad got home, the black Police car was gone. The two men had finally left. They sensed that something was not right at their home, Alf sitting at the table just as he did when Conrad had last seen him. Olga prepared supper. Quiet and remorseful it was that evening at home. Alf did not go to the pub, he did not yell at the boys, Olga still had tears in her eyes.

"Ok boys sit down, supper is ready" Mom commanded. The plain potatoes with some butter and jam were not necessarily the boys' favorite food, but it filled their bellies and that was better than going to bed hungry. The meal was taken without any spoken words. However, if you had a fine sense of what is right and what is not, you could feel that something was just not the way it was supposed to be.

Tess and Liz, their older siblings, and Alf junior were just sitting there, and instead of the usual teasing, hitting them on the back of their heads, and the usual name-calling of the older brother and the two sisters, all was silent and strange.

After supper, it was Conrad's duty to walk down to the milk store and get some fresh milk for the next day. At about seven o'clock at night, the farmers brought their fresh milk there, and the villagers would go to pick up what ever was needed by them. Conrad picked up the five-liter tin can and strolled down to the milk store as he did every night. It was almost dark when Conrad made his way to the milk station; it was getting dark sooner close to the mountain, because the mountain was blocking the sunbeams, so Conrad did not see the two boys from the village, as they were hiding behind a rose bush waiting for him. They were a couple of years older than he was, he knew the boys because he had seen them in the schoolyard, and suddenly they were there, unexpectedly, and they scared Conrad senseless, so much that he started shaking.

    As they stood in front of him, they started to tease the little guy, for no reason at all, just because he was there and he was smaller, but he was not to easily give up what was his. He had no money anyway, as the milk was paid for once a week. He had nothing that could be of interest to the two older boys. With a big swing, vrooom, the milk can in Conrad's hand landed on the smaller boy's head and at the same time, Conrad started to run, and made it to safety down to the milk station, where there were a lot of other villagers to get their milk. Besides, the boys were no real threat to Conrad, he himself played the 'chicken-out game'; this was just a little teasing, and after all "help yourself and you will be helped" was the motto. His only problem now was to get the dent out of the milk can, and well, he had plenty of time, as the people waiting in line were many. When it was his turn to get his milk, "Five liters please" he said politely, handing his milk can to the fat lady behind the counter.

The woman with a big wart on her nose took the can, filling it up and said to Conrad, "Please tell your mother to give you the money tomorrow for the past week's milk."

"Ok Mrs. Adler, will do, don't you worry I will have the money." Conrad rather liked her, she was always friendly, and sometimes when she was in a good mood, she gave him a little container filled with fresh, fat whipping cream. That was a special time, when Olga, his mother, would wait until Conrad had harvested enough wild strawberries from the mountain forest, and then she would whip up the cream and spread it over the fresh berries and it made a delicious dessert, free of charge.

As Conrad approached the house, he saw Liz, Tess, Alf junior and Wren sitting on the wooden bench in front of the house. Alf, the eldest of them all, fifteen years older than Conrad, had a very important look on his face. He was sitting at the end of the table and he was sort of a second father figure to the two younger boys. Down in the big city, Alf had just ended an apprenticeship as a watchmaker, and next year he was to go into the Army. All young men had to serve the Army at the age of twenty. Tess, sitting next to him with Wren in her arms, was crying…it seemed to be a commodity in those days for people to have tears.

Conrad did not pay too much attention to her, as he figured girls always had a reason to cry. Tess was thirteen years older than Conrad, she was not his favorite sister, not that he minded her, but she was not home too often, therefore they did not spend much time together. Tess also was busy in the big city, she was working as a housemaid for some business family. Liz, only ten years older, worked as a watchmaker apprentice where Alf, the oldest, was working. Conrad liked her she was always funny and ready for some kind of silly games to play with the boys. What Conrad did not like was the fact that Liz started to bring home this boy, he was about her age, and whenever he was visiting Liz, Conrad was sent away, "Go and play in the bush," that young man would say, or "go and get lost." Conrad noticed a change in his sister Liz, whenever this "big, stupid, city boy" as Conrad called him, came to visit.

"Conrad!" Alf, his older brother commanded. "Bring the milk to your mother then come down here and join us."

"Ok," he said, " be right back." He did as ordered and then joined his brother and sisters down on the bench. Once they were all assembled, Alf started.

"Ok listen up. Dad will have to go away for a little bit," he said. "At this time, being the eldest, I will take his place and will look after you, so you better get used to it, and do not think it is going to be a holiday, we still have to do our chores as before, or we are not going to make it through the winter. Is that clear?" Alf said.

"Why is Dad going away? Wren asked.

"Because he is sick," Liz answered.

"At this point, it is not clear when he will go and for how long," Alf continued.

"I hope he never comes back" Tess, the eldest sister said. She had reason to speak those words, she who had been violated by her own father.

"Well, that means no more beatings for a while" Conrad added with relief in his voice.

"Don't be so sure" Alf said with a smile. "You still have to make sure that your chores are done, and I want them done just as it was before, and rest assured little guy, I do look after it that all will be done. You know that I do not beat you up if I don't have to, but I do need to enforce the rules and make sure that you do your duties just as Wren has to. If we don't stick together now, we will have a rough time during next winter, you know how cold it can get, and if we have not enough wood stored because you did not do your duty, I will have to give you a hot bum to stay warm, clear?" Alf said. Now that made sense to Conrad, and somehow he felt a little grown up too, because he had now duties, which he understood. "No wood, means cold. No wood means hot bum"… now he understood.

"Wren, Conrad," Alf continued. "I still give you two enough time so you can go and play, but the garden needs to be weeded, the wood has to be hacked to the regular size, as you boys did over the last couple of years. Then you have to bring the wood up to the attic."

Using the crane mounted under the roof, with a long rope, and a basket filled with wood, the boys could easily hoist it up.

"Moreover, make sure that Wren is not standing under the basket again; he could get hurt as he did last year. I give you boys all next week with the wood, but the garden needs to be taken care of every day, the best thing is to do it early in the morning; it is not hot then, only takes about two hours and if you do it every day, one hour should be enough. Then you are free to go and play, I want you home by five, don't make me come and look for you." Alf, one by one, instructed his siblings with their new duties. All agreed to help wherever needed, somehow they felt safe in their new alliance. Besides, mother was still here too. Conrad and Wren, not really understanding what was going on, needed a little convincing every now and then, which Alf followed up as promised.

As the kids were sitting on the bench, they did not notice that it was getting dark, then Alf, their father, came out of the house. Tess was looking the other way, Liz was busy with a bug on the table.

"Conrad, Wren, go upstairs and go to bed!" Alf ordered the two boys. "Alf, come with me to the pub." They left and the boys went upstairs as ordered, accompanied by their two sisters.

Night settled in, mother still had a candle going in the living room and did some knitting, while Conrad and Wren went to bed. Liz and Tess were spending some time with their mother as they waited for the boys to go to sleep. They shared the same bedroom and usually wanted to do some girl chatting without interruption from those two "little monsters" as they affectionately called them.

It promised to be a gorgeous day, the rising sun in the east painted the mountain red, looking as if drenched in blood. The birds' excited chirping, the smell, oh that smell of fresh bread from the bakery below, the handling of a milk can in the distance, a farmer's dog barking, the sound of the river rushing over some boulders, the water from the mountain following its bed as it did for thousand of years. All this wonderful sensuality, gently blown into the bedroom by a fresh summer wind, coming down from the almighty mountain, slowly entered the minds of the two little boys still sound asleep.

Conrad was the first to wake up rubbing his eyes, in his cotton nightgown, he got on his knees, sinking the bedding down. Then, leaning out of the window, crossing his small little arms and resting his head on them, he greeted the new day. When he looked down, he could see the baker working away in his domain, just across from his bedroom. From that spot, he could see the big stone oven where the baker, with a big, long wooden shovel, just now pulled out some fresh, hot steaming bread. Now the smell of fresh, hot milk chocolate came from the kitchen, where he could hear his mother preparing breakfast. He loved this time of the day, the little guy. Here he could dream, here he could be lost for a little while, lost into a world where no one could follow him. He also loved to look up to the peak of his mountain, where he could spend endless days playing.

  Gently the door opened, not noticed by Conrad, who was still taken away by his daydreaming. His mother, slowly entering the room said, "Come on boys wake up, breakfast is ready." Conrad slowly turned his head toward her and with a gentle smile, he gave his mother a kiss on the cheek accompanied by a big, reassuring hug. The day had a perfect start.

  Wren also was awake now, kissed and hugged by their mother, bare footed, the boys followed her in to the kitchen, where fresh bread, jam and butter and steaming hot-chocolate were ready for them on the table. Their older brother Alf, and the two sisters, had already left the house for work down in the big city, and father had been gone to work since four o'clock to start his shift in the big factory.

  Olga sat down with the two boys at the breakfast table. Her eyes, red from crying all night, had dark circles around them. In despair, she looked at the two boys.

  "What are we going to do?" She thought to herself. Great sadness had overcome her. But then she pulled herself together; she even managed a smile as she said to the boys, "What are you up to today?"

"We wanted to go fishing" Conrad mumbled, with his mouth full. "Just behind the dump in the small stream. However, Alf told us we have to weed the garden, and then bring the wood to the attic by next week."

"Well" Olga said with a hint of a smile, "I give you two boys the day off. You can start tomorrow." It was obvious that she wanted the kids out of the house for the day.

"I have to do laundry today, and you know what that means don't you?" Olga asked. "I have to stand over by the wild river and wash dirty laundry all day. So why don't you boys go on and play, use the day as much as you can and enjoy yourselves. Just make sure you are home before it gets dark." In excitement, the boys nodded, wildly shaking their heads.

Conrad meets MARY!

They packed some apples and potatoes, which they wanted to roast over an open fire together with the fish they planned to have on the hook. Hook? Oh no, nope, no sir, they used their bare hands to get the fish, it was a practice which the boys fully mastered. It was an old practice, taught by the older village boys, handed down from generation to generation. So after breakfast they were quick to help their mother to bring the old wooden bucket down to the river's edge, where she would do the laundry. Off they went, it was still early in the morning.

The two were in no hurry as they had all day to themselves. It was not unusual for the boys to wander off some ten to fifteen kilometers away from the house. Both with bare feet; *who needs shoes I ask you?* Slowly they made their way past the old church then leaving the last house behind them they were in the open. A farmer on top of a hay wagon waved to the boys.

"Good Morning Mr. Adams how is the hay?" Conrad politely asked.

"All is well boys, if you want you can go to the cherry tree, but I could use your help later on in the week if you have the time. I have just received a large amount of wood, and it needs to be stored above the barn."

"Of course Mister Adams," Conrad yelled. "We will take the cherries and let you know about the wood later." He knew darn well that he had no time at all in the near future to help the farmer, but the boys did help in the past. The two approached the horses that pulled the farmer's hay wagon; they loved to be around animals. For a little while, chatting with the farmer, the two were sitting on top of the horses pretending they were cowboys, but eventually got tired of the game, jumped down from the horses and went on their way.

The dusty road wound itself along farmers' fields, towards the small community of Lommiswil in the distance. The Jura Mountain to the right, they also could see the Swiss Alps to their left in the far distance. It was a perfect setting for the kids, they felt safe wherever they looked.

They could now see the smoke rising from the dump, and they could also smell it, but that did not bother them too much. A farmer with his garbage wagon, pulled by four horses, just left the dump as the boys approached.

"Hey boys!" The garbage-man yelled. "What are you up too? There is a lot of stuff I just unloaded you sure will find the odd thing you could use. You know boys these city folks just have too much stuff, how else would they be able to throw out so much?" People those days always had time for a little chat. The man rolled a new cigarette as he looked for some time to pass with the boys.

"I have just recovered an old stove, see? There it is on the back of my wagon, my wife will be happy with me tonight, and I can fix it up and replace our old one, which is always filling up the kitchen with smoke around dinnertime."

The boys and the old man chit chatted a little while longer and then went off on their separate ways, the boys fishing, and the old fellow collecting more garbage. After spending a little time at the dump, the boys finally remembered their real purpose for going there. "Fishing." Dirty and smelly from the dump they looked forward to getting into the river and wash off the dirt a little bit. Not that the two minded the dirt, they had to go in to the river anyway so it served two purposes at once.

Slowly the two made their way across a meadow, the smell of fresh wild flowers mixed with the boys' stench from the dump surrounding them. They could see the small stream making its way through the forest, then, following the forest's edge, the river made a bent back into the deep dark bush. Then suddenly something caught Wren's eye; there were a boy and a girl in *their* territory. He could see that one was a girl as she had long black hair. Boys did not have long hair in those days.

"But what the heck is a girl doing there?" Wren asked Conrad.

"Don't know but let's go and find out. This is our stream after all."

"Hey you two, what are you doing in our river?" Conrad demanded to know. "Moreover, what is this girl doing here?" Conrad crossed his arms over his tiny chest that made him look very important. He had seen this kind of behavior before by the grown ups and it impressed him very much.

"Where are you two from?" Conrad wanted to know.

"We are from Bettlach, just about five kilometers from here."

"I know where Bettlach is!" Barked Conrad. "I want to know what you are doing in our territory."

The little girl's eyes grew in fear over such a loud voice, but could not irritate her bigger brother Will.

"That is my little sister Mary," Will answered. "I am Will, we are here to do some fishing, and you do not own that river, it belongs to all of us." Conrad noticed that Will was not willing to give in easily. He looked somewhat strong too; Conrad never was much of a fighter, so he looked for a way out of a potential fight.

"Hmm…" Conrad said. "What do you have with you?"

"Well we have some chocolate with us, bread and a little bit of cheese. What do you have?" Will wanted to know.

"We've got some apples and potatoes that we will grill on the fire."

It was a good day the four kids had on that river. Mary, the little girl, proved to be quite understanding and helpful, gathering wood for the fire. Conrad showed Will how to fish with his bare hands.

"Here you see?" Conrad said. "You stand in the middle of the river, slowly bend over, spread your arms and open the fingers wide" he instructed Will. "See that trout there? Just a little below us? See that it is swimming upstream?"

"Be quiet" Conrad said, "stay still, and wait. When the fish swims between your legs grab it fast and throw it on to the riverbank."

Will's first time fishing that way was not very successful, but Conrad and Wren knew all the tricks, and in no time, they had six shiny midsize trout on the river's edge. The fire was going with the potatoes and apples baking in the ashes. They shared the little chocolate they had, the cheese, the bread, apples and potatoes. An adventurous and playful afternoon was spent by the four. They played Indians and Cowboys all afternoon. Hide and seek and the chicken-out game, where they had to find out who could stand bare-footed in the cold fresh water the longest.

Slowly the shadows started to grow longer, over by the mountain it was already starting to get dark. The kids could not tell the time, but they had a good sense of it. So, the four strangers in the morning, and friends before nightfall, parted. Little did they know that one day they would be all together again but under different circumstances!

Conrad and Wren slowly made their way back home. They could not help it but had to pay a visit to the cherry tree, where they stuffed themselves full to the rim with good sweet and juicy cherries. The boys even stuffed their pockets with them till they burst. Eventually the two made it home long after nightfall.

Worried, Olga threw her hands over her head as she had seen the two approaching home. They had already finished supper, but the boys where no longer hungry anyway. Emptying their cherries on to the table, for all to share, they were the center of attention once again.

The boys were safely home, they had all their limbs still attached to their bodies, no broken legs, arms or any other visible injuries, so all was well and that called for a good laughter as the two boys were standing in front of the assembled family, smelly and dirty like little rats, tired to the bones. All they wanted now was go to bed and have a good night sleep, so they would be all powered up and ready for tomorrow.

"Conrad, Wren I told you yesterday what is to come, remember?" Alf, their eldest brother asked. Tired, the boys just nodded, not paying too much attention. "Well your father is now gone for a little while and as we discussed yesterday, we need everybody's help now."

"Where did Dad go?" Conrad asked.

"He had to go to the hospital, but it will be a couple of years before we see him again" Alf replied. "So tomorrow, we need you boys to help as much as you can ok?"

"Oh, now I remember!" Wren stepped in.

"Mr. Adams the farmer asked us to help him with the wood he just received. I am sure he will pay us with some sausages or a chunk of ham if we help him."

"That is good" Alf responded, "I will talk to him. But first, you must bring our wood up into the attic, and then you can go and help Mr. Adams, ok boys?" At that Moment, he was proud of his two little brothers.

Early the next morning, Conrad and Wren went right to work after they had breakfast. It was not such serious work that they boys could not have some fun as well. Conrad weeded the large garden, starting with the vegetables and slowly worked his way down to the strawberries. Wren started to water, but not without having, Conrad sprayed extensively.

"I will get you later" Conrad said with a smirk.

It was almost noon when the two finished their chore in the garden. Now this meant that some heavier, more serious work was coming. Bringing the wood up in to the attic was no child's play. They had to be very careful with the basket, if they overloaded it, it could very easily be dropped from half way up; it was not the first time and the boys knew that.

On top of the house, just under the roof, there was a wooden wheel with a heavy rope pulled through it. At the other end of the rope the boys would fasten the basket, then pulled up about ten Meters, while their mother would stand just at the edge of the window ledge and pull the basket full with heavy wood inside, where it had to be stored for the winter. It was a dreadful workload for the boys, but they were all wrapped up in their duty as they wanted to please their older brother. Before they were aware of it, Alf showed up from work. He really was surprised by what his two little brothers had done and praised them accordingly. Now that was something new! Big Alf, their father, would have no more to say then a grumpy "ok." He was never a man of many words, hard work was normal for him and he expected no less from his two boys, regardless of their age. Not so Alf the big brother.

"Conrad, Wren, tomorrow you boys can go and play, take the day off have some fun. If you carry on this way, you have the wood up in the attic in no time." Exhausted and tired, but proud of themselves, the boys went to bed that night way before their bedtime. However, not without promising one another that tomorrow they will carry on and surprise Alf once again. Proud and with satisfaction, the two fell asleep.

As promised, the next morning the boys went right to work, and by evening they had more than half the workload done. Just once, there was almost an accident. Both Wren and Conrad did not pay attention both were on the rope pulling hard, when the basket was caught on a window ledge. They just pulled harder without looking up, and suddenly the basket tilted and all the wood came flying down back to the ground, close to where the boys were standing.

"So that is enough" Alf said when he got home. "Soon enough the holidays will be over, so tomorrow you guys will take a day off." Gently he stroked their heads reassuring them that all was right.

"By the way," he said, "I have talked to Mr. Adams, he is willing to give you some time to bring in the wood, he believes that the weather is stable, and that it will not turn to rain anytime soon. He will pay you boys fairly, half of that you can share with each other and use it for whatever you desire." Now those were big words, their little chests growing, their big brother made them proud.

The next morning, the boys were sleeping late, Olga did not want to wake them up as she figured their sleep was well deserved. By eight o'clock, finally the boys got up, almost one hour past their usual time.

Conrad's brother gets hurt!

Still sleepy at the breakfast table, they made plans to go up to the round hole. The "round hole," as they called the cave, was way up on the mountain on a bare wall, and you could see it from miles away. The cave could only be reached over a very narrow steep ledge; the mountain wall on some places had a drop of way over 180 meters straight down. That did not scare the boys or any other boys in the village. The reward was well worth the effort. Standing in the cave one could see almost all of Switzerland. The really big city of Zurich, to the south east, the kids had learned about in school, or, if you looked straight forward to the south you could see the capital city, Bern, and way beyond that the Alps.

This great majestic mountain range is famous around the world. On a clear day, they could see the Eiger, the Moench, and the Jungfrau. To the west, they could see as far as Biel, the little town where the French-speaking population of Switzerland started. They could look down on the big city where Alf, Liz, and Tess worked. Oh what a feeling to stand on top of the world!

"Boys please be careful," their mother had told them. She always felt uneasy when she knew the boys were up there. To forbid them to go up would not help either, as they would just go there in secret.

"When you are up there please give me a sign, make up a fire so I can see the smoke," She asked. So they promised, and with the usual supply of food, they were on their way. In a cool, refreshing breeze the tall pine trees gently swayed back and forth, singing their never- ending song as the two boys strolled through the old forest.

After a half hour walk through the bush, at the feet of the mountain, they reached the start of the steep, narrow path, which would lead them up to the cave. It was there that the boys decided to take a short rest, before they would go into "the wall" as they called it.

"Look over there" Wren whispered, "a deer." For a while, the boys watched the lightly dotted deer as it peacefully grazed. Then with a swift and sudden move, it threw back its head, as it got wind of the two boys' scent and with an elegant, sporty jump, it disappeared into the deep of the forest.

Now refreshed, the two boys started their climb; the beginning was easy, slowly securing their foothold, and gradually they made their way up. After about five minutes into the climb with Conrad in the lead, they were just past the tree line. A sharp bent ahead of them, the path now only about half a meter wide, they could touch the top of the last trees. Suddenly Wren started to slip over a moss-covered stone.

"Hold on!" Conrad yelled, "hold tight, grab that opening there to your right just there in the wall can't you see it? Hold on!" He yelled again, but it was too late, Wren lost his hold and fell into the tree just below him. Luckily, the tree was only about three and a half meter below when he slipped. His arm was stuck between two branches and so he tangled in mid air. The only way Conrad would be able to rescue him, would be to go back down below the tree line, then climb up the tree and help his brother down.

"My arm is getting numb" Wren said with tears in his eyes. "Help me please, help me" Wren pleaded with Conrad. Conrad started to panic and he started to yell for help on top of his lungs. Unable to move out of fear, Conrad was fixed in his position, with his back to the wall he watched his brother dangling from the tree.

"Help!" Conrad yelled again, and again, and finally, after seemingly endless hours, the forester responsible for that territory finally heard the boys' pleas for help. Slowly the man made his way up to the two.

Without wasting time, he assessed the situation quickly.

"First you," he said to Conrad, "give me your hand, I will lead you down, then get your brother." Conrad, shaking down to every bone in his small body, slowly made it back down with the forester's help.

"Boy you wait here, do not move, I have to go and get some help for your brother, there is no way that I can help him by myself. I'll be back in no time," the forester said, running down the path to get help. Conrad was well aware of the mess they were in.

"Wren hold on, you hear?" He pleaded with his brother. Nevertheless, Wren had enough to do by himself; he was in a lot of pain right then. With his free hand, he tried to ease off the weight; lifting himself up a bit helped, but only for a short time he was able to loosen the grip on his arm. After an endless time the boys heard the fire siren in the distance. Then it was quiet again. Suddenly with a lot of noise, some fire fighters came running towards Conrad. They carried a large ladder with them and lots of rope. After several attempts from below, they finally realized that they had to get the boy from above. The firefighters had to drill a hole in to the mountain wall, then fasten and secure a steel ring into it. On a heavy rope, one man went down on it, draped the end of the rope around the boy, and then slowly lowered him in to the arms of the waiting firefighters below the tree. They comforted him and put him on a stretcher then carried him out of the bush into the waiting ambulance.

"I know you boys," the forester said to Conrad. "You are Alf's boys are you not?" He asked. Conrad chocking back tears, nodded helplessly.

"Ok we have to bring your brother to the hospital; he has an injured shoulder and will need a doctor's attention. You come with me, I will bring you home, besides, your parents need to be informed." Conrad followed the forester, he was afraid of the things to come. He knew they had let their big brother down, he knew he would never be able to hoist the wood up to the attic by himself.

It was early in the afternoon when Conrad arrived home with the forester. Olga was working in the garden when she noticed the two coming down the mountain road. She leaned her rake onto the stonewall, and with both hands pushing into her back stretching it back and forth, it looked like she wanted to give birth right then and there.

"Oh Jesus," Olga started to lament. "What is the matter now, and where is Wren? What did you boys do? Did you hunt a deer? Come on boy, talk!" Olga demanded. The forester could not help it, he had to smile over being bombarded by so many questions at once.

"Easy now Olga," the gray haired man said.

"It is not as bad as it looks, the boy here is ok, and the other one we had to bring to the hospital in Solothurn, he has a dislocated shoulder at best" he explained.

Olga, turning from white to gray, then to a red face and back to ash again gulped for air. Frantically waving her arms as if she was learning to swim, she looked at the forester with eyes as big as saucers, WHAT had the boys done? She wondered.

"Well they wanted to go up to the round hole, as you know the ledge is very narrow, and thank God, they were just at the beginning, when Wren slipped on a moss-covered rock. Luckily, the tree stopped his fall, but he got caught on a tree branch. Well you better get ready to pick up the other fellow in the hospital," the forester finished the conversation. "I will be back tonight to take a statement." Whenever an official did something, they needed a report, without a report they had no work. No matter where you were, it seems as soon as somebody was wearing a uniform he needed a report for everything he did. That was what was making them look important.

Just as Olga left the garden, the baker man approached her and said, "Olga, you know I have a car; I will gladly drive you to the hospital and pick up Wren. Conrad may come with us too." Happy not to have to take the city bus, she accepted his offer. Conrad all excited, "Can we go and see Dad too?" He asked.

"No" Olga said, "Your Dad is in a different hospital, but on one of the following Sundays we will go and see him ok?" Conrad was happy that all went so well after all, all he needed to face now was Alf his older brother, when he got home from work. As it turned out, all Wren suffered was a dislocated shoulder and a few scratches on both legs and a little on his face.

In disbelief and excitement, Conrad wandered around in the hospital. He looked at all the busy nurses and doctors whisking by him. Everything was so clean there, so quiet, and Wren sported a very good-looking cast, which made Conrad a little jealous. Sooner than he anticipated he would have his very own, but that is another story. Soon they all were on their way home, glad that it ended in such a good way.

When Alf and the two sisters got home from work, Conrad was already his good self again, and started bragging about how brave he was, and how he helped Wren to be rescued. Of course, he was the star attraction that night when he told everyone how he helped the firefighters to lower Wren from the tree, and how he, at the last minute, tried to get a hold on Wren, but Wren let go, otherwise he himself could have saved him.

"What are you going to do now with the wood?" Alf wanted to know, after he had enough of Conrad's heroic story.

"I will talk to Hans, I have helped him before, and I am sure he will return the favor," Conrad said.

"Well then so be it, please make sure that it is getting done." Alf could not bring himself to punish the boys, as he himself had been up there by the round hole more than once when he was their age.

Shortly thereafter, the forester arrived to take the statement. Olga made a fresh pot of coffee, the forester made himself comfortable at the table preparing to finish his story so he could present it to his chief in the Village Hall, where all the important business took place. Conrad had to repeat his story once more, which he did with great pride.

"Well" the important man said at the end "I," and he pronounced **I** with such pride, as he himself was to make decisions.

"I will suggest to the village that we block off that ledge up to the round hole, it is just too dangerous, and it is a real accident waiting to happen."

"You can place the whole Swiss Army there, we just will find another way up," Conrad thought to himself.

It was quite late in the evening when the forester finally left, but not without promising Olga to look after her every now and then; he knew exactly that she was without a man in the house. He did not count Alf as a real man, since he had not been in the Army yet. That was wrong thinking on his behalf.

The next morning Conrad went straight to his neighbor hoping he could get a hold of Hans, who was about his age. A short and friendly-faced woman, Hans's mother, opened the door.

"Good morning Mrs. Friedrich," Conrad said politely, "is Hans home? I need to talk to him."

"Sure Conrad, just wait a minute, he is just finishing breakfast." Hans was more than willing to help Conrad, because he owed him big time. Hans knew exactly that if he did not offer his help to him, the priest would know in no time who had painted the funny faces on his house. 'One hand washes the other,' so the old saying goes.

So the two went to work, Wren sitting in the sun enjoying himself. By nightfall most of the wood was up in the attic, which was happily noticed by all family members. Alf paid Hans two full Franks into his bare hands. That was a lot of money in those days. The two older sisters also each paid the little guy one Frank for his effort to help Conrad. Of course, Conrad took note of what he thought was an unfair trade.

"I will walk Hans home," he quickly offered. On their way to Hans's home, Conrad explained to his buddy how angry the old priest was over the paintings. Hans understood only too well, and willingly shared his four Franks with Conrad. Both boys, happy with the deal, parted. If you had nothing, as a kid, you had to learn how to earn…that was their philosophy.

When Conrad arrived home, there was a big wooden tub with steaming hot water on the kitchen floor. The little guy knew what that meant; it was Saturday night, time for the weekly bath. To have a bath every night was not economically feasible, too much wood was used to heat such a big pot of water. Besides, a little dirt on the skin keeps you warmer, and most of it will rub off on the bedding anyway.

"Tomorrow we will go to visit father in the hospital. You, Wren and I," Olga explained. "I want you boys clean when we go to the big city." The two older sisters and Alf junior declined the offer of accompanying them. They had their own reasons. Alf was not too fond of his father right then, and would rather go hiking in the mountains. Liz, that sneaky bugger, had a date with that snob from the big city, and Tess plainly had not exactly the best memories of her father.

Conrad goes to the big city!

Sunday morning, right after church, they left on the big yellow bus, which would bring them down to the city. Conrad and Wren had a hard time sleeping all night, as they were looking forward to take such a journey on the bus, and Wren was proud of his cast and wanted to show it off to his father. After a half hour bus ride, they had arrived in the city.
"But Mom that is not where the hospital is," complained Conrad. Wren also noticed that. This was not the place he had his shoulder fixed a couple of days ago.
"No," their mother explained. "I have told you, Dad is in a different hospital, this is only for grown men, and because there are so many there, they have to be guarded by the Police; you boys know how angry a grown man can get, so they have to take care of them."
Finally, they stood in front of the "grown men's hospital". Funny it was, in front of the hospital, there was a Policeman standing guard, and all windows had steel bars in front of them.
"Why do they do that?" Conrad wanted to know.
"So nobody can get inside," Olga explained to the kids. They seemed to be ok with it and did not ask any more questions. They had to wait in a room before they could see their Dad. Then after what seemed an endless time, a Policeman in what

looked like a brand new uniform, with a sword dangling on his side, picked up the trio and accompanied them to their Dad's room.

"Dad must have been an important man," the boys figured.

He had a room all to himself; to protect him, the windows had steel bars in front of them, and in the door to his room there was an opening cut out, also with steel bars, so nobody could go and bother him when he did important work such as knitting an area rug.

Dad was happy to see his boys, but between him and Olga, there were still some unanswered questions.

After a little while, the boys figured time went by too fast and the important-looking Policeman opened the door and escorted the three back out. Dad got a hug from the boys and a shy kiss on the cheek from Olga. They left with the promise to return soon, if it was not too inconvenient for him. They did not want to interrupt his important work. Olga promised to wait for him also and so they parted.

After the visit, mother promised them a special treat in the city. They would go to a café, order hot chocolate for the boys and a coffee for Olga, and she was also able to buy some cake, as she had saved the money bit by bit. Eventually the boys got tired of the city, it was boring. Nothing to do there and the other boys they could see, were all dressed neatly and behaved like little monkeys, well behaved, too well behaved for the two country boys.

"Stupid boys they have down here in the city," the two concluded.

Happy to be back home in their own world, the two quickly changed into more comfortable clothing, meaning their leather pants and of course no shoes which would restrict their little feet from feeling the softness of the grass.

"Conrad," Olga said to him, "next week you are likely to be finished with the wood, then you need to go up to Mr. Adams and bring his wood into the barn. I want you to be careful you hear me now? I know he will give you the old mare to pull the wagon, but still be careful," his mother pleaded.

"Ok Mom I will, don't you worry" the little guy reassured her. "I am going too," Wren explained, "I too want to work with the old mare, she is lame, and no threat to us," he pleaded with his mother.

"I don't know" Olga hesitated.

"But I still have one good shoulder. I can hold the horse with one hand, no problem" he said. Finally, Alf helped the boys out.

"Let them go" he said. I know the horse is almost blind and will not go anywhere if it is not forced." Still hesitating after a while, Olga finally agreed to let both of them go. But she worried for nothing, the boys were really careful, with all the enthusiasm all kids have when they want to please, they went to work for the farmer Adams.

Slowly, the worry-free summer came to an end. One week to go until school would start again. Wren did not look forward to it, but Conrad liked it. There was one big event to come, into the little village. For years, the priest had pleaded with his community that the church needed new bells.

"Just listen to the Bell of Death, it sounds like it has cracked and it has an awful sound to it" he said. It was custom whenever someone in the village passed away, to ring the bell for fifteen minutes at seven o'clock in the evening. It was then that the old women in the village silently lowered their heads, and the men respectfully threw their hats, stopping whatever they were doing. The kids stopped playing, and so the whole community mourned the loss of a villager; they cared for one another.

There were also happier times to communicate with the sound of the bells, like the wedding bells, or the bells on Sunday morning when the priest called his sheep to mass. It was usually the boys like Conrad, Wren, Hans and German who would ring the bells on a Sunday morning, as they were also altar boys, believe it or not. To ring the bells was always fun for the boys. It took quite a bit of a pull by the four little fellows to bring the bell to sound. At first you would only hear a tiny "bim" then slowly increasing the swing of the bell, the sound got louder and louder, until every Farmer in the community could hear the sound of the bell. Gently the wind carried the sound over the fields, to the even most remote farms, to call them for mass. When the boys pulled the heavy rope, which was connected to the bell way up in the tower, they swiftly held on as they could be lifted up as far as 3 meters into the air. The trick was not to let go hold of the rope until they were back on the ground.

    Finally, they had enough money to order new bells, six in all. A big celebration was planned for the occasion. The Community Music Band would start two kilometers below the village, in a row of six men and ten rows deep, sixty men strong they played their march music in perfect synchronization. The main road was closed to what little traffic there was. They looked impressive, these men, with their deep, dark blue uniforms, and the red stripe down on the side of each pant-leg. Proudly they marched in perfect synchronization with the fast-paced march music.

    Flower girls walked ahead of them, smiling and proud to have such an important job. Behind the band, the elder villagers walked together with such important officials as the Mayor, the teachers and all officials in the village. Then, pulled by twelve heavy strong horses, the especially prepared wagon with the bells on top was to follow. With flowers draped and garlands wrapped around the bells, it was a beautiful sight as the shining bells blinked in the warm afternoon sun.

    The four boys waited in the bell tower for their signal to start ringing the old bells one last time. As soon the music band was within sight of the church, the priest was to give the four a sign.

Nervously the boys waited peeking outside for the sign. Then there it was, they could hear the music in the far distance, the old priest almost forgot to give the signal as he was excessively excited.

What a peaceful time it was, the old bells ringing one last time, the music playing, the decorated wagon with the new bells, the proud flower girls, the very important-looking officials and honoraries. The heavily sweating horses with the six bells in their pull, signaled the end of the procession. For now, the new bells would be stored in the church's courtyard, until fall. The bell tower was in need of new wood beams as well, or they would not support the weight of the new bells. The whole tower was to get a complete overhaul; since they were getting new bells, "...They may as well restore the whole tower" the priest used to plead.

"He should have been a politician," the elders mumbled behind his back. To have different ideas than the priest was dangerous, as the priest had a direct connection to higher powers.

All went well in this small little village, that late summer afternoon. It was a celebration; the whole community celebrated. At nightfall, after singing and dancing, it was time to go home and care for the livestock. Peacefully, the sun slowly glided down behind the mountain's peak.

As Olga tucked her two youngsters into bed, she knew all was well and her little world was somehow restored. The two had spent most of the day beside Alf, Liz, and Tess. It was a perfect family harmony as nothing looked out of place.

Mary's family in trouble!

Ten kilometers to the west in the tiny community of Bettlach a small tragedy took place just around the same time. It was at Mary's and Will's home where all hell broke loose. Thomas their Dad, remember the painter I told you at the beginning? Not that he was much better than Alf senior, oh no don't get that wrong, just because he was not where Alf was, it did not mean he was any better. He got home on this late Sunday afternoon, like he normally did, he had a little too much of the good stuff. You could see it by the way he walked home, swaying from side to side, he used the whole sidewalk, a little out of balance he was, the good old Thomas.

Unfortunately, he was a little early that afternoon, he lost one game after another at the pub, quite a bit of money too. Therefore, he was in a lousy mood, and ready to pick a fight, any fight just give him a reason. Just as he entered the apartment they lived in, a working buddy of his opened the door, ready to go home to his lawful wife. As I said, Thomas was a bit early this Sunday. The encounter with another man in his apartment did not go over too well. A heavy argument started between the two men. The two disagreed to whom the women inside the apartment belong. Thomas, a little too weak from too much alcohol, and his opponent too tired from his demanding duties with the woman inside, all they did was argue back and forth until another tenant finally approached the two and demanded an end to their loud conversation, in which he was not interested.

Mary and Will, her brother, were out on the prowl all afternoon. Encouraged by Elli, their mother, to stay out as long as they wanted, she gave the two an extra supply of chocolate to make sure they would not be home too soon on that Sunday afternoon. She knew damn well that Thomas would be at the pub all Sunday to play cards, and all she wanted was a little bit of fun of her own. She got more than she bargained for, that night.

One must know, there was also one brother, Max, he was way older than Mary and Will, already on an apprenticeship program in another town, and he rarely came home as he was in disagreement with his parents' lifestyle. Then there was Lilly, the youngest sister, but she was always on her own with her grandparents. Two years earlier Elli also had a miscarriage, and that did not help her relationship either.

However, it was a hefty and loud evening, after which Thomas somewhat sobered up. Thomas called Elli every name in the book, and his repertoire was quite impressive that night. Elli herself did not want to stay behind, and had a colorful repertoire too. The loud, dry sound of Thomas' fist landing in Elli's right eye underscored his argument. Elli therefore did not look too pretty the next few days, which prompted her to call it quits. That was the end of their relationship. Elli quickly found an apartment in Zuchwil, a community twenty-five kilometers east of Bettlach, and fifteen kilometers northeast of Oberdorf. Just at the other end of the big city. That is very important for you, the reader, to know, so keep it in mind.

The next month she would pack up her three kids, and head out on her own. Will, Mary, and their youngest sibling Lilly, now back from the grand parents.

At this point I like to point out, that not all families were like that in tiny Switzerland. To think that would be as silly as if the Swiss would think all North American people live in tepees and hunted with bow and arrow.

What the hell was wrong with these people? With the Second World War just finished a few years earlier, the future did not look too bad. They all had enough food, they were healthy, they survived and they knew the difference between right and wrong. What was it they wanted? Maybe they had to live in fear too long with too little, too long with almost nothing. Now, they were hungry for life, hungry for love, and hungry for everything they could lay their hands on. What was it they forgot?

Oh yeah of course, it was their kids who now had to pay for their misfortune. "Oh not so," they would disagree with you, if approached.

"All we want is the best for our children. We hope a better future awaits them" they would say; ask them, I am sure they will tell you. However, I will not write this book to judge this generation, that is not my place. All I can do is look back and hope to make it better.

Little Mary did not have a much happier childhood than other children, as many kids in those days suffered from some sort of violent abuse, sexual or mental. It was no surprise to her, that one Sunday Dad picked them up for a visit. They had spent a relatively happy Sunday afternoon with him. By the time they got back home to their Mom, her new boyfriend was present. Well, that did not go over to well with her ex. Thomas lost it completely, Will standing closest to Thomas was about to get the scare of his short life. Thomas grabbed the little feller by the neck, lifted him up, and shook him like a wet cat.

"Do you see what I will do with your little bastards?" He yelled. "How do I know these kids are mine?" He continued. Having said that he stepped out on the balcony stretched his arm right over the rail with little Will dangling helplessly in mid-air. Needless to say that the Police picked him up rather quickly, and locked him up for a while.

Let us skip a few years; Conrad as well as Mary still were happy kids to some degree. Many tales still could be told; two different kids, growing up with just about the same family troubles.

A few years went by, Conrad, Wren, Liz, Tess and Alf were on their own, and they managed well. Olga was a little happier during those years, if only she could stop going to the city, and care a little more for the two youngest ones. They were carefree those days for the boys, but they did their duties well. They no longer had to fear the almost daily beatings by Alf. No more yelling and fighting by Alf and Olga. No longer did they have to look on as Olga got beaten up every now and then when Alf came home, full to the rim with alcohol.

    Of course, during the few years Alf was in the "hospital" the two boys eventually found out the truth. They were teased enough, branded by their teacher, and foremost, the priest. Oh yeah, of course it was the boys' fault, and as a good priest he had to let these two little bastards feel it, right? Was this not the priest's job after all? It was his duty to bring kids like that to the right way of living. This could only be done by letting them know what their father had done. This could only be done by putting the blame of everything that went wrong in the village on them.

    The night the farmhouse went up in flames after a heavy thunderstorm, just to name one example, of course it was their fault; were they not, the day before at the farmer's and played up in the barn, in the hay, pretending they were helping the farmer? Did they or did they not? Of course they did! If parents or somebody else in a family did something wrong, of course then it was their kids' fault. They need to be punished, as often as possible; they need to learn respect those little bastards.

    Then the big day arrived. When Conrad and Wren came home that afternoon from school, big Alf, their Dad, was sitting at the table with a big bowl of soup in front of him, Olga sitting beside him, pretending to be *sooo* happy. Alf greeted the two with a nod of his head.

"Well boys, happy I am home again?" He asked. The two admitted to be happy, sat beside Alf and shared a bit of the soup.

Early that evening, a young, fat man with a big bike waited in front of the house. Tess came storming outside with one suitcase, just as Conrad and Wren got home from their daily routine.

"Well boys" she said, "I am sorry but I have to leave, I can no longer stay at this house, it is not your fault little guys. One day you will understand why I had to leave." With that, she jumped on the bike, wrapped her arms around the man's waist and that was the last to be seen of Tess. The boys missed her terribly, but as all kids, they forgot quickly.

It was as if Olga and Alf were back on track again. Alf spent more time in the pub or at work than he should, he never spent time with the two boys; after all, that was Olga's job.

One day Alf came home from work around two-thirty that afternoon, then after his meal, he went up into the mountain to cut some wood, which the boys would have to bring home the next day. After that, he went straight to the pub and got loaded. When he finally got home late that night, he picked a fight with Olga. With this arguing going on, the two boys woke up, but only Conrad had enough courage to go and find out what was going on. All he saw was that Alf raised his hand to give Olga a good beating. Conrad, afraid, got in between the two. He wanted to protect his mother the little guy. That did not go over too well; a well-aimed foot from Alf catapulted the little fellow right through the room where he crashed against the door. With a bleeding nose and crying on the floor he did not dare to move. Some more words were flying back and forth then finally Alf left to go back to the pub. Of course, Olga kept quiet, she did not want Alf to go back to jail. *Welcome back to the good old times boys!*

   The following Sunday there was a regional music competition. Every community had its own Music Brass Band. Once a year they got together to compete. That was a big event. All those uniforms, sharp-looking men, the shining instruments; the whole atmosphere was very exciting. Well, the band from our little village took the second prize, and on Sunday afternoon they were to arrive back home. As custom had it, they would assemble at the edge of the village, then, like a well-trained Army Band, they would march into the village, playing their instruments like professionals. Proudly accompanied by flower girls, there were also the village flag, the regional flag and the Swiss flag in the center. Proudly the men marched. Heads up, eyes straight, in synchronized forward march. Then in the center of the village they would be forming a circle and perform just for the fellow villagers. Everybody would be there, cheering, clapping, and having a good time, of course followed by beer, lots of it, and dancing all night. Alf, Olga and the two boys were standing in front of the house to watch the parade. It was just across the place where the band was performing.

Suddenly one musician, he was in the last row, turned around and yelled something across the street, something directed at Alf. The kids could not understand what the man said, but it must have been something offensive. Alf, without hesitation, crossed the place, grabbed the man by his neck, and before anyone was aware of it, the musician had his head stuck out the other end of a hedge. Beside him lay the brass horn, which he so proudly played just a minute ago, damaged and unable to sound properly. Oh yes Alf was a strong man.

Of course, the Police once again had to take a statement, somehow Alf got away with it, but it was not a pleasant thing to be around him.
That was the end of it. Alf junior figured that there was likely no more peace to be found in that little town of his, the place where he was born where he learned to walk, played and had made friends. It was the place they called home, every corner of the village, the mountain they were so familiar with and fond of.

What about Conrad and German's plan? They wanted to be chefs on a big boat when they grew up. They wanted to travel the world together. What about that?

Alf junior had enough money saved to buy a small house in Biberist, just about five kilometers south of Solothurn, therefore, the family moved on too, out of that small little town where they dreamed their dreams, made plans, had friends and knew every single tree on the mountain. They knew every little path, leading through the bush, every cave up there on the big mountain wall. That was the village where they knew everybody and everybody knew them.

One Saturday morning they packed up their belongings onto a big wagon, which the old man borrowed from a farmer, and a horse to pull the heavy load. Down the mountain road they went, through the city, with Conrad and Wren sitting on top of the wagon.

A friendly little place the new house was, and Alf junior could call it his own. Olga and big Alf got the big bedroom, Alf junior, as the proud owner, had his large domain upstairs, while Wren and Conrad shared a room just beside it.

Slowly the old wounds closed, the old man grew more and more silent, and Olga finally had not much to worry about anymore. Liz, Conrad's favorite sister, got married to this geek from the city, and no word from Tess, the oldest girl.
Slowly Wren and Conrad grew apart. Wren had different ideas than Conrad, yeah they still were together, but each made his own new friends, and they had different interests.

It was a new and exciting world the two boys entered. They had to make new friends, and had another big forest they could discover. Besides, they still had sight of the mountain, and all Conrad had to do was look out the window; on weekends he still could take the train or the bus to visit the mountain he loved so much. Things started to get better.

One day the news came that Alf junior wanted to get married, and wanted to start his own family. Alf and Olga of course had to move once again. This time they went to Bellach, fifteen kilometers to the west of Solothurn. Olga, Alf senior, Conrad and Wren were now on their own. They found a four-bedroom apartment in a high-rise building. Still at least they had their beloved mountain within sight. One day, Olga took Conrad aside.

Young Conrad!

"Conrad," she started, "next month you will be out of school, you know you have to start working then. I have talked to someone at a factory, over in Solothurn, the big city. You could start as an apprentice there. Next week you and I will go there and look at the place, ok? You will also have to go to apprentice school; in three weeks you will be sixteen years old, that means you will be a young man then, and fully able to start working."

The day when Olga and Conrad went to the factory where he was supposed to start as an apprentice finally arrived. Conrad took a shower, and then got dressed in his Sunday suit, complete with a tie; handsome he looked the young fellow. Proud he was too. The day when he would be accepted into the grown-ups world was just around the corner.

  The two had to wait by the receptionist for a little while, Conrad's future boss was busy at the Moment but would see them as soon as he could, they where told by the friendly and very pretty receptionist. Conrad already had an eye for such pleasant things. The man they were waiting for finally came to pick the two up. He was an old man Conrad figured. "At least forty or so," he thought.

  The boss had a friendly nature and was pleasant to talk to. Conrad and his Mother got a tour of the factory. There were long rows of machines, with busy people rushing back and forth between them. The young fellow was very, very impressed. After the tour in the foreman's office, Olga had to fill out many forms for the program.

  "Do you think that you would like to learn how to set these machines Conrad?" The man said.

  "You know we are making parts for our famous Swiss watches, and they have to be very precise. I know your older brother Alf very well," he added. "He is working upstairs as a watchmaker. Do you think that you can work as reliably as he does?" the man asked.

  "Yes Sir!" he replied, a little shyly.

  The foreman, impressed by the boy's friendly and polite nature, finally agreed to let him into the working world.

  "Now there are a few rules you have to follow. First, once a week, we will send you to school, which you will attend. We will start working at six thirty until four-forty-five in the afternoon. Make sure you are on time, being late is a no no. All older coworkers you will address as Mister; you will listen to them and follow their orders. I will assign an apprentice in his last year to you; you will pay him the same respect as you would pay me. You also will be addressed as Mister, but you will loose certain privileges should you decide not to follow all the rules. Are we clear on that Conrad?"

"Yes sir!"

"Well then, I will see you in two weeks time, the first day you will be here at eight in the morning sharp for an orientation. See you then."

Conrad was a little nervous although his future boss did not appear to be mean, and the men in the factory also were rather friendly. What made him nervous was the unknown, "...But give it time and you will fit in," he thought to himself.

Then came the day when Conrad, the second last one to grow up suddenly, was catapulted from childhood into adulthood. It was the beginning of his contract as apprentice, he had just turned sixteen that day. When he got home from work, the friendly Mrs. Mueller, a neighbor of his, was in the hallway.

"Good afternoon, Mrs. Mueller" Conrad greeted her. "How are you doing?"

"I am fine, thank you Mister Weiss." Conrad stopped at once.

"Why do you call me Mr. Weiss? You know I am Conrad," he asked.

"Well," Mrs. Mueller said, "it is your birthday today, you are now sixteen, you are working, and therefore, we are respecting you by calling you Mister Weiss."

"Well thank you very much Mrs. Mueller," Conrad said. "That is very nice and thoughtful of you. Do you think they will let me sit at the round table at the pub? Conrad asked, swallowing hard.

"Don't push your luck young man," Mrs. Mueller said laughing. "When it is time, they will let you know."

"Well then thanks again and I will see you later on tonight, I am sure Mom made a birthday cake, so I would like to invite you and Mister Mueller for a coffee and a piece of cake. All right?" Conrad asked.

"Yes, gladly" the lady said," we will be there."

Conrad was worry-free then; he was liked by his coworkers, and was well respected because he was always working, was never late, and did his share.

On weekends, especially in the fall, he liked to hike the mountains. That was always his favorite time. With a couple of new buddies he made at work, Heinz and Franz, they went up early Saturdays, at 4:00 o'clock one morning. They met at the foot of the mountain, then hiked up to the 1200-meter high summit. They especially liked it when there was fog covering the valley, better yet, when the whole of Switzerland had a blanket of fog as high as 1000 meter on it; that was a special feast for the eyes of the three young men. Close your eyes and imagine this.

Right below your feet at 1000 meters elevation, there is a blanket of fog in the far distance, the sun slowly and shyly rises over the horizon. Way to the south, they could see the majestic snow covered Alps. Nothing else but the blanket of fog covering the space between the mountain range of Jura in the west, to the Alps in the south; the fog looked like an ocean, and one felt like wanting to take a dip. It was a little chilly, this early in the fall morning.

The boys, sweating from the one-hour hike, covered themselves with heavy coats. Sitting on the edge of a high wall, dropping straight down for about 180 meters, they were waiting for that special Moment. To the left, at the end of the hiking path, there was a six and a half meter high steel cross. It marked the spot where a man with a horse on a winter night, fell to his death, as he had misjudged the path. To the right they could see as far as the little city of Biel, where the French-speaking population of Switzerland started. Straight ahead the Alps; the young men could even name the most famous peaks; the Matterhorn, world-famous with its narrow shape, and feared by mountaineers, followed by Eiger, Moench, and Jungfrau.

Then there it was. Slowly the sun started to greet the three young man, round and red as blood, it dipped behind the snowy mountains into a faded red at first, then with all of nature's power, the full beauty of the mountain range was visible as blood covered giants.

Slowly even the fog beneath them started to look like a sea of blood, so red and beautiful, so perfect in the making, one could not help but to thank God for the beauty they were able to witness. After this nature's spectacle, Conrad and his friends would pack up and hike up to a mountain farmer's in the distance. There they would have a hearty breakfast; crusty, deep, dark bread, hot coffee, homemade jam by the farmer's wife, fresh creamy butter and cheese.

Early in the afternoon, the young men would hike down into the little village of Oberdorf, Conrad's old hometown. No one could remember him unless he would state who he was, though he was not too interested in being recognized, as he knew that his father had not left too good of an impression. There they would have a couple of beers; after all they were old enough to work, so they were old enough to have a beer, and most the time, all they did was quench their thirst. If they were in the mood, they could drink a few too many.

Mary the young Lady!

"Mary, now that you are fifteen years old, it is time to make a decision," Elli said to her daughter. "I just don't have the money to support all of you so I will send you to a place where you are safe and where you can learn how to keep a household in order. You can eat and sleep there, and on weekends you may come home. Will is already working to help support us, now it is your turn."

"Mom I would like to be an apprentice hairdresser, that is my dream and you know that," Mary pleaded.

"Too bloody bad!" Elli's boyfriend said. "It is your mother's decision and that's that."

Not much poor Mary could do, she was a minor, and it was her mother's decision. After a year went by, Mary had learned to take care of a household; she knew everything to keep things rolling smoothly. She learned how to cook and how to clean, how to look after a family. She pleaded with Elli, her mother, to let her come back home. Finally Elli agreed, but only if Mary would be willing to go to work at the nearby factory, so she could help support her.

"Well then," Mary thought to herself." Better than being a slave," and so she agreed to go to work in the same factory as her mother's. It was a well-established big company, where they made big weaving machines, and large Diesel engines for big tankers, which steamed through the oceans all over the world. It also was the same company where big Alf worked the morning shift.

Wren, who could not decide if he wanted to start as an apprenticeship, also worked there, and coincidentally started the same day in the same department as Mary, but they acted as if there was no memory of their encounter in there early childhood, that summer afternoon by the little stream.

Conrad established him self not too badly at work. After all, he learned how to work early on in his childhood. The first six months or so did rather go well for him, no complaints from his boss or fellow co-workers. Mind you, Conrad had a slight drinking problem, as on the weekends he liked to get together with his friends and throw a party. The longer that went on, the better they could handle the amount of beer they drank. Olga, his mother, lived in fear he could end up like his father, but Conrad had sworn early in his life never to beat a woman, and never to abuse his children, should he ever have his own, and never get to the point where he would come home to his family drunk.

Right then he was young, reckless and the world was his for the taking. Saturday nights also meant dancing, especially during the warm and cozy summer nights. A band would have put up a dance floor somewhere on a lake, or in the forest, with a beer stand, a barbeque and the band would play till the early morning hours. That was Conrad's domain, he loved to dance with all the pretty girls, and that was all he wanted in his hay days. Girls had the nasty habit of asking the boys not to drink too much or they would not dance with them anymore.

"Girls," they used to say, "nothing but problems, nothing but complaining, girls are stupid, do you hear? Let us have another beer, the girls can dance by themselves, so there you go." Not that the young men disliked the company of the ladies, but there were other priorities in their lives.

The young women could not understand what was so funny in the young men's competition to see how fast one could empty a pint of beer and then, with a disgusting burp, make room for more. They used to call them pigs; now that was not very lady-like was it? Besides, the young men were warned by the older ones once, about the girls.

"All they want is to put a string on you, then before you know it they get pregnant and you have to get married. No more beer guzzling nights with the buddies" so they were told, and of course the older guys were way, way smarter, they knew what was going on. ...*No, thanks for the flowers, but no thanks. Who wants to end up like their parents? Father at the Pub, Mother with a boyfriend. Who needs this?*

Those were Conrad's happy, careless days, days of exploring life, its possibilities, camaraderie, fun and sometimes a little stupidity. Hey, they were young, they worked, were respected, and best of all, they had friends and were free of the sometimes-nasty days of childhood. Now young adults, they could no longer be touched. Besides, they grew stronger too and maybe, just maybe, would hit back in defense.

"Just try it Alf, come on!" Conrad thought.

One Monday morning, Conrad still had a little cloud of dust in his brain, but he was at work. The eldest apprentice came to see him.

"Mister Weiss" he said, "the supervisor would like to see you, right a way."

"Ok" Conrad nodded.

"Ah, Mr. Weiss, before you go to see him, a bit of advice if you care. Stop drinking the weekends away, it is not good for you." Conrad looked startled.

"Hmmm" he mumbled, "are the weekends not my own time? Have I ever missed work? Have I ever been late?"

"No" Heinz, the eldest apprentice replied, "but that you are drinking a bit too much is quite obvious on Monday mornings, and besides, your grades in school have dropped; you have been a top student, and we don't like what we see right now."

Hanging his head low, Conrad slowly made his way to the supervisor's domain, a large office at the front of the building. Worst of all, his big brother, Alf, whom Conrad very much respected, was sitting across from his supervisor. That did not spell something good. "Oh shit" he thought to himself as he knocked on the Supervisor's door, waiting for the solemn "Come in please."

There he stood, head low, with an expression on his face that said, "I am grown up, and you guys can't force me stop drinking… besides you guys drink too, I have seen it, so don't give me the third degree here." The Supervisor and Alf both heard the knock on the door. They chose to ignore it for a while. That was a good trick, which engendered respect, which made the young men at the door think; you could see it, as Conrad nervously stepped from one foot to the other, curled his lips, uncomfortably looking up and down the aisle. "Can anyone see me? Do they know why I am here?" he thought. Finally there it was.

"Come in Mr. Weiss." Conrad opened the door and shyly stood in front of the two men, knowing damn well that he had let them down; he knew he was wrong, but to admit it was something different. He got the scare of his life.

"Mister Weiss," the supervisor's thundering voice echoed through the office. "What in the world are you thinking? Almost every Monday you come to work as if you still were drunk from the weekend, your grades have dropped dramatically in school!" Conrad never heard him talk like that and he was scared, confused, and stubborn. On top of it, his brother agreed with the supervisor.

"Mister Weiss, I told you up front what your duties would be, what we expect from you. You are not holding up your part of the deal. We give you two months, so smarten up, polish up your grades, show us that you care."

Ashamed, Conrad left the office, red-faced but stubborn like a mule and he returned to his workbench.

"Conrad!" He had not seen Bruno, the eldest apprentice, approaching him from behind. Gently he placed his hand on Conrad's shoulder.

"Listen" he said, "on Saturday we would like to go up to the mountain, hiking, why don't you come with us? I would like to spend a little time with you, what do you say?" He asked. After a moment Conrad nodded in agreement.

"Deal" he said. "I will come with you."

Conrad was in his rebel years. There was not much that could convince him that, with a solid apprenticeship, his future would look much brighter. He would go on for a while but the job eventually got the better of him.

Saturday rolled around and as promised, he, Bruno's protégé, would meet him at the foot of the mountain. Early in the morning they started to climb up the long and steep winding trail, up to the summit. The air was crisp and fresh, the two in good spirits. They were greeted by the birds, singing with all their might. It was a perfect setting. As they arrived at the mountain's restaurant, which was no more than a piece of land that the farmer had changed into a chalet, and converted part of it into a pub. The farmer's wife would wait on the guests and cooked whatever meal the patrons desired. The two young men were ready for a good hearty breakfast. Sitting outside in the early, warm summer sun, it was easy to forget why they went up there.

"What do you think Conrad," Bruno asked, "do you think we can make it over the ridge by the cross, and then climb down the other side? It is steep there and the descent is hard and long, but it is well worth the effort as the scenery is just outstanding."

"I know," Conrad mumbled with his mouth full, "been there done that" he said. They both agreed to give it a try. He was right the older fellow, the scenery was outstanding, as you could see the Alps with their snowcaps in the far distance. They could make out the Emmental, with its lovely rolling, hilly landscape. Best known for its famous cheese, the Emmental, the one and only cheese with the big holes in it.

The two had a wonderful day. Tired mind you, but who can stop a seventeen year old? When they arrived back home, there was a local dance night in the forest.

"Want to go?" Conrad asked his friend.

"No that is enough" Bruno replied, "and I think you should go home too now. Remember what we were talking about? Remember, more learning, more school, and less beer? You know," he continued, "it would be nice to see you back on track." Conrad liked him, he was not bossy, nor did he push him around, but nevertheless he could not help it, as soon he was out of sight, Conrad got thirsty. It was there where Conrad found his old school buddy, German. German, a heavy drinker himself, was already deep into the liqueur and ready to get some more. German was an apprentice at a hotel down in the big city. He wanted to be a cook; both when they went to school together always dreamed of being cooks on a large boat while sailing the world.

During his apprenticeship German got the taste of heavy liqueur, and a few years later was an alcoholic and eventually he shot himself at the old cemetery, where they used to hang out together as kids.

Needles to say, Conrad did not make it home until late Sunday night; they had too much fun. Monday morning again, with a buzz in his head, he went into the foreman's office to report in sick.

"Well, Conrad," the supervisor advised him, "it may be better if you quit the job and when you think that you know what you want to do with your life, then maybe we will hire you back, as you always did a good job when you were sober."
Adios, good by see you later.

So it was that Conrad went on his way to the worst and it did not get better for a couple of years. He labored here and there, but something was missing in his life, he was unable to figure out what it was. Just something was not there. Oh yeah, he had tons of fun, with many friends. And yet, he knew that something was just not the way it was supposed to be. Alf, his old man, was almost ready for retirement, and he did not care about much any more. As long as he had his peace and could go to the pub, why would he care? He was not accustomed to show that he cared, but maybe he did, the old man. Olga seemed happy with the situation more or less that is, again, who knew?

Conrad worked hard. He never missed work, because he could not afford it; that was one thing Alf taught him well. "If you can drink," Alf used to say, "you can work."

Alf grew a lot more quiet in his old days.

"Leave me alone and I leave you alone," was his motto. Liz and that geek she married now had three children and often they visited Alf and Olga. Family ties started to get stronger again, and for a while one would think it had always been like that. If by coincidence Alf junior, Liz and all the children would visit it always ended up in a big party. There was no more hitting by the old fellow no more yelling and screaming by Olga. Things where just fine, yet something was missing in Conrad's life, but WHAT?

It was one year later, late in the summer Wren and Mary still worked at their jobs in the big factory. They were never more than just friends working the same old boring job, day in and day out. Wren had become a loner, he never was one for company he wanted to be by himself, he was not even looking for a girlfriend. Olga had dropped a couple of hints to Conrad.

"Do you think he likes boys rather than girls?" She used to ask him.

"Don't know," Conrad used to reply, "why don't you ask him?" that was about the extent of it, Conrad did not care for him and Wren did not care for Conrad. Things were just fine the way they were. Nevertheless, that Friday afternoon Wren asked Mary to go swimming at the public swimming pool. He needed all his courage, as it was the first girl he asked out, but it was a public place so he figured that it should be all right. At first Mary did not know whether to agree or not, would Mother allow her to go?

Conrad meets Mary again!

"Tell you what," she said, "I will meet you by the big pool, it will likely be about one o'clock in the afternoon, all right? The two liked each other as friends, they never had much more then a friendly word, romance was not in the cards.

As promised, Mary was by the pool that Sunday afternoon. She wore a full bathing suit with stripes, which made here look even slimmer. Wren was pleasantly surprised to see her. The two spent a couple of hours swimming then Wren invited Mary for a strawberry dessert at home. It was a nice walk home through the suburb, then passing some farmers' fields. Just at the outskirt of the big city was Wren and Conrad's new home.

"Well come on up," Wren invited Mary.

"Mother is home, I know it. We can listen to some records belonging to my older brother, have dessert and then you can take the city bus to go home. The bus stop is just over there; I will walk you there when it is time."

Mother was home, or Mary would have left. So they were sitting in the living room, listening to some records that Conrad collected. Conrad was very picky about his records. He cleaned them on a regular basis, he sorted them, and had each one listed. Unfortunately, Conrad just got home when they were listening to his favorite song. Wow, would you look at Conrad! Red-faced and mad as hell he started to yell at his brother.

"What the hell do you think you're doing?" He demanded to know. "You know damn well that these are my records, you know damn well that I don't like it when you handle them, you never clean them or put them back in place. Get the hell out of my records!" Mary, surprised by so much uproar over so little, got very quiet and shy.

"Well it is time for me to go home anyway, Wren could you please walk me to the bus stop?" Mary said.

"What was that?" She asked Wren on their way to the bus stop. "He can really get angry over little does he not?"

"Oh don't worry," Wren replied, "he is a loud mouth I will handle him when I get home."

Conrad did not notice Mary's lovely figure, her warm personality, her hair, or the way she walked... or didn't he? When Wren got home, Conrad picked a fight with him.

"What in the world was THAT?" Conrad wanted to know. "That girl has more make up on her face than a clown in the National Circus, her hair is held together with a layer of hairspray so thick, a hurricane would not be able to move it out of place."

"Oh shut up you idiot," Wren said with no emotion, "she is a nice girl. There is no reason for you to flip out like that. The next time I will knock your noggin flat, you dickhead, you are nothing but a hooligan." The two brothers went on for a little while longer until Alf demanded peace and quiet.

Not much longer and Conrad's life would change forever. It would turn around like a raging bull in the arena chasing a torero. Sometimes life can play tricks on you and you don't even realize it. Conrad knew that some things had to change. The Army was just around the corner to pick him up. Every young man at the tender age of nineteen would be physically examined and, if found able, at the age of twenty he would serve the Army for seventeen weeks, then three weeks every year thereafter, for eight years. It was a time not too many were looking forward to, but there was no way around it. It was not much different for Conrad. He knew his time was coming.

Summer went by pretty fast. It was early fall, when Wren asked Mary out again. They wanted to go and see a movie. Mary did not really want to go but did not want to disappoint Wren, so agreed to meet him downtown on the following Sunday.

"Conrad do you want to come with us? I have invited a girl from work and she is taking her sister with. I don't want to go alone," Wren asked.

Conrad, having already forgotten the previous encounter with the girl, agreed to go. They got themselves ready for the movie. Conrad knew how to behave around girls when he wanted to. So dressed in his Sunday suit and even a tie, the two approached the movie theatre where they were supposed to meet the girls. It was then that Conrad's life changed forever, so fast he did not know what happen to him. All he noticed was that beautiful girl in a pink dress. The sight of her hit Conrad like a speeding train. Her black, shoulder-length hair, curled at the end, complementing her soft, slightly oval face. She was the most beautiful girl he had ever seen. All these years she was right under his nose and he could not see further then his own shoes! *What was the matter with you Conrad, were you blind?*

Like all young men, Conrad blushed, not really knowing what to say to her, but one thing he knew for sure. "I am going to sit beside her," he thought to himself. He started to stutter a bit, he was so nervous. His brother Wren and Mary's sister did not even exist anymore. Best of all, it seemed that Mary felt the same way about him. So it was that the world around those two ceased to exist. Conrad knew right then and there, he would not let that beauty get away. It was different with this girl. She had kind of sad eyes, and the way she walked, talked, and laughed just electrified him. For the next couple of weeks he would walk around with the saddest eyes whenever he could not see her for a day or two. He had that stupid look on his face as all young men do, when they fall in love.

He was not hungry any more, had a hard time sleeping and one could only talk to him by hitting him first a couple of times to wake him up. Mind you, this also had its good impact. Suddenly he could not find much interest in getting together with his friends and getting drunk. He wanted to be left alone whenever Mary was restricted by her mother from seeing him and that was rather often. It was then that Olga started to sleep a bit better as she had seen the change taking place in Conrad; he stopped drinking, he started to pay attention to how he dressed; to make a long story short, he was a young man who had fallen in love so badly that it changed him for the better.

It got serious the two started to date steadily; every Saturday they were together, went to see a movie or went dancing, and were not to be separated again.

"Mary," Conrad said one Saturday evening while slowly dancing.

"I would like to introduce you to my parents, how do you feel about that?" He asked.

"I don't know Conrad," she whispered, "what if they don't like me?"

"Not like you? Who is there in this world that would not like you? Besides, it doesn't really matter anyway," he said. "I am going to marry you whether they like it or not," he added quite sure of himself. Mary just looked at him and said, "What makes you so sure I want to get married?" Conrad almost got a shock, he could feel that cold, ugly feeling crawling up his spine, he almost blacked out, as what she said was more than clear to him.

"I am just kidding!" Mary was quick to add when she noticed the surprised look in his face. "Of course I want to marry you, you know I love you Conrad, and there is nothing in this world that can keep us apart. You know we are a little young just yet, I am only seventeen, you are eighteen and you still have to go into the Army, so they can make a man out of you…" she carried on smiling after her last remark.

"I am scared my father constantly hit my mother, my mother always had boyfriends. I am scared that we could end up the same way, and I want to have a good family you know?" Conrad nodded in agreement.

"Yes my Love I know how you feel, I have the same problems at home, and I too want better things for myself and my family.

"Besides," she continued, "was that a proposal?" She tilted her head slightly and looked at him with the smile he could not resist.

"Oh, I am sorry Mary," Conrad quickly tried to better the situation for himself, "Mary, for me it was clear the Moment I saw you that I would only marry you or stay single forever."

"Conrad," Mary answered, "It will be you; no other man will walk me down the isle, I do feel the same way."

Conrad, relieved, squeezed her a bit tighter, so as if to say, no one shall ever come between us. So the two slow danced until the early morning hours, then Conrad walked her home, gently kissing her good bye on the doorstep and then he was on his way home. Happy and wide open to accept all that was to come their way Conrad knew that, as long as Mary would be by his side, nothing could go wrong. If only they would know the future! But it is a good thing in life that one cannot see into the future, or he would have packed up Mary right then and there and would have run away with her, far, far away where no one could come between them.

On one of the following Sundays, Mary was invited to Conrad's parents for Sunday dinner. That was quite a step it was a big hurdle. Conrad, for days, pleaded with his mother, "Oh please" he would argue with her, "she is such a nice, beautiful girl and I know you would like her." Finally Olga agreed to have this young lady over for a Sunday meal; after all she had seen the change in him over the last months.

When Sunday finally came, Conrad picked Mary up at the train station. It was a fair bit to walk, but that gave him more time alone with her, and she did not really mind either. At least, this way they could be by themselves, holding hands and talking the same nonsense all young people talk when they're in love. No matter whether they are as far away as China, Russia, Siberia, or America. Whatever the language, the words are the same, the look in their eyes, the way they hold hands, so why should it be different here in small Bellach at the feet of the Jura Mountains?

Mary left quite an impression on Olga, and Alf… well Alf was Alf. He was nice to Mary and friendly and that was all Conrad wanted from him. Mary politely got up after dinner, cleaned the dishes, helped Olga however she could, and Conrad was so proud of her.

Mary and Alf never met at work. It was such a big company. With thousands of people, it was impossible to know them all, but now after that Sunday he knew her, he was very fond of her. That girl could have asked big Alf any favor, and he would have been there for her.

Conrad and Mary's love was sweet and innocent, that was a time in which the two grew closer together. Of course, Conrad wanted to discover more, but a quick slap on his wandering fingers quickly reminded him where to stop. The heavenly violins played nonstop around the two.

They spent their spare time hiking or dancing. Every single minute they had to spend, they would spend together. Sometimes they would share a Saturday night with Alf and Olga, but not too often as the old couple had very little understanding of their need to kiss whenever possible.

It was strange, Mary never asked Conrad to her home, and when it was an issue with Conrad she would say, "Later my love, right now Mother has other plans."

"Oh well so be it, sooner or later she will meet me"... anyway so he thought.

The day came when, for Conrad, Heaven, the world and all things broke apart, literally. It was on a Friday night, when the phone call came to Conrad's house. It was Mary, her voice trembled, she was chocking back tears. Conrad just listened stone-faced, shivering with anger. What he just heard could not be true it was a voice from another world, so unthinkable so unreal so inhuman. He was not able to speak for a while, he just listened, unable to hold back tears himself. Finally after pulling himself together he said, "Mary don't worry I will come and get you, wherever you are, just hold on trust me I'll be there."

Olga noticed a sudden change in Conrad.
"What is the matter Conrad?" she asked.
"WHAT'S the matter?" He yelled at her.
"WHAT'S the matter? I tell you what the matter is. Mary's Mother apparently does not like me. She made arrangements to move Mary up into a small village over by the Alps, far, far away, but I will get her trust me!" He was quick to add.

"Jesus Conrad, don't get in trouble, think about it, the pain will go away and you will eventually find another girlfriend." *WRONG.*

"Oh no, not me, you so-called grown ups, you short-sighted monsters. You heartless individuals, you have presented me with a bill I am not willing to foot. Besides you can trust me, I will find the house of the aunt where my Mary is, if I have to walk from here to the moon and back!" Which, of course, was nonsense since even the Americans had not arrived there themselves yet. He was dead serious though, and Olga sensed that something was going to happen.

Conrad was a walking nightmare over the following weeks. Then out of the blue he announced to his parents, "I am going to Zurich, I have landed a job at Swiss Air. I have to go there to find myself." Conveniently forgetting to mention that it was a hell of a lot closer to Frutigen, where Mary was, as he found out. It did not take him long to find out where his girl was; her younger sister, Lilly, knew Wren, and Wren was willing to help Conrad, since he was in so much pain.

    Conrad did not waste much time; the first day at work he had already made a new friend, and the best thing about this new friend was, he had a car, and he liked Conrad. Conrad talked constantly about Mary, his lost love. He talked about her so much, and seemed to be in such constant pain that his friend agreed to drive with him the next Saturday up to the village of Frutigen, in the Alps. It was only about a two hours drive, but Conrad was not able to sleep all week and on the weekend, he was a complete wreck. He had a plan, and he was not willing to share it with anybody. He would stick to it, no matter what the outcome would be; consequences for his actions did not exist for him, and if they came, he would brush them aside. His one and only goal was to get Mary, no matter what.

    Early Saturday morning the two friends were well on their way before sunrise.

    "Eight o'clock is soon enough," his friend tried to bargain with Conrad the night before.

    "Are you nuts?" He replied. "What if Mary wants to go hiking, or she is going to have to work on the farm? No way man, make sure you pick me up at four o'clock in the morning at the latest, or I clock you one on your stubborn forehead, you hear me?" Conrad pleaded. His friend finally agreed to pick him up at four. He realized that there was no bargaining with this crazy, mad man but he liked him, otherwise he would have stuck to his way, because he had to work till midnight at the airport. That argument was not good enough for Conrad and he knew how to plea bargain, he even asked him to go home early, then Conrad would pay him for the hours lost. Oh no, no more games, he almost went nuts, he was close to collapse, but he would not give up.

"If there is a will, there is a way." Which Conrad changed to: "If there is a will, there is a Mary." Day by day that was all he was able to think about. Poor little fellow, a world so big and he was so alone, oh how he hated all these so-called grown ups.

On Saturday morning at three-thirty a.m. Conrad was already outside waiting for his friend to arrive, checking his watch every five minutes. It was heart breaking if you could have watched him. Finally, five minutes late his friend arrived.

"What the hell took you so long you sleepy head?" Conrad nervously asked jumping in the car. "Let's go, let's go we don't have all day." Like a crusader Conrad was sitting next to his friend, all that was missing was the shining armor.

"Is this all this old piece of junk can do? We are on the Autobahn and you are going 130 kilometers an hour; step on it you lame duck!"

"Listen if you don't stop pestering me you can walk," his friend said. He did not like it if someone put down his beloved car, friend or not friend. Conrad sensed the seriousness of it and finally shut up, at least for a while. Then it was already nine o'clock Saturday morning, they arrived at the little mountain village where he knew Mary was.

"Let's go for breakfast," Conrad suggested, "there I can ask my way to Mary."

"WHAT? You don't even know where she is?" His friend asked.

"Nope," Conrad said, "but I will find her." And he sure did, after asking his way around, he finally found the farmhouse where Mary was supposed to be.

"Park the car over there by the restaurant," Conrad demanded of his friend, "then wait there, I will come and get you when we are ready."

"What the hell do you mean, by 'when *we* are ready?'" His friend asked with a hunch not promising too much good. But by now he was in with Conrad, and had to stick to him come what may. He made the sign of a cross on his forehead, rolled his eyes and made his way over to the restaurant where he waited patiently, willing not to be too surprised of the things to come.

Conrad paced the street up and down in front of the place where he knew Mary lived. The minutes slowly drifted by, Conrad knew that Mary had to go grocery shopping for her aunt, but he did not know where. Any minute she had to show up. Finally there she was! He almost fainted, when he saw her coming around the corner. She had no idea that Conrad was about to approach her. Slowly he made his way across the street, and then she saw him. Her knees wobbly as if they were filled with rubber, she put her grocery bags down and started running towards him. They flew into each other's arms. Hugging and kissing, looking at one another in disbelief.

"Oh my god Conrad, what are you doing here? Why did you not call me? When did you get here? How long have you waited for me? What are we going to do?" The questions just rained down on Conrad, some questions he had no answers to, all he knew was she was in his arms, nothing else mattered, she was his again and he was not willing to let go, ever. They did not realize that the people stopped walking and watched them, some with a smile on their face, some in disbelief at how they hugged and kissed, and hugged again. Gently stroking her hair, "Mary, I have not seen you in two months, look how beautiful you are… Oh my love," Conrad stuttered

"What are we going to do? I cannot let you go again you have no idea how much I missed you," Mary said. Conrad slowly gained back his self-confidence.

"Don't you worry my beautiful, wonderful little dove, we will find a way, and this time I will not lose sight of you again trust me." And trust him she did.

"First" he started to explain, "we will go and talk to your aunt; I will tell her that I like to invite to go hiking for a couple of days, and if she asks who else will be with us, we tell her that there are fifteen people with us; that will convince her that nothing is going to happen, and that you do not need a chaperon. It also gives you a good excuse to pack up all your clothes, and most necessities. What you must leave behind we will go and shop for in Zurich."

"Zurich?" Mary asked wide-eyed.

"Mary we are standing here in the middle of the street, let's go and introduce me to your aunt, then you and I will go for a short walk, and I will explain to you what's coming, ok?" He said.
A little disconcerted over so much secrecy, she agreed.

Aunt Elizabeth was no problem for Conrad, as he was neatly dressed and well mannered. Conrad convinced her that there would be no problem going hiking, as they were a whole group of young people.

"So, now Mary and I would like to go for a short little walk, as we have not seen each other in over two months, and have a lot to talk about." Arm in arm the two left the house, walking towards the restaurant where his friend excitedly waited for them to come back. He was in the Garden Restaurant as the two approached him.

"Could you please wait a little while longer? We will be right back," Conrad asked, forgetting to introduce Mary to him.

The two lovebirds went off. Holding each one other so close as if to say, "Nothing shall come between us anymore." You could see the love the two shared, the passion, the electrifying energy between them. They had no eyes for their surroundings, or what was going on in front, in the back or right and left of them. All they were seeing was each other, you could have run them over with a truck and they would not have noticed. Such love and passion was made in heaven. They were nervous and trembling, as they walked about the little town.

"I cannot let you go again," Mary stated. "If you leave me I will go crazy. What are we going to do?"

"Don't worry my love I have a plan, all will be well, I will never again let you out of my sight, you will be by my side for the rest of our lives," Conrad stated passionately. He did not have a plan, but that was all he could say at the Moment. He still had a few hours to make one up; he had to think fast, time flies when a young man is close to the woman of his dreams. Nevertheless, it did not take Conrad too long to develop a strategy, a plan so perfect it could in no way go wrong. He just knew that this was the right thing to do; as a matter of fact it was the only thing to do.

"How is your aunt Elizabeth?" He suddenly asked.

"What do you mean by that? Surprised, Mary questioned him back.

"Well how is she toward your mother, is she nice to you? How does she treat you?" Conrad explained.

"She does not like my mother," Mary stated. "She never agreed with her. She does not like her lifestyle, but she treats me nicely, and is always fair with me. But what does she have to do with us?" Mary wanted to know.

"I need her to like me, and I have my reasons for it."

"Of course she will like you Conrad," Mary assured him. "Why would she not like you? Tell me."

"Mary, I need you to trust me one hundred percent; are you willing to move with me to Zurich?"

"Yes of course," Mary said, "next time you come up here I will be ready."

"What do you mean 'next time'?" Conrad almost collapsed. "Today sweetheart, this very afternoon you will be with me in that car heading for Zurich."

Mary blushed. "How can we do that? She hesitated.

"That is easy my love, just trust me. Max get your car ready, we will meet you in about half an hour in front of the house, right under their nose," Conrad said to his friend as they walked by the restaurant.

"Conrad please don't forget, I have to start work at eight o'clock tonight, we need to leave here at three at the latest," his friend said.

"All right all right, no need to get nervous, you just have to drive faster," he said with a smile.

Back at aunt Elizabeth's house, Conrad started to talk to Mary's aunt about the hiking route that they had planned to take. He talked about how wonderful a weekend it was going to be. Mary, shy as always, sitting besides Conrad at the kitchen table, had a hard time not showing how nervous she was about the whole thing, but she wanted to be with Conrad, and there was no way to convince her otherwise.

Finally, Conrad stated that Mary should go get ready packing so they could meet the rest of the group. That was the time when aunt Elizabeth asked Conrad to give her a quick hand over by the stable.

"I have some heavy wood there I need in the kitchen, and would really appreciate it if you could help me. In the mean time Mary can go and get herself ready. Mary," she said, "make sure to pack enough clothes, it is getting cool now at night, and one never knows what comes their way. Better to have too many clothes than not enough." You know how fast the wetter can change in the mountains.

So Aunt Elizabeth and Conrad walked over to the stable, leaving a relieved Mary behind. Quick she was to get upstairs to her room and pack as much as possible into her suitcase. She had to leave quite a bit behind but that did not matter now. The main thing was that she was by Conrad's side.

Short before the stable, Aunt Elizabeth turned around, looking at Conrad with a friendly but stern expression on her face.

"Listen young man," she said, "that you are going hiking is the biggest bull I ever heard in a long time. I was married for many, many years, and my husband had made up more excuses than you will ever dream of. I always caught him in his tracks, but that is not important now you hear? There is no group of fifteen people in town to go hiking, and you know that damn well" she continued. Conrad's face turned from green to red, then back to white as fresh snow, his knees started to get soft as butter in the warm afternoon sun.

"However, don't worry" she added, "I will be with you two all the way, I am not quite sure what you have in mind, but you will tell me now and I will help you. I have seen Mary over the last two months and I know damn well that she missed you, besides, I like you Conrad you look like a young man who knows what he wants right? Now all you have to do is explain to me what you two are going to do." A stone so big fell from Conrad's chest that he was afraid they could hear that a mile away. He wanted to trust the friendly aunt, but did not really know where to start. He searched for words. He was looking for an explanation, but could not really find the gateway. Elizabeth had a good sense for what the young man needed.

"Tell me Conrad, why did you let Mary go away from home to come up here? Why did you not stop her right there? Here, sit down and tell me your side of the story, come on, let's talk."

Mary, up in her room, peeked out the window, and, afraid someone would see her, was hiding behind the curtains, looking down at the two by the stable. She could not understand what was going on down there, "why are Conrad and aunt Elizabeth sitting down now? There is no time to sit down," she thought to herself. "What do they have to talk about?"

"Well," Conrad started to explain, "there was really no time for me to do anything; Mary called me one evening and said that her mother was sending her away, as she did not want me to date Mary. By the time I went by their house, Mary was long gone. I have talked to Mary's sister outside, but she was not allowed to tell where they brought Mary. My brother Wren finally found out and told me. So I went to Zurich to work for Swiss Air, as it is closer to Frutigen than to my parents' house. Now I am here, and I want my Mary back." Conrad was almost in tears, as he explained his side of the story to aunt Elizabeth and she never stopped him from talking, she just listened to the young man's story, and what his plans were once they arrived in Zurich. What she heard convinced her enough to help the two. It all made sense, what he had told her.

"Well Conrad, let me tell you one thing" she said after a long, nerve-wrecking minute. "Your story fits exactly my sister's story. You two look to me as if you are dead serious, and I know that if I wanted to stop you two, you would find another way, right?"

"Yup" was all confused Conrad could say.

"So here is my plan. Go and get your friend over by the restaurant, I will cook dinner for all of you then, well then," she said, "it is up to you and Mary."

What was it with aunt Elizabeth? Conrad had never seen a grown up that agreed with him so much. Maybe it was Elizabeth's way to get back at her sister down in the big city, maybe she just loved a good love story. Maybe she dreamed of her younger years, when she waited for her prince to come along like that and take her away. Maybe she just knew that working against the two would only have made matters worse. She had seen Mary for two months now and she knew that the girl suffered from a broken heart, and to fix a broken heart, well, that was no easy task.

Mary, still standing behind the curtain, watched in horror as Conrad walked away. Aunt Elizabeth was on her way back to the kitchen, and she saw Mary up in the window.

"Come on down Mary!" She yelled as she entered the kitchen. "Don't worry, Conrad will be right back."

A relieved Mary came down the wooden stairs.

"Where did Conrad go?" She asked.

"Don't worry he will be right back, in the mean time you may give me a hand to get dinner ready, otherwise you will never be ready to leave for Zurich with Conrad.

Mary, of course not knowing what the two had talked about over by the stable, almost fainted. Fainting is a thing all lovers have in common and it is the best way to get out of almost anything. Just faint and all is fine.

"Don't worry," Elizabeth was quick to add, "Conrad told me what is on his mind. I have watched you for a while now and I just know that there will be no harm in letting you go."

"But what are you going to tell my mother?" Mary wanted to know.

"Nothing," her aunt replied.

"Nothing?" Mary asked with disbelief in her voice.

"But, somehow we have to tell her that I am there and not here anymore" Mary added.

"You are so smart, you little, wonderful girl," Elizabeth said with a smile.

"Conrad promised me that within a week he would have straightened things out with her; no matter what, he does have an idea on how to turn things around for you two. As far as I know, he has also talked to his parents, and they are fully supporting you two. It seems that only my sister has no clue about how much you missed each other."

Conrad and Max had entered the kitchen, overhearing the last couple of words.

"Don't you worry Mary," Conrad ended the conversation, "I have it all figured out. We will be all right."

It was sort of an adventure for aunt Elizabeth. She was crazy enough to help the two to escape…If only she knew that Conrad had no idea yet where to put Mary; he had no room for her, but he booked three days off work to find her a room, and he was so sure that all would be ok, there was no doubt in his mind. In addition, he forgot to mention that he had not talked to his parents in over four weeks. Nevertheless, who would guess that he would be able to lie?

"So now sit down or dinner will get cold," aunt Elizabeth demanded, "and if you two could be polite and keep your lips apart while you are eating, then maybe you will be able to get some food down your throats" she added smiling.

Suddenly Mary, with a shudder, asked, "What if my mother calls before we are able to straighten things out? She would be furious."

"Oh don't worry she won't" Elizabeth assured her, "she never called the last two months, why would she call now?"

"She is too busy with her new boyfriend anyway" Conrad added. That cleared Mary's last doubts.

"So, now it is time to get ready" Conrad demanded. "We have to go now, or Max will be late for his shift."

"Mary, if you have to leave some things behind, don't worry, you can come back and get them later," Elizabeth explained.

"Just make sure that you are all right, and you Conrad, take good care of her you hear?"

"I sure will" said a smiling and relieved young man. He liked aunt Elizabeth and almost, but only almost, felt sorry that he had not told her the whole truth.

The packing went fast, all they could stuff into the small car was a suitcase and a couple of cartons, which contained the bare minimum that a woman can live with.

Early in the afternoon, the three friends were on their way to Zurich. Could you have watched them, you would have seen them beaming with excitement, hugging and kissing in the back seat, the two were in their own world. Nothing, and I mean absolutely nothing, could be done to make those two any happier. If Shakespeare had seen them, he would have thrown out his script for *Romeo and Juliet*.

"So, what are you going to do now?" Max asked, as the two took a break from a long, intense kiss. Conrad thought for a Moment then with a smile said, "Max you will drive us to the airport; right now I don't have a room but come Monday, it will not be hard to find one." Mary looked at him with a big question mark on her face.

"What do you mean you have no room?" Mary asked.

"Well," Conrad replied, "I do have a room, but there are five more guys and the old landlady will not allow girls up in our room. Come Monday, you and I will go and find a room for you, my love. In the meantime, we will stay at the airport for a couple of days. Nobody will ever question us, many travelers sleep on the benches. In the morning, we can have a shower in the public washroom, disappear for the day, then come back at night."

Mary was excited, she had never seen the big city and its bustling life, and after all it was an adventure! Conrad seemed so strong, so sure of himself that she could not help but give him a big hug followed by "…Oh I love you sooo much."

Conrad was proud of himself.

"What are we going to do about my mother?" Mary kept asking.

"Oh that is easy my dear, tonight you will call her, and I have a story for you to tell her. You will tell your mother that you and your girlfriend have found a job in Zurich and that you would like to go there. I am sure that she will agree, since she does not care too much about what you are doing as long as you are away from me right?" Mary nodded in agreement, impressed that, obviously, Conrad had it all under control.

Late that afternoon they arrived at the airport. Mary had never seen so many different people.

"Chinese people, Africans, Americans, Russians, you name it," Conrad explained proudly.

So the two settled in, Conrad was all proud and beaming with excitement, showing Mary the whole airport, big planes taking off or arriving at the other terminal. He knew all the ins and outs, and Mary said to herself, " I know I can trust him with my life, nothing will keep us apart anymore."

"When are we going to call my mother?" Mary asked.

" Not here Mary, there is too much noise from the intercom and she maybe get a hint when she hears it. We have to go to the city, which is only half hour away by bus. There we will find a nice quiet restaurant where you can call." So it was done. As Conrad predicted, Mary's mother did not care too much about where her daughter was. She was too busy with her boyfriend and did not want to spend too much time over something she could not control, that was too time consuming for her.

"Ok then Mary," her mother said. "If you think that you can make it in Zurich, go ahead, but please keep me informed on what you are doing, I am just glad I got you away form that Conrad."

"It was as Conrad had predicted. Nobody cared about the two. Why should they? They had their own worries, besides, what they did not know could not hurt them.

So the two started living on their own and that was just ok with them. The first couple of days Conrad and Mary were busy looking for an apartment. At night they would settle into the airport, using the public benches to sleep on, acting like travelers. They would pretend to have just arrived and were waiting for the connecting flight. With a suitcase beside his or her bench, no one ever even dared to question them. Every other night, the two used another terminal, just to make sure that security would not get too suspicious.

It was rather easy for Mary to find a room, a friendly family was just eager to take her in. They were very fond of Mary, as she was a polite young lady. They would allow Conrad to visit as long as he did not stay overnight. They had sensed that something was not quite right with the situation, and started to question Mary. Slowly the whole truth came out. Mary could not lie to those nice people. Conrad also started to trust them and the two spilled their guts. The couple roared laughing, over so much enthusiasm; they admired their adventurous minds.

"Ok," the man finally said. "We will watch over you two. Mary, you can stay with us as long as you want. Conrad, you may visit Mary anytime. At this time we do not want you to stay over night, as we have small kids of our own. If you need anything, let us know." The two were more than relieved, now they had something they could call a home.

Mary got a job as a sales associate at a big department store where she sold toys. Conrad kept working at the airport, and to improve their finances, worked part-time as a security guard. He would sometimes work the night shift, when he would stand in front of a jeweler's store, pacing up and down the street all night. It was kind of a scary thought for Mary to know him all alone out there, facing the dangers of the night. Conrad needed to do that to help both of them out; Mary did not have the means to support herself.

Finally, life had acquired a meaning for him. He had someone to take care of, someone who loved him, and thought the world of him. Life was just wonderful for the two and, as expected, nobody from back home really cared for what was going on in their young lives. There was the occasional phone call home, other than that it was quiet and Elli, Mary's mother, had no idea that the two were together again.

Sometimes Mary would baby-sit the two children of her landlord, but not too often. Most times she and Conrad were occupied with exploring the city and life itself. Saturday night dancing was a given as the lovebirds were excellent dancers, and seemed to be one when together on the dance floor. Conrad loved to hold her in his arms, swaying to the wonderful soft music. The two never liked the trendy hard rock, The Beatles, or The Rolling Stones. They enjoyed the kind of music they could slow dance to, holding each other close, feeling each other's warm, soft body. Every minute they had a chance they would kiss, long and demanding. On one occasion a passerby made some remark, Conrad, now a little more secure of himself, just turned around and said, "Life saver, you know?" The Lady kept walking. Oh how wonderful life can be when you're in love, in love with so much passion, know that your partner is the one and only one you will ever love and care for. You have made the right choice and you know it. Oh no, not the foolish sex-driven love, where you never get out of bed, and then eventually you get tired of it. No, not that one. Rather the one you know it is the right choice for now and for all eternity. Sure, the two had hard times, not knowing where to turn for their desires, for a love that burned so hot you could grill a steak on it. It was reassuring to have such a love and, as the old saying goes, "Where there is a will, there is a way."

  The only real hard time was around Christmas. That was the time when Mary's mother would like to call Mary and ask her to come home for the event. It was the same with Conrad's parents.

  "**Now what**?" They asked each other. It was the older couple that came up with a solution, a solution so simple the two could never have thought of it themselves.

"Why don't you two just take the train back home, then short before you arrive to your hometown you separate, spend a day or two at home then come back, suggesting that you have to work. You think you are able to make it, one or two days without seeing each other?" The older man asked. Finally, they agreed that they were not likely to die if they separated for a day or two. Off they went and as discussed, shortly before arriving in their hometowns they separated, but only a short distance, as they could not stand to lose sight of each other. It was not likely that someone would be at the train station, but the two wanted to be sure not to be surprised. Sure enough, no one was there to greet either one, which left the two with a chance for a last kiss before taking off in different directions.

It went smoothly for both of them, nobody suspected anything and two days later they were in each other's arms again. The train had not left the station as they were entangled with one another. The people around them were non-existent. After all, they had not seen each other for two days, and that is a long, long time. Actually it was only one and a half day, because on their way home they chose the last possible train, and on their way back the first one, that made up for a full thirty-three hours fifteen minutes and twenty-five seconds. One breakfast with the family; one lunch, and one dinner, but who was counting? If you are in love that much, going to the corner store alone is a long time.

Back in Zurich, it was now close to New Year. The weather was cold and fresh snow covered the streets. Conrad still patrolled the streets at night, when he would rather be with Mary, but he had no choice as they had to pay rent and food had to be bought. Mary always cooked for both of them, and Conrad was so proud of her, because she could cook like a pro. She would ask the couple to use the kitchen.

"I want to cook for Conrad," she always explained. On some occasion, she put candles on the table, and they had dinner like a real married couple. It was then that the older couple started to put some romance back in to their lives. It almost seemed as if they learned from the two how to be romantic again. Suddenly the older fellow started to surprise his wife with flowers. The wife surprised him with a little extra makeup or a new sexy dress. So the arrangement was a good one for all involved. Conrad knew that he had made the right choice.

For New Year's Eve, the two had plans. It was their first real New Year's Eve party together, dancing, laughing, having fun all night with their new friends from the big city. Life was lived to the fullest, as if it would end tomorrow. One could feel the excitement the two shared, the love for life in general and for each other in particular.

Life can also be harsh, cruel, and unpredictable. It has its own twists and turns and when least expected it can hit you with a force you never thought possible. Life can also lift you sky high, where all colors are one: "pink," the air filled with the sound of heavenly violins, with Cherubs circling you. Then with brute force can throw you back down on the ground and into the ditch so hard that you just have one and only one thought. You want to die, right then and there. Such a life-threatening event took place with young Mary and Conrad, in the form of a letter from the long forgotten Swiss Army.

When Conrad got to Mary's home that night, she was sitting at the kitchen table with the people with whom she lived. The two kids were in bed, as they were not allowed to watch such tragedy. Mary had the letter, which was actually addressed to Conrad, picked up at the post office, and with butterflies in her stomach, opened it. It was a friendly invitation for Conrad to join the Swiss Army for full seventeen weeks. The problem was they did not ask him to join, oh no, they ordered him to join. Conrad was supposed to be in Biere March the 12th, 1969 at exactly twelve pm. This was a remote site, three hundred kilometers away, and Conrad would only be allowed to go home every other weekend. Do you have any idea how far three hundred kilometers is, when two people miss each other? They made it quite clear that he was not to be late, or else. *Or else* meant Army jail-time for starters, then go home and join the Army with the next batch, the coming summer, which was much harder than in the spring. Of course this was no tragedy, but you tell that to two young people that are so much in love. Besides the

Army issue was not a favored one among young people in Switzerland.

Franz, the older man, his wife Joanne together with Mary were sitting at the kitchen table, when Conrad arrived that night. Right away he sensed that something terrible must have happened. Mary with a long face just got up and greeted him with a big hug, not wanting to let go of him. Finally he pried himself loose and asked, "what's wrong my dear? Did your Mother find out about us?" But then he spotted the letter on the table. He knew it was coming, and for a while now he tried to prepare Mary for the event, but she usually brushed it off, and sealed his lips with a smacking kiss.

"Come on you two," Franz interjected. "It is not that bad to serve the Army. Believe me it also can be fun at times, and you will make a lot of new friends. Besides it is an honor to be able to serve the Army. Not everybody is eligible, like a man with criminal record, health problems and so on.

"Mary can stay with us until you come back. And we let you sleep over on the weekends when you can come home. Now that would make good sense, don't you think?" This sounded good and the two almost agreed. When you are that young, and that much in love, it's as if there is a chemical in both the male's and the female's body that prevents their brains from thinking rationally. You are smart enough to see the consequences, smart enough to agree with what the "older" people tell you. But this chemical just shuts you down, telling you that no matter what you have agreed to, it is all wrong.

The discussion went on for quite a while, as the two were not really convinced that leaving Mary alone in the big city was such a good idea. Then suddenly Conrad said, "Mary my love, maybe it is best that you stay here until I can come back. I have to go and have no choice in that matter, you know as well as I do. I am not really too fond of going to jail, the Army jail is well known for being not too people-friendly."

The sudden change of mind should have alarmed Franz and Joanne, but it was getting late, tomorrow was another day, and by then the two would have accepted what was not in their hands to change.

"Oh Con," she whispered in his ear, hugging him under the arch of the door and kissing him good-bye for the night. She always called him Con when she was upset over something.

"What are we going to do now? I don't want to stay in this big city all by myself, I know we have a lot of friends, but it would not be the same without you. I do not make enough money to pay for rent, food and all the other things. And you are not making any money in the Army." So what were those two thinking?

"How can we get through this?" they asked themselves.

Mary said, "When you can come home on the weekends, you are on the train for six hours, you will be here at ten o'clock on Saturday night, and you have to leave Sunday by three o'clock. That is an awful situation.

"I cannot and will not go back home either; Mother would find out that we are dating again, unless we don't see each other on the weekends. That would ultimately lead to the situation that we don't see each other until you have finished your service in the Army, and that is not until late June. We just have to find another way."

"Sweetheart let me think this over till tomorrow, I promise you I will find a solution for us that will work," Conrad said. Did Conrad just say, "let me think?" yes indeed he did, and that in itself is a contradiction in terms. Young men in love do not think, period. They believe that they think, but that special chemical in their bodies is working contrary to rational thought.

Overnight, Conrad brainstormed about what to do, and in the early morning hours he found a solution so great and so perfect that he was absolutely sure that no one could prevent them any longer from being together. Not Mary's mother, not Conrad's parents, not the Army. Not that he would have tried to avoid going into the Army, that was unthinkable, but he came up with an idea so great, he just knew was better than anything that had been discussed the night before. He was sure that Mary would agree. Just as long as the two kept their mouths shut until they decided it was time to fill-in the rest of the world.

The next morning Conrad placed a phone call to his mother, Olga.

"Mom" he started, "do you remember Mary?" He asked.

"Oh uh yeah why do you ask? Have you not forgotten her yet?" Olga replied.

"Oh no, no way" he replied. "As a matter of fact we are dating again."

"What do you mean by that?" Olga demanded to know. "What if her mother finds out? You are going to be in big trouble young man!" Olga lamented.

"You know she does not like you and there is nothing you can do. Leave Mary alone and come home, you know I like Mary very much, but under the circumstances, it is best to stay away."

Now that was not what Conrad wanted to hear. He sensed that his plan had to be changed. There was no counting on the old folks for support, so slowly he started to change direction with his mother.

"You know" he continued, "I have to go into the Army in two months, they called me in for service up to Biere. On the weekends I would like to come home, it is too far to drive to Zurich every weekend, and it would make more sense for me to stay with you folks."

Olga was delighted, as it seemed that there was not much behind the story of the two dating again, otherwise he would be insisting on going to Zurich.

"So what is Mary doing then?" She asked.

"Well, she has a job near Zurich. I am not quite sure, I have seen her once or twice that's all." Conrad made up his story as fast as he was talking.

Olga was convinced and agreed that he should come home over the weekends.

"So that is settled," Conrad thought to himself. The next phone call he placed was to Mary at work.

"My love," he started, "I pick you up tonight after you finish your shift, I am off work for the next two days, I will invite you for dinner at that romantic restaurant, remember?" He asked. Mary all happy that they had a little time for each other, agreed to meet him at the entrance by the big door, at the department store where she worked.

After that phone call, Conrad took a long, hot shower. He paid extra attention to details as he shaved himself clean, took out his best Sunday suit, and then went for a leisurely walk down by the river. He had a lot of thinking to do, oh not that he did not know what to do, but how to explain his strategy to lovely Mary that was his main concern right then. Shortly before it was time to pick up Mary, he went to a flower shop just around the corner from her place and bought a dozen long-stem roses, red as blood.

That was the way Mary saw him standing there on that cold, snowy winter day. She flew into his arms, happily accepting the roses, which earned him an extra kiss and a long hug.

After Mary had a quick shower, she returned to Conrad who passionately waited in the living room. She was dressed in a knee-high gown that fit her body so nicely, as it was tailored just to her. Somehow she felt that it must be something special what was on Conrad's mind, and she wanted to look her best.

The setting at the restaurant was very romantic. Dimmed lights, tables for two all around, a large aquarium with tropical fish in the center, mood- setting music, flowers placed all over the restaurant. Discreet waiters and waitresses whisked them to a table in a far corner, as they had enough experience knowing about who wants to sit where. This young couple definitely needed to be left alone.

"What is the occasion?" Mary asked, after they placed the order for their drinks. "It is not my birthday or yours, and it is in the midst of January with not much going on."

"First of all" Conrad started, "you know how much I love you and that nothing in the world can keep us apart anymore right?" Mary nodded in agreement, her eyes all lit up. Conrad was a little afraid of what he had to bring to Mary's attention, but he had made up his mind earlier and now short on words he worked to clear his throat, so he could talk in a normal voice.

"Mary" he started again, "do you want to marry me?" The waiter who just approached the table and overheard Conrad's question stopped in his tracks and returned to his place, waiting until they would call him. He knew that to interrupt now would have been trouble. Mary blushed with excitement, lowered her eyes and softly but determined said, "Yes, I do Conrad." He almost fell off his chair, it was never in question for him that she would not say yes, but now that she said it, it almost blew him away.

"Waiter, could we please order a bottle of wine, the best you have?" Conrad added. "We have to celebrate."

"May I be the first to congratulate you?" The experienced waiter said. Both accepted, a little shy and blushing.

That was step one in Conrad's plan, the next step would be a little harder as he needed Mary's cooperation to go a little further. Conrad waited until after dessert. He did not want to have too much stress put on the issue, so, "One step at the time, don't rush, let it sink in," he thought.

After a delicious meal of "Zurich Gschnaetzlet," a delicacy in Switzerland made of chopped veal in a wine sauce, blended smoothly with cream, and together with the wine the two consumed, it had its impact on the way their brains worked. Slowly, Conrad worked his way toward the big question he was about to unleash onto unsuspecting Mary.

"Darling" he started, "in two and a half months I will be in the Army, and I will miss you terribly. I can't stand the thought of you all alone here, I won't see you for weeks, but there is something we can do so nobody is ever able to keep us apart.

"What do you have in mind?" Mary asked. "Well" he continued, "if we can meet in our hometown, when I get home on the weekend, then we are able to have four more hours to ourselves."

"My mother would get suspicious and I am sure she also would have some questions for me," Mary argued.

"You see my love," Conrad picked up the conversation again, "I thought you could move in with my parents, they have an extra room, and I know they like you very much. Besides" he continued, now he was ready to drop the bomb, "if you are pregnant then I just know they will help us." Mary gasped for air, pregnant? She repeated as if she had a hearing problem.

"Yup," Conrad said, "pregnant." Mary thought for a little while then smiling she said, " That is not a bad idea." Now it was Conrad's turn to gasp for air. He did not expect such an easy outcome.

"Conrad," Mary whispered, "it is in the midst of the winter, there is snow on the ground, we don't have a room to ourselves, so how do you want to achieve that?" She asked. Then with a grin on her face that Conrad loved so much she added "Oh I know, I just go to Franz and Joanne, tell them hey listen up you two, I need your bedroom for a while because I want to get pregnant."

"No" Conrad smiled, "I have another idea. We will spend a romantic two days over the coming weekend, out in the country, rent a motel room and never come out of it until Sunday night."

"Hmmm" Mary smiled, "you really have thought of everything haven't you, you little bugger? But yes, I already want to marry you, why not go all the way to make us happy. And a little one will only add to our lives."

They were all excited, and were more than willing to make it work. Late into the night, the two spent time at the restaurant, discussing how it all would work out for them and that both parents would not have a choice but to go along with it. By the time Mary would have the baby, she would be past the age of eighteen, then nobody could prevent them from getting married.

Conrad escorted Mary back to her home; now they shared a wonderful secret, which they would not discuss with anyone.

The week dragged on as both looked forward to the weekend with excitement. Mary told Franz and Joanne that the following weekend she would not be there.

"We want to go to a friend's place down by the lake." They reminded her to be careful, but did not worry, as they knew she would be in safe company with Conrad.

Conrad was by himself anyway, therefore did not have to make excuses for anybody.

Early Saturday morning, Conrad picked Mary up. What happened that weekend I won't elaborate on, but they tried hard, and the owner of the motel had a big smile and a lot of sympathy for the two as they left after paying the bill on Sunday night.

Conrad of course accompanied Mary back to her place.

"How was the weekend?" Franz and Joanne asked the two.

"Oh we did a lot of dancing, singing and playing games," Conrad explained.

"We had a real good time," Mary added with a smile. Mary had changed, only a little bit, but Franz and Joanne could not help noticing it. She seemed to act a little more mature suddenly, a little more dream-like also. They had no explanation for it, they just knew something had changed. Conrad also showed way more care when picking Mary up, his first question always was "How do you feel my love?" That had changed from "What are we going to do tonight?"

As if it could happen overnight, everyday Conrad asked Mary, "Do you feel anything yet?" to which Mary just answered with a smile. Then about a month later, of course way too early to predict anything, Mary said, "Conrad my love, I believe we have succeeded, I am late, and I just have that feeling that something has changed inside me."

Conrad almost flipped, he was so happy, he danced around Mary, kissing her, hugging her, and it was just a given that Mary was pregnant. Such is young love, and nobody has the power to change the course of things.

Over the following weeks the two observed every little change that happened, nothing went unnoticed!

"We are going to be so happy!" The two whispered in each other's ears when they were by themselves. Franz and Joanne never suspected anything, and they were never to find out either.

One week before Conrad had to go to serve his country, they started moving out of Zurich. Conrad brought all his belongings to his parents' home, Mary to her mother's. Of course they did not move back with their parents at that very Moment, no way; there was a full week they could spend together, why would they miss that?

Conrad was supposed to report Monday at noon. That meant he had to leave his hometown at six in the morning. So if they took the first train out of Zurich at five in the morning they could spend the time together until they arrived in Solothurn one hour later. Conrad would stay on the same train, and Mary needed to go home. But not for long, it would be at least two weeks before they would see each other again, should Conrad be able to go home at that time that is.

The train was packed with travelers in that early morning hour. There were many young men Conrad's age and they were all heading in the same direction. The last twenty minutes or so, Conrad and Mary spent to work out some more details such as, what if Mary's mother finds out sooner than planned?

"Mary, all you have to do is go and see my parents, tell them that you are pregnant, and need a place to stay. I know they will not refuse to take you in. Besides, before my Army time is up, we can talk to them together."

If only life could go by the script, instead of side tracking all the time. As you can see, it was all well planned. It worked for the two at the time, and people most of the time do what seems to be right for them at that very Moment. Eventual casualties may be sorted out later.

Mary made her way home slowly. She was in no rush, standing for a long time at the train station, waving good-bye until they could not see each other anymore. Mary had five days before she would have to start her new job, but she had to be careful, she could not show any sign of morning sickness, Elli would sense the trouble right away.

Nobody was home when Mary arrived. She could not even enter the apartment where her mother lived. Both Mary's mother and her sister already went to work to the nearby factory. So she spent the morning sightseeing her old town. Nobody remembered Mary anymore. Mary had grown quite a bit, changed her hair, as all women do, and also had gained a little weight, not much just a little. By nightfall she finally made it home, she was tired from all the walking, looking around, and from all the thinking she had to do. But it paid off.

When Mary's mother and her sister got home that night she had her perfect little story straight on the table. She missed the old town, hated the bustling big city life in general, and just wanted to be home again. Elli was not too pleased, but had no choice for the Moment, as Mary made it clear that soon she would be out of the house again, as she was now used to be on her own. Mary went to bed early that night, she missed Conrad terribly and she needed time to shed some tears into her pillow, for reasons only she knew, and was not willing to share with Elli nor Lilly. Not at this point in time.

To Conrad and Mary it seemed that they were the only two in the whole world that had to go through such cruel treatment. The two had been standing a long long time at the train station, that morning, very close in each other's arms, it was a scene right out of a love story, and whoever passed by the two, would think, "What kind of tragedy is happening here?"

Now, Mary could nourish herself from that last hug and good-bye kiss as she lay in bed all by herself feeling very lonely.

After four hours of an endless train ride, the fresh recruits finally arrived at their destination, in a remote village just above Geneva. Not that Conrad had forgotten Mary, not by far, but if a bunch of young men were just about to arrive at the Army base, they had a lot to talk about, and time was flying for Conrad and his comrades. Besides there was beer on the train, because when you are just about to be a Soldier, you do need beer. The young men were greeted at the train station by friendly officers of the Swiss Army, as if they were little boys and the officers did not want to scare them off too soon.

"Let's just see and wait until tomorrow," Conrad whispered to his neighbor. "I would not be surprised if they start to yell at us like mad anytime soon." He did not have to wait too long for his prediction to come true. A little shy his neighbor nodded in agreement.

"I am sure all hell will break loose tomorrow; I have heard enough of that shit back home. Where are you from?" Conrad asked.

"I am from Zurich, and all I did so far was attend the university, I have no idea what they want from me. I have no ambition to be a Soldier, nor do I want to learn how to shoot people." Conrad felt sorry for the fellow. "Listen just stay close to me I will help you through this. I am not really a friend of all this Army shit either, but you know as well as I do we have no choice in this matter. I have a bride at home, and I miss her terribly," Conrad explained proudly. "I don't want to be here any more than you do, so let's go through it together," Conrad added, well prepared for the harsh times ahead.

"Always yell" his older friends back in Zurich said, "but never louder than the Sergeant, always stay straight up, eyes straight forward and most of all do not move if you have not been asked to. Don't ever be late, never you hear?" his friends pounded into him. "Never talk if you have not been addressed." Conrad was scared before he even got there, but now he knew there were people his age who were even more scared than he was. At least he was not alone; he was just a tiny little boy amongst many.

"ATTENTION!" The command, yelled by one of the officers, came unexpected, loud, demanding. It echoed over the young men's heads, and in that instant erased their private lives for the next seventeen weeks. Slowly, not used to acting too fast yet, the crowd of young men started to turn their attention towards the officer, halting whatever it was they did at the moment.

"Listen up," the officer continued. "We now march together through the village, to the camp. I expect you to behave as young men and not like idiots. Pick up your belongings, form a row of six, then follow me so you won't get lost. From now on I am your Mother."

Of course he yelled because he had to. All Sergeants in the Army have to yell, that is a given, they need to do that so they will be understood by all. Besides yelling confirms their authority and earns them respect. How else could one make real men out of boys without yelling at them?

For the next day or so, there would be not much time to mourn the loss of their girlfriends back home. Things had changed for them, it was time to move on, time to grow from boyhood into manhood.

After a half an hour march, dragging their belongings with them, the new recruits arrived at the base camp. It was a colorful event. Young men from all walks of life gathered in one place for the one and only purpose to serve and protect their tiny little country in the heart of Europe. There was the one looking scared and lost. His father, a rich entrepreneur, had never let him out of his sight. He was a spoiled brat and could not understand that he had to be there; or the one to Conrad's left, a poor farmer's boy from a small village up in the mountains. It did not matter where you were from or who you were. All were one and one was all.

To the right hand side of the five hundred some new recruits, there was a large assembly of high brass; Lieutenants, the Major himself and other high-ranking officers were at the scene to greet them all. Only the Sergeant was busy yelling some orders to his fellow corporals, as he tried to bring some meaning into the chaos. The young men now needed to be dressed in Army gear, shown their quarters, and in general make them aware of the fact that they were now in the Army. The first important thing they had to learn was, hurry up then wait.

The first day at the camp was not too bad for Conrad, he quickly learned how to react to orders yelled to him or others. He had not much time to miss Mary, his love, busy with receiving his Army gear, shoes, pants coverall, helmet, and so on. At night though, just before ten, when all lights were to be turned off, he placed a picture of Mary that she had given him at the train station, into his locker. He loved it, especially because Mary had hand written a note down below: "I love you, my thoughts are with you."

Then at five o'clock the next morning, unexpectedly, the corporal on watch duty burst into the quarter.

"Get up you lazy bums, it's time for a little exercise! Come on, come on," he yelled as if he had to wake up some mummies. "You lifeless bunch have ten minutes, and then you will all be assembled in front of the caserne." Of course they were all not used to such harsh treatment on their first day in the Army.

It was cold that mid March morning. Snow still on the ground the young men were shivering as they awaited further commands. Finally the "Mother" showed up.

"Good morning! He yelled. "First we will have a little warm up, we don't want you guys to get cold, so lets go for a little walk, follow me." With that he turned around and started running over to the exercise field.

"What is this shit?" Conrad's neighbor asked him. "No Breakfast and already running around?"

"Be quiet" Conrad replied, "If he hears you we are all in trouble." It was that spoiled brat with a rich father.

"Oh yeah you think so eh? He said. "Watch me." With that he yelled at the Sergeant, "Hey where is my breakfast?" The Sergeant stopped in his tracks the ones following him too closely almost ran him over.

"Who the hell was that?" The Sergeant demanded to know. No answer. Conrad just looked at his neighbor, but kept quiet. "Already then, follow me you milk faces," he yelled "I am going to give you a Mother's special; instead of running around the track, we run up that hill in the distance then run around the track. Anybody else who needs breakfast right now?" He yelled. It was, as expected, all was quiet. One hour later they arrived back at the camp, pumped out, gasping for air.

"Ok boys," the Sergeant said. "Now you can go and have breakfast." Unfortunately, breakfast time was over, the kitchen was closed, so they had to wait till noon for their next meal. There was no time for a quick snack. As soon as they had arrived at the kitchen, the Sergeant was already there, standing in front of the door, commanding them back to the field where it was time now to receive further instructions.

"Listen" Conrad said to the loudmouth, "next time, I will personally take care of you, should I miss breakfast again." A couple of others, standing around them, quickly assured Conrad to be of help should that guy need any further advice.

The following two weeks were all exercise, running, listening to instructions on how to approach an officer, how to pay attention when spoken too, and so on.

"We will teach you how to show respect towards your fellow Soldiers, your superior officers, how to be on time, how to make a bed properly, how to clean your shoes, pants and all other belongings," the Sergeant said. There were two weeks of constant yelling, running, waiting shivering in the cold and getting used to each other. They were not Soldiers yet, they were recruits, the lowest rank in the Army.

"First we have to pry you loose from your mother's milk," the Sergeant used to yell at them.

"We have to get you guys loose from Mommy's apron. I AM YOUR MOTHER; from now on I take care of you. I will tell you when to eat, sleep or go to the washroom, IS THAT CLEAR?" Sure it was, like always, the young men had gotten accustomed to the new situation rather well. If not, their new "Mother" was quickly to remind them with a little extra exercise. Then there it was, the first weekend they were allowed to "go home to Mommy," as he explained. Oh no not just like that; first you had to be clear on how to behave when in public with the uniform.

"You will always respect any civilian when on the train, bus or any other public transportation. As members of the Army you don't have to pay, therefore you will stand up, and offer any one of the opposite sex your seat. You will behave properly at any given time during your two days out of camp. If you walk with your bride in the city arm in arm, and an officer approaches you, you will drop whatever it is you are doing and salute the officer as you have learned. There will be Military Police out on patrol, and they are more then willing to bring you back to camp a little prematurely, then we will deal with you here. All clear?" He yelled. "Dismissed!"

Off they went to the train station, back home, for a full thirty-two hours. After a long four hours back home by train, there she was. Standing next to the train track, among other girls, she waved all excited when she recognized Conrad for the first time in his uniform. Conrad almost ran over a couple already engaged in the usual greeting ceremony. Then he had her in his arms. Oh how good that felt, to hold her close again, to look her in the eyes, feeling her, touch her face like a blind person, assuring himself that it was her. Careless, the two left the train station having only eyes for each other; nothing else around them mattered anymore. It did not exist. They were all alone, all to themselves.

Mary had to be back home by midnight, so the two went to a nearby restaurant to exchange the latest developments of the last two weeks. Mary's mother had not suspected anything yet, but it started to get close to when she had to fill her in.

"We give it until next time I come home, and then I will approach her and have a talk with her. Is this all right with you my love?" Conrad asked and a relieved Mary agreed; at least she knew she did not have to approach the problem by herself. Shortly before midnight, Conrad escorted Mary close to her apartment, not too close, just to the street corner, but he would stand there and wait until she was home, then walk by her house to make sure she was home safe. Mary would keep the light in her room on for a while, so Conrad could be assured she was home safely.

The next day, there was not much the two could do. After a nice meal downtown, they went for a walk in the park, followed by coffee and cake at their favorite café, always making sure not to get noticed by people who may fill in Mary's mother. But life is unpredictable one never knows what's on the path ahead. Only too soon it was time to say good-bye for another week. Provided that Conrad was not getting into any trouble during the week, from now on he could go home every weekend. Every Sunday night, the same tragedy unfolded at the train station. For generations the young ladies accompanied their boyfriends there to say good-bye for another week of loneliness, another week of suffering, oh how cruel life can be! Conrad and Mary were no different; long hugs, endless kisses, while one would think they must have been suffocating any minute, as there was no way that one could hold their breath for so long, but they survived.

The following week went fast for Conrad; he had no time to think of anything else, as he received training on the machine gun, which he hated, and the large artillery tank, which he hated even more. He had a bad time being cramped into such tight spaces with six others.

It was a little different for poor Mary. On Wednesday morning she had a hard time keeping her breakfast down which, of course, got noticed by her mother. She did not say anything until the evening, when she got home from work.

"Mary," she started. "Are you pregnant?" She demanded to know.

"I, I don't know" Mary replied stuttering. She caught her by surprise.

"Did you see that Conrad again? Is he the father? Did you see him in Zurich?" Question after question she fired at poor Mary.

"Just so you know, someone I work with saw you two in town last Sunday, you were at the Café Bruegger in Solothurn. No you're not going to marry him," she continued. Finally, Mary caved in and told her that yes in fact they were together ever since she left Frutigen and that they had been living together for the last few months or so in Zurich.

"And just so you know" Mary continued, "we are going to get married as soon as I turn nineteen, and that will be soon, June the 8th just in case you have forgotten!" Mary let loose. She had enough of all that and wanted to get out. Oh if only Saturday would be here and Conrad would be by her side!

Saturday, as soon as Conrad arrived home, Mary greeted him with such enthusiasm that he could not help but know that something must have happened. Mary quickly filled him in.

"Well then so be it," he said. "You are coming home with me, you will live with my parents from now on until I am out of the Army, and then we will get our own apartment." Conrad started to take control of both their lives again. He took Mary by her hand and together they went to see his parents.

"Mom Dad," he started. He did not waste any time to explain that suddenly Mary was back in his life; to him it was clear that she belonged there and there was nothing anybody could change. Should they not like what he had to tell them then he would find other arrangements.

"Mom Dad, Mary is pregnant. After my time in the Army we will get married, we still have time until October before the baby arrives. Mary's mother is giving her a hard time and does not want us two to get married. I would like Marry to take my room until I am out of the Army, then we will look for our own apartment. I hope that this is all right with you two otherwise I will have to make other arrangements. It would not be easy but I am sure it can be done" he ended his plea.

Although Olga and Alf were not thrilled to hear the news, they never disagreed with him, as the determination on Conrad's face made it quite clear that he hade made up his mind. Besides, the Army seemed to have its impact on him. He appeared much more grown up than when he left for Zurich over six months ago.

"Ok then "Alf agreed. "Mary you are more than welcome to stay with us, we will look after you." With that it was settled.

"Now for tonight, you can stay here if you are not comfortable going back home. You can stay in Conrad's room since no more damage can be done anyway. Tomorrow, I will go with Conrad in the morning and get your clothes and all that is yours, you don't have to worry," Alf was quickly to add when he saw Mary's concern on her face.

"Conrad and I will take care of your mother while you do the packing." With a big sense of relief, Mary hugged and thanked Olga and Alf. Conrad was happy with the outcome; it was as he had planned and he never for a minute had second thoughts about it. The only hurdle he had to face now was Mary's mother the next day, but that was tomorrow, and not now. Mary was in his arms, "...So we deal with tomorrow, tomorrow, end of story," he thought.

Mary, Conrad and Alf left rather early the next day for Mary's place.

"Where the hell have you been all night again?" her mother charged ahead, not paying attention to Conrad and Alf.

"She was with me and she will stay with me," Conrad answered, pulling Mary away from her mother and putting her behind his back for protection.

"She will stay with us until Conrad is out of the Army," Alf interrupted. "There is no way that she will have an abortion as you demanded. Besides you and I will go and have a little chat while Mary and Conrad are packing up her belongings." For some reason Alf must have had something over Elli to convince her that it was best to listen to him. So the two went outside as Mary and Conrad went packing.

When Alf and Mary's mother got back, she just sat down in the kitchen and did not talk to Mary anymore, nor did she interfere with the packing. The last words she had for Mary just before they left were "Do not come back home again, you hear?" Of course Mary was devastated by such words, but now she had Conrad and that was all that mattered. Off they went to the new place.

Early in the evening, Mary accompanied Conrad back to the train, which would take him away again for a full week, but now she had a home again, life looked good and the future bright. Alf and Olga treated Mary nicely and were always looking out for her welfare. Mary felt at home and started to love her future in-laws. They had a good relationship, Mary helped out whenever she could, and Ellie, her mother, was not to be seen again for years to come.

Conrad was then a lot happier at the Army camp. Knowing his love was in safe hands he started to get a little too cocky at times. A big relief it was for him to know her safe. So he started to get more involved with his comrades at the camp, only trouble was, sometimes instead of shutting his mouth as he had learned, he started to mouth off. Not a lot, not directly to the Sergeant, just like any other of his friends. They were more like murmured disagreements to himself very, very careful, always on the look out. He did not want to jeopardize his weekends, which could end up in having to stand guard in that small guardhouse. Then one day, unexpectedly it hit him; they were exercising out in the field, the Sergeant, chasing them through dirt and mud puddles, had it with Conrad that day. Just out of the blue it was Conrad's turn to get nailed. The Sergeant, standing beside a big mud puddle, started to yell at Conrad.

"Get your lazy ass over here, show me an attack right along this line here. Move it, move it!" He yelled. Conrad already pumped up recognized his opportunity to get back at the Sergeant. He started to run straight towards him and with all the power put into his jump, Conrad landed right in the middle of the mud puddle splashing the Sergeant full of dirt. It was fun at the time, and his friends of course had a good laugh about it. Conrad was their hero, at least for that day. Not so the Sergeant, he had absolutely no sense of humor, but did not react for the time being, well aware that his time for justice would come. He just stood there in silence, nothing indicating his mood. Then suddenly, "You are under attack!" He yelled. "Do not move! I will let you know when the enemy fire has stopped." Needless to say the "attack" lasted a full forty-five minutes.

"Hold your head low," the Sergeant yelled from time to time when Conrad wanted to lift his head out of the puddle for more comfort. Dripping wet he finally let Conrad come out of the mud, but that was not the end of it. Back at their barracks, Conrad received the Sergeant's uniform for cleaning, to be delivered as soon as possible. He got help from his friends, and soon could deliver the uniform back to the Sergeant. With a grin on his face he could not help himself, he stood attention as the Sergeant opened his door.

"Your uniform sir" he reported. The Sergeant just looked at him took the uniform and with a rather friendly "dismissed" he ordered Conrad out of his sight. Relieved, Conrad headed back to his quarters glad that was over and done with. Far from it! The Sergeant, that bastard, had his own way of making sure what happened would not repeat itself in the near future.

Thursday evening, in front of the whole detachment, the recruits where receiving their orders.

"Recruit Meyer, recruit Sanders, recruit Silberman, three steps forward!" He yelled. "You guys will be on guard duty this weekend, inform your girlfriends and make sure they leave you alone." Conrad already relieved was sure he got off easy. Then suddenly, "Recruit Weiss, three steps forward," the Sergeant yelled.

"Recruits attention!" He yelled on top of his lungs. "This is master cleaner Weiss," he continued. "He cleaned my uniform spotless, I was impressed. As a special recognition recruit Weiss will help to spot clean the whole caserne." A whole world collapsed right in front of Conrad; and he had thought he was safe. He managed to call Mary that night. Both were devastated but there was no way out was there?

Mary in the meantime had started a loving relationship with Conrad's parents. Alf felt sorry for her, so, quickly he organized a Sunday afternoon trip up to this little village where Conrad was stationed. Alf was familiar with the Army, so it was no problem for him to find out what time it would be best to meet Conrad.

He did not tell Mary what his plans were, and Mary was more than happy that she did not have to spend the weekend all by herself. Early that Sunday morning Alf, Olga and Mary went for a little train ride, and soon, it dawned on Mary where they were heading.

"Oh thank you Alf," she said, and rewarded his efforts with a kiss on his cheek and a big hug for Olga. They arrived there around noon; it was a warm and pleasant Sunday up in the mountains. The three went to a nearby restaurant to have lunch.

"Do you think we will be able to meet him?" A restless Mary asked.

"I will see what I can do" Alf replied. "Wait here, I will be back soon." With that Alf left in search of Conrad. It was not hard to find his son. After talking to the lonely guard at the gate, Alf made his way through to the commanding Sergeant who, just as lonely and bored, was happy to kill time talking with the older man.

"Oh Conrad is killing time with a broom, just behind the housing complex." Alf convinced the Sergeant with five Franks, which were enough for at least four beers down at the restaurant, that it was imperative for him to see Conrad. The Sergeant of course, had forgotten he had to fill out a form and do much paper work, which allowed Conrad to get out of the facility.

"…But only for an hour" he reminded Alf. " If they find out I am in the gutter before I know it," the Sergeant said.

"Of course," Alf assured him, "been there, done that." The two parted as good friends reaffirming to one another how hard it was to serve and protect. Alf, a Sergeant during the Second

World War himself, knew how to handle issues with authorities in the Army.

It was not hard to find Conrad. Lonely and bored, sweeping up some left over dust with a broom he carried out his weekend duty. When he saw Alf approaching him from the main house he was more than surprised.

"What are you doing here Dad?" Conrad asked with a smile.

"Well we are going to have a beer together" Alf replied.

"Is Mary here as well?" Quickly Conrad asked.

"Sure is!" Alf was quick to reply with pride.

"But Dad I cannot leave here, you know they are going to put me in jail if they find out."

"It is ok son, I have talked to your Sergeant and right now he is very, very busy with paper work. I was told for at least one hour he will be occupied with inspections and other important stuff. So there is an unguarded exit, right at the end of the complex. Out and back in one hour, you hear?"

Conrad's head was fluttering, he knew only too well that if caught he would be locked up at least three days in the "hole." On the other hand, there was no one else at the camp over the weekend, just the lonely guard and a friend of his and just as mad that he had to stay. So the risk to get a surprise was low. With a racing heart, he planted his broom in to a corner, took a dash to the unguarded exit, crossed the street, and then with shaking knees entered the restaurant. There they were, sitting at a table in a back corner, his Mom, Dad and most importantly Mary. She was beaming with excitement when she saw Conrad entering the restaurant, and so did he. Conrad as happy as he was to see them all, was uneasy, but Alf assured him that all was ok, and he was a Veteran so Conrad trusted him.

"Olga let's go for a walk," Alf suggested, so the two elderly left the lovebirds alone. Of course Alf was very proud of himself as he was always ready to play along if he could play a trick on the authorities.

"One day you guys are going to get caught in one of your escapades" Olga lamented. "You know for yourself what Conrad has to face it if he is discovered."

"Don't worry" Alf assured her, "all is well."

"Why did you do that you big dummy?" Mary asked Conrad in reference to his act of bravado, with a smile.

"Because, he deserved it and it was just too inviting," Conrad said. "Well it won't happen again" he reassured Mary.

"Hope not. I would like to see you on the weekend. Right now I do need your support you know. Women don't have a great tolerance for men's need to play."

The one-hour the two had to themselves went by too fast. Olga and Alf came to pick up Mary, it was time to head to the train station, and Conrad needed to go back to camp before it was too late. Reassuring Mary with a last hug and a kiss that he would be home for sure the next weekend, he headed back to camp. The Sergeant kept his word and never saw Conrad leaving camp. Conrad picked up his broom, which now seemed to be a little lighter, the sun shone brighter and his work was not so bad anymore. He even managed to whistle a song while grooming the yard. So, all went well that weekend. Six more days and he would be back home again, but as Murphy's Law has it, it would not be the last weekend he had to stay at camp.

Mary, now on her way back home, happy to know that Conrad was well, could not stop talking about their future together. She did not see the beauty of the countryside the little train passed through. The beauty of the mountain, the Alps in the far distance, the awakening of spring all around her, the meadow just starting to bloom. Of course not, she was a young woman in love and her mind was everywhere but with her surroundings.

She constantly bombarded Alf with questions, and all he wanted was a little nap. Suddenly he said to Mary, "Good thing Conrad learns how to be in the midst of rapid fire." With big eyes Mary, unsuspecting, asked, "Why? Is that dangerous? Why rapid fire? Tell me Dad." By now she called him Dad.

"No there is no danger in it, but I mean that by getting used to rapid fire, he will be able to deal with the way you talk," Alf explained with a smile. Eventually Mary settled down and it was a peaceful trip home.

As promised, Conrad arrived home the following weekend. It was time to get a little more serious. The two needed a marriage license, and Conrad was tied up until his release from the Army, and that was still thirteen weeks away.

"Mary you will go to the City Hall next week, and get all the necessary papers. When I come home next weekend I will sign them, at least this way we are getting a head start" Conrad suggested. If only it would have been that easy! Neither one had given a thought about how things really work. Mary was just about to find out no sooner than when she entered City Hall demanding a marriage license.

"Ok" the man behind the counter said. " Young lady, here is the paperwork, please fill it out then bring it back. It takes about six weeks to process them, we are not in Las Vegas here you know", as if Mary knew where Las Vegas was.

"Fine Sir, will do." Mary went to work on the papers right away, and by the time the weekend was there she presented them to Conrad. He himself not used to all this paperwork, signed them, asking Mary to return them next week, so they could be processed as soon as possible.

"First thing Monday morning," Mary promised. Oh if they only had any idea how things work when government employees are involved. First, the man behind the counter noticed that poor Mary was not even of legal age to get married without her mother's written consent.

"Young lady, you will turn nineteen on June the 8th, you want to get married May the 15th. You are not even of legal age at that time. To marry is impossible, unless you have your mother's written permission." Now it was Mary's time to get desperate. She knew that her mother would never give her the necessary written permission. As a matter of fact she had not even seen her mother since she left to live with Conrad's parents, and she did not want to see her either. Now what?

Turning nineteen in June, the baby was due in October, there was plenty of time, but try to tell that to a young couple in love who want to get married **now**. Devastated Mary had a lot to complain to Conrad the following weekend.

Conrad just laughed it off, and said, "We will get through that don't you worry my love." As all loving and caring fathers-to-be, to him it was more important to put his ear onto her tummy and listen to the progress of the unfolding wonder of Life.

"We will just put things off for four weeks; by then you maybe have a small little tummy but that is all that's visible. Nothing to worry darling," Conrad assured her.

"We buy the wedding dress a little bigger and no one can see it," Mary agreed, but the following week there was another setback, with which even Conrad had a little trouble. Back at the office, the same man assured Mary that he couldn't process her papers until she was of legal age to get married. That would mean the two had to wait until

June the 9th to present the paper, then six weeks of processing, then marriage counseling at City Hall again. That could end up being six months later than planned, and the baby would not be born into a legal marriage. That was important to both of them, so Conrad had to find a way to convince Mary's mother to sign the paper.

"Don't you worry I will get her to sign" Conrad reassured his young wife to be.

Sunday morning Conrad left early to see Elli, Mary's mother. His head pounding and a nervous wreck, trembling he knocked on her door awaiting a slew of nasty words coming from her. Instead a stranger opened the door. Seeing Conrad in his uniform, he politely asked, "Yes sir can I help you?" That gave Conrad the necessary push to be self-confident.

"I am here to see Elli sir," Conrad responded just as politely. "I need to talk with her about her daughter Mary."

"Oh so you must be Conrad then" the man replied.

"Yes Sir I am" Conrad said.

"Come on in, I will get Elli for you, please have a seat on the couch." Of course Elli heard who was at the door and that he wanted to talk to her, but she was in no hurry and took her time.

"What do you want from me?" She asked as she entered the living room. "Did you not do enough damage already?"

"Madam there are no bad things we have done; Mary and I love each other deeply and all we want is to spend our lives together as a couple. You know very well that Mary is pregnant and we want to get married whether you like it or not. Sooner or later this will happen with or without your permission. Mary turns nineteen June the 8th the baby is due in October. Please ma'am we do need your written permission to get married July 4th. That will still give us enough time so the baby can be born into a legal marriage with a father and mother.

"Yeah and should I sign the divorce papers right with it?" She fumed. "You two have no bloody idea what marriage is all about, marriage is about work, love, commitment and everything else that comes with it."

"Well you should know," her new beau interrupted her.

"Listen Elli, you may have had a bad marriage, but I don't think that you are the right person to give a lecture here." Conrad did not want to argue with Elli, he tried to stay calm as he needed her signature, and as it seemed her new man was about to take Conrad's side.

"Well Elli," Conrad continued, hoping to bring this to an end as soon as possible; he had no intention to waste his short time he could spend with Mary on this.

"Here are the papers I need you to sign so we can get married in time. That is all we want then we will no longer be a bother to you." Elli was not about to give in and sign it. She wanted the young man to have as much a hard time as she could possibly give him.

"What makes you so sure I will sign?" She asked. "Why the hell should I? In the past you two did everything you could to blindfold me."

"Well" the other man interfered, "why don't you just sign? It doesn't cost you anything and you get them out of your hair."

"Yeah for now, but you just watch, sooner or later they will come and ask for help, and I am not willing to support them now or in the future."

"Elli" Conrad pleaded with her, "rest assured that we will be able to look after ourselves and do not need any support. All we are asking is that the baby can be born in to a functional family and that he or she can bear my name." With that he placed the paper to be signed on the table, right in front of her. She just kept harassing the young man.

"You asshole, have you not brought enough shit into my life? When do I ever get rid of you?"

"As soon as you sign the paper ma'am," Conrad replied politely. He was more than ready to give her a piece of his mind, but first he needed her signature.

"Ok you dumb shit!" She finally gave into his plea. "Here, signed, over and done with" she said. "Just never come back to seek help, I am not available."

"Sorry Elli but why the hell would we ever want to see you again?" With that he took the papers and secured them in his uniform. Now they were safe; after all he was in full uniform, which also meant his side bayonet, which he never thought of using, though it gave him some kind of protection.

"Just remember, there will be a day when you may want to see the baby; just remember that madam." As if in the Army, he stood attention for a minute then turned around and left the apartment, followed by Elli's latest boyfriend.

"Listen young man" the fellow started, "She doesn't mean it that way; she is just concerned about Mary."

"Yeah well she has a funny way of showing it," Conrad countered. "Do you think Mary likes the situation Elli has brought on us, sending her away so she could not see me again? Elli did not show too much concern when we were in Zurich, because she didn't know Mary was with me all along. Sir I am sorry but I have to go now, my time is limited as I have to go back to my Army camp tonight. Goodbye sir and thank you for your support." With that Conrad turned around and just let the man by himself. He had no intention whatsoever to waste more of his time than it was necessary.

Proudly Conrad presented the signed paper to Mary. She was happy but she had concerns while he was gone. She was worried that something would happen to him, or that her mother would not sign the papers, but now all was well. Relieved and happy that night Mary saw him off at the train station, promising him that first thing Monday morning she would go to City Hall again and tackle further paperwork.

Finally the government official moaned behind the counter.

"Young lady, next time you want to get married make sure you have your paper work in order first."

"There will be no next time," Mary said with a firm voice. "We will stay married."

"Yeah, Yeah," the man said, "have heard that one before. Regardless you have the papers, we will process them and in about two weeks you will be able to pick them up."

"Two weeks?" A surprised Mary asked, "I thought it was going to be six months?"

"Nope, but what's the use of making it easy for you young folks? As soon as spring is around all you want to do is get married." Oh it felt so good to tell someone off. Maybe his hemorrhoids were bothering him, so he had a reason to let off some steam to whoever came to his office, and, in that case it was poor little Mary.

In the meantime Conrad's unit, back in the Army, had to move out of their comfortable housing. They were in the process of learning the game of war, first hand, up in the mountains. There it was where they had been told that the enemy would attack them, and they had to defend their range. It was there that Conrad got hurt. It was far after midnight when their unit got word that the enemy had just entered their territory, and they now had to defend it. Conrad, in the midst of charging forward with his rifle pointed toward the "enemy," heard the corporal yelling, "FIRE, down, down!"

Conrad let himself fall to the ground, as he had learned and twisted his ankle between the broken wood of a tree stump. It was so bad they had to airlift him out of the mountains and into the nearest hospital. For two full weeks he had to stay there, it was not the most pleasant of things but he had no way of changing it.

Of course Alf, a big softy by now, felt sorry for Mary and took her for another trip to see Conrad. Bedsides he was mighty proud of his son, as he got injured in training and that was something he could now tell his friends at his favorite pub.

Shortly thereafter, at about mid-term of Conrad's Army time he got called by the highest-ranking officer.

"Soldier Weiss," the officer yelled as Conrad stood attention in front of the Major's desk. The Major just ignored the Soldier for a while, and when he saw it fit to say, "At ease Soldier," Conrad relaxed. Then out of the blue the Major started yelling without any warning.

"What are you doing here Soldier?"

"I was told to report to you sir," Conrad yelled back.

"That is not what I meant," the high-ranking officer said, now sitting down and lowering his voice so that even normal people could understand him.

"What I meant is, why are you in the Army?" "Sorry Sir, the question was not quite clear to me."

"What?" The officer started yelling again. "Are you telling me I don't know how to communicate?"

"No Major sir, sorry sir but I believe that I have a hearing problem sir. Just this morning I was at the shooting range, and forgot my hearing aids." Conrad was not stupid he knew damn well how to react without getting in to too much trouble.

Anyhow, the officer had tested Conrad enough.

"Sit down Soldier," he said with a smile.

"Thank you Major sir," Conrad answered as he took the chair in front of the humongous desk.

The Major loved the military; all over his desk and on the walls he had lead Soldiers, canons horses and other military equipment. A display case showed a wonderfully handcrafted set of duel pistols; the Major could not help it but to notice Conrad's admiration for the display.

"Do you like it Soldier Weiss?" the Major asked.

"Yes Major sir I do!"

"To get back to my original question Soldier, why are you in the Army?"

"Sorry Major sir," Conrad countered a little more careful this time, "but I do not understand the question. It is mandatory and an honor to serve the Swiss Army, and to help to protect this wonderful country of ours, Major sir."

The Major seemed satisfied with the answer.

"So what are your plans in the future with this Army Soldier Weiss?"

"Well Major sir, I will be back next year for another three weeks, and every year thereafter until I have served my country Major sir."

"Well Soldier Weiss, the Army has plans for you" he said, with his eyes locked on poor Conrad, who was sweating by now.

"Oh shit," Conrad thought to himself. "That is the last thing I need right now." Conrad replied, " Major sir that is an honor but I am afraid I don't know what you are referring to Major, sir."

"We have observed you as well as all the others in your battalion; we have found that you would be a good professional Soldier. You have shown good leadership and were always willing to help others. Besides, we have made a man out of you and we think that you should serve the Army as an officer."

"Watch out," Conrad said to himself, "this man is out to get you by the balls." Out loud he said, "Major sir I have proven to be a man before I was a member of this Army sir Major sir."

"Oh and how is that may I ask?"

"Sir, Major sir, my bride back home is pregnant Major sir."

A red-faced Major jumped up from his chair.

"Give me fifty for that stupid answer Weiss!"

"Yes sir, Major sir." With that, Conrad dropped to the floor to give the Major fifty pushups as demanded, while thinking, "Watch out my friend, this man is going to fry you." When finished, Conrad got up and stayed on attention not moving an inch, as if rammed in to the ground.

"So mister wise guy, what makes you think that THAT makes you a man?"

"Major sir, nothing sir, I apologize." Conrad managed to stay straight-faced all the way through, but now he knew that he had to be on alert, on high alert.

"Soldier Weiss," the Major continued, "just because you know how to battle a woman, that does not make you a man…but, if you can battle a woman without casualties that is what makes you a man, understood?" He yelled. Conrad wanted to tell him that the *battle's* outcome was intentional, but he kept his mouth shut, and instead just yelled, "Yes sir Major sir."

"Well Soldier I will give you two days to consider the offer, two days from now at exactly noon you will report back to me, is that clear Soldier?"

"Yes sir Major sir!" Conrad barked.

"Dismissed for now!" The Major said, and with that Conrad slammed the edge of his hand to the side of his head to salute the Major, and made a perfect circle leaving the office. A guard in front of the office had a big grin on his face, which prompted Conrad to say, "Stupid" but not too loud though, just so that only the guard could hear him.

That same night his unit had to go on a march, fifty kilometers straight, with full backpack, rifle and full combat gear. They had eight hours to complete the task or face another march up the hill. Conrad and two of his best buddies were just about to prove to themselves and their comrades once again that they were determined to finish the heavy and demanding march as one unit, without any trouble. Heavy rain did not make it any more pleasant, as they marched through the night. After about four hours into the march Conrad's friend noticed a change in the man ahead of them; he started to stumble, as if he was drunk.

"Hey pull yourself together," Conrad's buddy said to the man. "We have absolutely no intention to add on another ten kilometers or so."

"I cannot go on any longer" the man replied.

"Ok give me your rifle" Conrad said, "and give me your backpack," his friend added.

"We can help each other and make it through the night, but before we cross the checkpoint you have to take over again you hear?" Conrad added.

"Ok guys thank you."

After another half hour the man was completely exhausted, one could see that nothing the other man did would help him. At this point the man, with one hell of a jump assaulted the leading officer in front of him, took the officer's pistol out of the holster and aimed it at him.

"Stop right now right here, I cannot go on any longer!" He demanded. It took the officer by complete surprise; with his arms hanging down low he started to calm the man down. He looked at him not moving an inch, it was quite clear that this man had lost complete control of himself. He was behind the officer, and Conrad and his two friends were standing right behind him. Slowly Conrad and his buddy lowered their gear and, as if they were one, they jumped the man whose backpack and rifle they had carried just a minute before.

He had no chance as the attack from behind by the two men took him by absolute surprise. They knew that the officer's pistol was "hot" loaded with six bullets, but they did what they were trained for, and it paid off. The man got arrested at the very instant, that was the most stupid thing he could have done, when more than half of the training camp time was over. Now he faced a hefty jail term, in addition he had to do it all over again the coming summer. Conrad and his two friends got themselves a long weekend they were dismissed on Thursday instead of Saturday.

"Well, well, well" the Major laughed as Conrad reported to him as ordered.

"Soldier Weiss!"

"Sir Major sir," Conrad saluted.

"At ease Soldier," the officer commanded. Once again, Conrad felt uneasy, he knew that something unpleasant was just about to be offered to him.

"Soldier Weiss," the Major started. "You and your closest comrades have proven to yourselves and the Army that you are indeed *Men*; Army material. We shall put in a recommendation for you and your friend to put you through Officers training. You men are absolutely brave and deserve to have an Army career. Poor Conrad's face changed from white to green, from red to black and in the same color pattern back to normal.

"Sir Major sir, can we talk this over again? Maybe under a different and more relaxed atmosphere?"

"What in the world is it that is so important to you that you do not want to serve the Army? Ok then let's go and talk this over in a more relaxed atmosphere. Follow me Soldier Weiss."

"Yes sir Major sir." Conrad and the Major left the office and the officer led Conrad on a leisurely walk.

"Now mister Weiss," the Major started. Conrad saw it as a good sign that the Major called him mister Weiss, and not Soldier Weiss.

"What is it that you do not want a career as officer with the Army?" He talked like a father now, putting Conrad at ease. He liked the young man and could not understand why he would not choose the Army over anything else.

"Sir Major sir," Conrad took his chance. "My bride is pregnant, that was not just a stupid remark, she really is, and Sir yes we had it planned. There were certain circumstances I do not want to reveal here sir."

A stunned Major shook his head in disbelief.

"What is it with you young people?" He asked. "Why always head first through the wall, not thinking, just straight forward; that was stupid, sorry Soldier but I cannot see that as a reason not to follow an officer's path in the Army"

"Sir Major sir," Conrad started, but the officer waved him off.

"Drop the rank Soldier, just call me sir. Now let's go over there to the bench to have a little chat. Explain now to me how you got into this mess."

"Sir I don't believe to be in a mess, it just is a little early in life to have a family but we will manage." Conrad started to explain.

"The very moment I saw this girl I knew that she was the one I wanted to marry. Everything seemed right to her and me," Conrad continued.

"When I finish my Army time I need to go to Zurich for two weeks to finish my job at Swissair, then I will pick up my job as an apprentice in the private sector, basically getting my life back in order and start a family sir." Conrad explained that wedding plans had already been made, for early July.

"Should I be forced into an Army career sir, many things may go wrong. I will not have the means of supporting a young family, besides the fact that I would need to be away from my family for another twenty-one weeks. I strongly believe in family values, and as a young father I have my responsibilities. I would… no I **need** to be there for our baby sir, I believe that any baby needs a father as well as a mother. I believe that should I be forced into the Army, I would not make a very good Lieutenant, would I sir?" Conrad tried very hard to convince the old man.

"My young family is of the outmost importance to me, sir" he continued. "I just know I have to be there, and I know that we are going to make it." So far the Major, just sitting there, did not interrupt Conrad for a minute.

"Now listen up Mister Weiss," the old man said. "I want, no I *need*," the Major corrected himself. "I need to know why you were thinking the way you did, how else can I make a good judgment call? So spit it out, come on talk!" he demanded.

"Sir about two years back, I met her for the first time, and fell in love with her right then and there. After her mother found out that we were dating, for some reason she did not like me so, she sent Mary, my bride, away. I discovered her whereabouts I went there, picked her up, then the Army time came. We did not see any other alternatives but to get married." So Conrad started to spill his guts out to the old man. When he was finished the Major just nodded his head.

"Well Soldier I do have some sympathy for you and will see your case through again. After the long weekend you and your comrades have well deserved, you will report back to me for further investigation, dismissed." Conrad got up from the bench, stood attention, saluted and went back to his quarters, where his friends were all sound asleep; after all it was two o'clock in the morning. The Major really took his time.

Thursday morning came around, Conrad and his friend got the order to report to the Lieutenant on duty in the Sergeant's office at once. The two reported in a minute's time. The Sergeant, the Lieutenant and a couple of other officers were assembled in the office.

"At ease Soldiers" the acting Lieutenant ordered. "First I would like to thank you both for possibly saving my life the other night. I really appreciate what you did. Now, and please correct me if I am wrong, WHAT THE HELL DID YOU GUYS DO WITH THIS MAN'S RIFLE AND BACKPACK?" He barked at the two right out of the blue.

"As far as I remember the order was, full backpack, rifle, and combat gear right? He yelled.

"Yes sir" Conrad and his friend replied at once.

"What if the pistol would have gone off? He would have killed me!"

"Sir that would not be possible," Conrad yelled.

"What the hell makes you think so?" The officer demanded.

"We had him in a padlock sir, arms tied around his waist, all he would be able to shoot was his own foot sir," Conrad's friend replied.

"Sir we noticed that the man was starting to faint," Conrad took over. "We wanted to help him and make sure we made it back in time, so we took over for him sir."

"You now damn well that this was against regulations! The officer said.

"Yes sir," the two agreed.

"Well then, just be glad, both of you that I am such a nice guy," with that he smiled.

"Gentlemen" he continued, he had his fun with the two. "Today at noon you both will be dismissed for a long weekend, you will stand in front of the unit beside me, you both will take their salute then I will personally drive you to the train station." Both men stood attention, saluted then with a "dismissed" left the office.

"Shit that was close!" Conrad said outside the office.

"This guy sure had his fun with us" his friend agreed.

"Well at least we got our long weekend, let's just forget the rest. We are off duty till 11:00 a.m., let's go have a beer."

"Yeah we deserve that one" Conrad agreed. "As long as we are back at eleven, or we are going to be fried once again."

At exactly eleven hundred hour they reported back to their unit, a little tipsy, but not drunk, from having had a beer or two. Oh no that (being drunk) would have jeopardized the well-deserved long weekend. The Sergeant did notice the small inconvenience of the two but kept his mouth shut, as he sympathized with them. It was quite a show the Army put on for the two. Their whole unit was assembled in their parade uniforms. The Major, all Lieutenants, the Sergeant the units' "mother" and right beside them, Conrad and his friend.

"Attention!" The Sergeant yelled. With one heck of a noise all feet were drawn together at once.

Standing attention the whole unit saluted the two, then all attending officers saluted them. They were mighty proud of themselves as they returned the salute; chests out so far they were afraid the buttons would come loose. Then with one command, the whole unit paraded by in front of the two, saluting them once more, then the show was over.

"Soldiers dismissed!" The acting Lieutenant barked. With a sigh of relief the two made a dash toward the waiting jeep, jumped in looked back and laughed. They were waved off by there friends off to a wonderful long weekend.

Of course, nobody expected Conrad to be home on a Thursday night. They were all sound asleep when he arrived, and that was good, so nobody could see that he had a little bit too much beer. The two went for a couple of quick drinks as they thought they deserved them and who could blame them?

Conrad went to sleep on the couch after assuring himself that Mary was sound asleep in his bed. It was quite a hello the next morning, when Mary discovered Conrad sleeping on the couch.

"What on earth are you doing here?" She wanted to know.

"Mom Dad, come quickly, look who is home!" An excited Mary yelled. The two could not believe their eyes when they saw Conrad on the couch, with sleepy eyes and an alcohol cloud surrounding him, but that was not important right then, the main thing was that he was home. Now he had to explain to all what happened, and that extended breakfast until noon.

Mary was so proud of him, but as a typical woman in love, reminded him to stay clear of such adventures in the future. Alf was beaming with pride. That meant a shortcut to the pub where he declared his son as a hero of the Swiss Army. By nightfall the whole community knew what had happened; Conrad was dragged to the pub, worried Mary beside him. She knew the outcome of all that, so she prepared herself to sleep alone that night, as Conrad likely would be sleeping on the couch again. Not that Conrad was drinking a lot, but every now and then, when the time was right and the opportunity was there, the alcohol seemed to take the better of him.

Then oh yeah, then it could happen that he swallowed one too many. Good grief, Conrad! And so it was. Conrad, a full member of the grown up men's group in the village, was sitting with Alf and his friends at the round table, telling his story over and over again. Olga and Mary left the pub early, knowing too well the outcome of all that.

Conrad had to tell his story over and over again and by past midnight the pistol was not a pistol anymore but an assault rifle. The attacking man was suddenly a whole gang, which the two fought off. It was funny to watch Conrad telling the story over, and over again.

The next morning Mary and Olga were not too pleased with their hero; the whole house smelled as if Alf had started his own brewery, but this was an exception, so the two women did not make too much of a fuss over it. By noon Conrad was halfway functional again and could now pay all his attention to his young bride.

They had spend a lovely weekend together, and too soon he had to head back to his unit. Monday at noon Conrad reported back to the Major's office.

" Soldier Weiss reporting sir Major sir."

"At ease, Soldier" the Major ordered. "Please sit down Mister Weiss."

"Thank you sir," Conrad took his old place in front of the desk.

"Mister Weiss," the Major started, "what have you learned in the Army?"

"Well sir," Conrad started, "I learned how to handle a gun, how to kill people."

"Stop, stop right there" the Major said.

"What I meant was, what have you learned as far as life goes?"

"Sir, I have learned to work with others, to respect others and how to stand up for myself Major sir!"

"What about dignity mister Weiss?"

"Well Sir, I have never been disrespected by any of your officers, they always treated us fairly Major sir."

"Damn he is not giving up," Conrad thought to himself.

"Well Soldier," the Major carried on. "I have given all this a long second thought. I believe it would be great to see you as an officer in this Army, I think it would also benefit you."

Conrad started to get uncomfortable, and the Major noticed that with a smile.

"Mister Weiss" he carried on, "there is no need to get nervous. I understood your values very well, and took that in to consideration. I am asking you one more time, are you sure that you want to serve in the private sector?"

"Yes sir Major sir, absolutely, I could not stand to be away from my future wife and my child for another twenty-one weeks, sir Major sir," Conrad answered as quick as he could. He did notice the change in the Major's voice.

"Well then Mister Weiss, I will put your case on hold. I will not process it. Should you feel a need for change please feel free to see my again." Conrad wanted to get up and give him a big hug, but then he wondered how that would look; a Soldier hugging a Major in the Army; the thought put a grin on his face.

"Dismissed, Soldier!"

Relieved, Conrad got up from the chair as if a tarantula was under his behind, saluted the Major and with that was out of the office.

It was as if there suddenly was a special sweetness in the cool afternoon breeze. For a while, Conrad paused outside, lit a cigarette and with wonder on his face watched the small blue smoke slowly disappear. He had to ponder the Major's decision, as he still could not believe that he dismissed him with such ease.

"Oh well, over and done with," Conrad thought to himself. "Just another hurdle on the trail of life." With that he returned to his unit. They only had to serve three more weeks in the Army. The second last weekend they would have to stay, there would be a parade of all Soldiers with their tanks, and other equipment, and all Soldiers would be dressed in full parade uniform. Rows of eight men, twenty-five men deep, and in sections of ten. All two thousand Soldiers, plus tanks, motor bikes, huge trailers, communication units and so on. What a show! They would proudly parade in front of their invited families, showing off their "stuff." The Army brass band would play march music and the Soldiers would march in synchronization. No one dared lose their step during the parade; everybody would notice that right away, especially the proud Major saluting HIS Soldiers.

The next week would only consist of perfecting their skills of marching as one unit; cleaning the equipment, counting and recounting all that was to be left behind for the next batch of new recruits. The rifle and a full box of ammunition sealed and carefully accounted for, was to be taken home by every Soldier, including their full uniform, which was every Soldier's personal pride.

Then that long awaited Saturday was upon them.

"Soldiers," the Major lectured them in the morning. "You are the pride of this unit. Today as you march in front of your families, be proud, be one, now you are full members of society, back in private life you may start your own families. *Did he think of Conrad?*

"Take with you what you have learned, and yes today is the day you can show off. AT EASE!" He barked. "Dismissed." He was never a man of big words, but rather of actions.

At noon the first families started to arrive. Olga, Mary and Alf were there too of course but Conrad was nowhere to be seen; as all Soldiers he was busy cleaning his shoes and uniform from the last dust. They could not dare to have some dust on their uniform or on the shoes. The rifle also needed to be looked at once more. Two hours before the parade, the Soldiers were already in formation, ready to march but, as it goes in the Army, hurry up and wait. Then there it was; the Army brass was assembled, the Major the officers and their "Mother," the Sergeant. The brass band started to play a march to entertain the crowd. With a big boom from a canon, the signal had been given; the parade had started.

Proudly the Soldiers marched by in front of the crowd, and while passing by the high ranks, they threw their heads in their direction and saluted.

"There he is, look Dad, there is Conrad right on top of that big tank! Don't you see him? Why is he not waving?" Mary asked. Of course Conrad saw her, but there was no way he could wave back to her, he was a Soldier, he was on duty and Soldiers in a parade don't wave. After a long two-hour parade they finally were able to see one another, but for a short time only, because they had to head back home early, though it was a proud and happy time for all.

"Soon I will be back home my love and then we can go ahead with our lives. Two more weeks and I will be home, we are going to be ok, don't worry Mary," Conrad assured her. Mary knew that it was all right.

The remaining two weeks went by fast and the last Saturday was finally upon them. Seventeen weeks that bonded those young men together transformed them in to *Men* with self-respect, dignity and respect towards others. Of course the excitement was written all over their faces while packing their personal belongings, on the last day that they would be wearing their uniform. Of course they had to go home dressed in the uniforms, they had no personal clothing.

A few beers started to make the rounds. Then a few more; it was time to celebrate. By the time Conrad and his buddies arrived at their respective hometowns, they were not quite themselves, but that was to be forgiven; after all coming back to a private life was not an easy transition.

At the train station, Conrad was so excited to see Mary, even though he had a hard time walking straight and he forgot his damn rifle on the train. One of his buddies handed it to him through the train's window, at the last Moment. Now that would have brought him three weeks of Army jail time; Mary was not too pleased to see him in such condition, but it was an exception, and so she kept quiet.

The next day, a nice warm sunny day with a little bit of a breeze coming down from the mountain, the two went for a long walk along the river and were busy all day long figuring out their next step. In one week Conrad had to go back to Zurich, he needed to finish his job at the airport.

"Two weeks only my love but I have to do it. I cannot just go there and quit and come back, you know that this is not how we do things." Conrad said.

Mary understood, at least he was able to come back home at night and that was all that mattered. Come Monday morning, first thing Conrad did was to go straight to his old boss, the one where he had worked as an apprentice.

"Sir I now have a family to support, and I would like to finish my job as an apprentice, picking up where I left off."

"Are you still drinking Conrad?" His old boss asked him.

"Sir I do have the odd beer, but now having the responsibility of supporting a family I did give up partying sir."

"Well then Mister Weiss, are you willing to go to night school instead of regular once a week school? I could pay you more money then."

" Sir that is more than I expected thank you very much. I need to go to Zurich for two weeks and then I will start here right away."

Seeing that Conrad had taken on full responsibility and the change in the young man the Army had made, Conrad's boss was glad to see him back. That night Mary and Conrad had reason to celebrate. All started off well for the two and soon there would be the wedding date.

The two went for a nice, quiet dinner to celebrate Conrad's new, "old" job. As usual they met with a couple of friends afterwards, and it seemed that the two were off to a good start.

The two weeks in Zurich were passing by fast, a last time Conrad made contact with his old friends, and they all wished him and Mary well for their future. Conrad's old buddy, with his old car, still laughed when they talked about the way they got Mary to Zurich.

And so Conrad left Zurich for good, heading back home where he belonged. Conrad had no trouble getting back to his old job. Most of his acquaintances from back then were still there and welcomed him back. Only his former ally was missing; he had finished his job as an apprentice and moved on in life.

July the 3rd 1969, the day before the wedding day came. Conrad invited his work buddies, including his boss, for a party that night. Conrad was afraid to have a drink or two in the presence of his boss afraid he would make a bad impression. As it turned out, the boss could get a cold one down pretty fast himself.

"...But you see Conrad," he explained, "I never missed work or neglected my duties."

Conrad took that to heart and by the end of the night the two were on a first-name basis.

It started as a nice Saturday morning, their wedding day, the most romantic day for any young couple. Mary wanted to get married in her small little town, in the little chapel where she got her first communion, not too far from the apartment where she used to live with her mother and her younger sister Lilly, just a stone throw away.

At one o'clock they were to walk down the aisle. It was a short, nicely arranged ceremony. All of Conrad's family was present and their friends too. Mary even invited her father as she understandably wanted to have someone from her side as well. She had seen him, in the past, a couple of times and Conrad had somewhat of a relationship with him.

Just after the ceremony, they all were outside for the obligatory wedding pictures. Mary's younger sister showed up at the side of the church. Lilly just looked at the weeding party, then locked eyes with Conrad. Now Lilly was only eighteen at the time and was instructed by her mother, but what she yelled across the churchyard was burned into Conrad's and Mary's minds for the rest of their lives.

"Your marriage will go to hell!" She yelled, "I will take care of that, just remember you two." Conrad, acting quickly, took crying Mary by her hand and ushered her onto the waiting bus that would take the wedding party to the reception. In the meantime Alf made sure that Lilly was no more a bother for the two during the wedding party.

The following week was a busy time for the two, Wren, Conrad's younger brother, wanted to move back in with his parents. He had just finished an apprenticeship for the ministry of transportation and he was now a bus driver for the local transit unit.

Mary and Conrad started their search for an apartment in the small towns around the big city. Mary, one night, all excited, said to Conrad, "I have found one in Zuchwil, not far from where I used to live. It is very nice, clean and affordable. Can we go tonight after your work and go have a look?" She excitedly explained to Conrad.

"Well yeah I guess," Conrad replied, "If you are comfortable living that close to your mother I don't mind it, as long as you are happy my love."

"Oh it will be ok" Mary explained, "I am sure they won't bother us, and we'll mind our own business, don't worry."

"Ok then" Conrad agreed. It was indeed a nicely located apartment in a small four-story building. Four weeks later the two lovebirds moved into their own place. Everybody was very nice to the young couple and helped them out whenever they were in need. Mary, by now a little rounder up front, made new friends; in the evenings they were all sitting together having coffee or the occasional beer. Alf showed up every now and then, making sure the two were all right. Sunday was mostly family time and they all met at Alf's place.

Family outings were the most important thing to the two, as that reassured both that they belonged. Mary started to have a little trouble walking up and down the stairs, especially on laundry day, but Conrad made always sure that he carried the heavy load up or down the stairs.

Then October the 29th of the same year came. It was close to midnight when the little one decided to enter this world. Strong and healthy, with a voice so loud it could entertain a whole town their little sunshine was born. Conrad could not resist, he had to go to Alf and Olga to break the news, which they then celebrated into the wee hours of the morning.

Conrad learned his lessons. He went to work straight from his parent's place, only to be sent home by his laughing boss.

"Go home Conrad" he said, "You will have today off with pay." He went home and after catching up on his sleep, he went off to see Mary and their new family member. He was so proud, holding the little girl in his arms. Glancing at Mary he said, "We are so lucky, the three of us." They hugged kissed and assured one another of their devotion to one another for the rest of their lives.

Two years or so went by pretty fast. Conrad spent all his free time with the little one and with Mary. Sunday mornings he took his little pride and joy with him for a walk then met up with his buddies for a Sunday morning matinee at the pub, while Mary was at home preparing a nice Sunday dinner. Life was good. They had many friends, a lot of fun and a lot of love to give to each other.

Conrad finished his job as an apprentice two years later and then moved onto another job, as it was custom not to stay with the company where one received training.

Then one Monday morning, Mary went with Monica, their little girl, to town to do her daily grocery shopping. It was then when she crossed path with her mother for the first time in many years. Her mother Elli did not make too much of a fuss over it.

"Don't you want to see and hold our Monica?" Mary asked.

"No thanks, I have no time, got to go." That was it. Mary was devastated when Conrad got home from work.

"Don't worry my love," Conrad tried to calm her down, "I understand the way you feel but it makes no sense to force the issue." About three days later, Lilly knocked on their door.

"I would like to talk to Mary" she demanded of Conrad, who had opened the door.

"What is it you want?" he inquired.

"I want to talk with my sister" she insisted.

"You know what?" An agitated Conrad countered, "we would appreciate not seeing you again, but I will talk to Mary and I will leave it up to her. Now get the hell out of here." With that he slammed the door shut.

Mary, once again crying said, "Why can't they just leave us alone?" We have our own little family now, they did not care before, why now?" She asked more herself than Conrad. But Lilly seemed to be determined; she was waiting to see Mary when Conrad was not at home.

"Please Mary, come with the baby to our home for a visit, Mom really misses you and the baby."

"Yeah what about Conrad?" She asked.

"Well he does not seem to be too fond of us" Lilly said. "But you can bring him too if he wants to come."

"I will talk with Conrad first, I will let you know, and now please leave us alone." That night Mary filled Conrad in on the news. He was not too pleased with their offer, knowing that Lilly had not too good of a reputation in the village. She was well known to most men. However, after a while of Mary's pleading he gave into visit them one evening, but, he said, "One more time, one more insult towards you or me and I will not tolerate it."

So one evening the three of them made their way over to Mary's mother's place. Lilly was present as well her mother's boyfriend. Conrad noticed that Lilly suddenly wanted to play nice aunt. She did get on his nerves and he had a hard time seeing his little girl in her arms.

Elli at first did not react too much to the little girl; she did not have the patience any more to deal with such a lively little bundle of energy. It did not go too badly that night, Mary and Conrad were willing to give some consideration to seeing them every now and then, but Conrad was on alert.

Lilly started to visit the two more often than Conrad liked. She came to visit almost daily, and Conrad started to get weary of her. Then Lilly started to visit with her boyfriends; sometimes she would show up with a couple of them. Conrad noticed that by now, Lilly started to influence Mary.

"Why don't you come out with me once a week, why don't we go dancing and have some fun?" She pleaded with Mary.

"No," Mary said. "I have a family now and have my responsibilities, please leave it at that." But Lilly was not quick to give in. One evening she arrived at their home with two of her friends. It was obvious that the two men were up to something, they started flirting extensively with Mary, and one even followed her to the bedroom as if he lived there. They were after his Mary,

"Oh no not with me boys!" He thought. Immediately Conrad threw the three out of the apartment.

"Now listen up Lilly" he said, "never show up here again you little slut. It is quite obvious to Mary and me what you are up to." Mary could not believe what she just heard; Conrad never used such language before. Conrad had enough of all that, he could just see what a nice aunt Lilly was shaping up to be.

"Mary I really don't like the way Lilly is trying to influence you, by now I am really starting to hate it here, I hate the guys she is hanging out with. They have no respect for family or anything else and I will never allow her to come close to you again. I am sorry but I cannot help it, I have a bad feelings about her."

"Conrad my love, you know that I will never leave you for another man. And this guy was not even a Swiss" she added with a smile.

"Yeah I know, but why wait for something to happen? Let's move out of here. I think it is time for us to move, I have heard of a really nice two-story apartment away from here." Mary and Conrad quickly left town, never seeing aunt Lilly again for years to come.

Conrad moved up in his job, they both worked hard to succeed. They had their struggles like any other young couple did, but their love and devotion to each other showed. Conrad admired Mary and little Monica. He did whatever was needed to make life as comfortable for them as possible. Mary worked on her end to provide Conrad with a loving home, clean and friendly, and Monica was his little sunshine, Conrad adored her.

One day Conrad got home from work and told Mary that his boss had quit and would start another job. Little did the two know that this was the beginning of what would alter the course of their lives in Switzerland forever.

It was on a wonderful sunny Sunday morning. Mary, Monica, and Conrad went hiking up the mountain, which they loved so much. In the

early afternoon they were sitting on the mountaintop, overlooking most of Switzerland with their hometown way below. Little Monica played in the grass a short distance away. Conrad grabbed Mary, planted a kiss on her cheek, and with a smile said,
"Don't you think Monica needs a little sister or brother?" He asked.
"Right now and here?" Mary asked laughing.
"No, no, I can wait until tonight" he said beaming with excitement.
"I agree Mary continued, "but first I need to see our doctor, I want my back pain checked out. Something is bothering me lately" she added.
"So nothing tonight?" He said, giving her a big hug with a sad face.
"That is not what I said," Mary countered laughing. The teasing went on a little while longer, they were a perfectly happy couple. Late that evening they made their way down the mountain, tired but happy. Conrad put Monica to bed and tired as she was fell right to sleep.
"So my love," Conrad picked up the conversation, again. "What do you think?"
Mary, sitting on the couch watching a movie, was not really aware of what Conrad said.
"Think what?" She replied absentmindedly.
"The Baby, the baby darling!"
"What baby? …Oh yeah the baby, right!" She said.

"Let me go and see the doctor first thing Monday morning ok sweetie?"

"Ok" Conrad agreed, "but what about *practicing* tonight?" And again he put on that sad look on his face, which Mary had a hart time resisting. She teased him by pretending she had fallen asleep.

"Oh no, not with me you sweet little monster," he laughed, tickling her. It ended up being a romantic evening after all.

The following two weeks would be stressful for the two. On a Tuesday afternoon Conrad got a phone call at work. Alf, his Dad, had suddenly passed away; he had gone for his daily walk in the bush when he suddenly fell over, he did not even feel the impact to the ground, It did hit real fast. At least he went out as he always wished, no suffering just "…Boom you're gone" as he used to say. Mary was devastated, as she always loved that grumpy old fellow. Life went on as it always does; without death there is no life.

Mary did go to see her doctor and the news were not very encouraging. Conrad had noticed in the past that Mary did have a big bent at the end of her back, but never thought anything of it.

"We have to go to see the doctor together," Mary informed Conrad. "It is nothing life threatening but he said we have to be careful should we wish for another baby." The news the two received from the doctor were not promising about having another baby.

"Mary's back shifted at the bottom after giving birth to little Monica, and a second child would put Mary's life at risk," the doctor added. That was quite sad news for the two, more so now that Mary had to go for an operation but what had to be done, had to be done. So Mary had an extensive back operation, which left her in a cast for over six months. It was hard for the two but, as always, together they managed.

Olga would take care of Little Monica while Mary was in the hospital, then after Mary was home again, Sonja, a life-long friend, would come over during the day to look after Monica and Mary.

Then when Conrad got home, he would take over. Cleaning, cooking, feeding Monica and Mary, and washing her every night. It paid off though. After six months in the cast, Mary recovered rather quickly, and within nine months, she was her quirky good old self. They brought little Monica over to Olga, her Grandma, who would baby-sit her, so her parents could celebrate.

For years to come, they worked hard and got ahead. By now, Conrad made top dollar and they could afford a comfortable lifestyle. There was nothing that could take the two apart anymore.

Mary's mother, Elli, in the meantime had left for Germany with the man she married. Lilly her sister was out of the picture. Then one evening, when Monica was nine years old, Conrad received a phone call.

"Weiss," he answered.

"Yes this is Haeberle, sorry to bother you at home Mister Weiss, do you remember me?"

"Uh, oh, not really I am sorry but I cannot recall you sir."

"Well I was your boss a few years ago."

"Oh yeah sure, I am sorry Mister Haeberle, now I remember! How are you sir?"

"I am fine, tell me Mister Weiss, how would you feel about a job change?"

"Actually sir, I am rather comfortable at the position I have and I am making good money. Why what is on your mind sir?" Conrad replied.

"Well I would like to make you an offer, but not over the phone."

"Mister Haeberle," Conrad quickly replied, "why don't you and your wife come over Saturday night for dinner? I am sure Mary would be only too pleased to see you again."

"Ok thank you very much for the invitation" Mister Haeberle said.

"Well then six o'clock sounds good sir? We are looking forward to seeing you."

"Thanks again and my regards to your wife Mister Weiss, good night."

"Good night Mister Haeberle."

"What did he want from you?" Mary asked.

"I am not quite sure my love, but I have the intuitive feeling he has something to offer. I have invited them over for supper Saturday night, he and his wife will be here at six, I have reason to believe that there is something good in it, something likely about a job. So let's make a good impression on them. That should not be too hard. The way you cook will set them at ease I am sure. I will get some wine I know he likes a good beaujolais."

"Why do you want to change job my dear?" Mary continued. "You are settled, make good money and you like what you are doing."

"No sweetheart, I never said I want to change my position but we can at least see what's in store and what he wants. Besides it will be a nice social evening. And you, sweetie," with that he turned to Monica, who colored some book on the table "Please remember, no worms, frogs or any other live animals on the table do you hear?" Conrad advised her.

She just nodded then with her bright smile replied, "Do I have to behave too?"

"You better or you are going to bed early," a stern father reminded her.

"C'mon now Conrad, you are overreacting, right now you don't even know what he wants," Mary said on her way out to the kitchen.

"Dad, I could have a sleep over with Susie, and then I would be out of it," Monica piped up.

"Nope you are staying home, I want my family together for the occasion."

"But Dad!" Monica started to rebel.

"No buts and ifs. That's the end of it ok?" her father replied.

By Saturday all was settled; Mary made her famous rabbit stew, the whole house smelled like paradise. Conrad was a little on the edge, not knowing what was coming.

"Oh relax hon," Mary tried to calm him down. "Of the two of you, you are in the better position; after all it is he who wants something from you and not vice versa."

"Guess you are right honey" a nervous Conrad replied. "Still I cannot help it, to feel something coming, after all he is the general manager for a large company, and if he takes the time to visit us, well you know we are just 'little' people."

"Not that little Conrad," Mary countered, "after all we have quite a good living, and you are working hard."

Like a Swiss clock, exactly five minute to six the doorbell rang.

"Now I really know he wants something," Conrad muttered. With that he opened the door. With the usual back padding and assuring each other of how good they looked, and how well they were doing, the party settled down for supper. Mary had outdone herself once again with her cooking, and Conrad was beaming with pride. Just once little Monica dropped her fork to the floor and when she got back up reminded Dad, "Daddy you have one sock on inside-out." - Conrad always had one sock on the wrong way - A stern look on her father's face quieted her down. After supper the two men settled in on the couch, the women had their own conversation and little Monica was ready for bed.

"Well Mister Weiss," the guest started. "You may wonder why I contacted you after all this years."

"Oh well" Conrad said, "I guess you just wanted to polish up an old friendship. After all we have worked well together." As predicted, Conrad needed to open up two more bottles of wine. After a while, Mister Haeberle started to dwell on the real issue of his visit.

"Well Mister Weiss" he finally started. "You know that I took over a large company in Grenchen, we are at the turning point of introducing new technology to the plant. Have you ever heard of CNC controlled machines, Mister Weiss?"

"Well uh, yeah a little, but only from magazines and such, we touched it up at evening seminars as well, but I have never worked with them," Conrad explained.

"In the next month we will receive two machines equipped with computer controls. One will be from France, the other from Japan. I would like you to give it some consideration to take over these machines and become our leading man with this new technology."

"Sir I don't even know what a computer is" Conrad explained. "I have heard of it but never worked with one."

"That's why I am here with you right now," Haeberle explained. "I want to send you for schooling to France, for the one machine, and for the Japanese one you will receive six weeks of in-house training, if you are willing to take on the task. I need you there Mister Weiss," the man explained.

"We need a man, who does not give up easily, and I know you are the man for it. Next week we will have an informal meeting with the president of the company, myself, all management and you. What do you think?"

"Hmm sounds good so far and I am flattered that you have thought of me Mister Haeberle. I will give it some consideration and will inform you of my decision next week." Conrad replied.

"Don't forget Mister Weiss, as it stands, we can offer you five weeks holidays, a good salary, all benefits paid, plus daily travel expenses to and from work; we will also expand the new technology into it's own department and you have the opportunity to grow with it. I just want you to keep this in mind. All the training you need will be provided to you, so I believe we can offer you a package that is hard to resist."

The evening went quite well, it was way after midnight when the couple left.

"What is a computer?" Mary wanted to know.

"Oh I am not really sure sweetheart, but I believe it is some sort of a machine where you punch in some words and numbers and this will control the machine."

Conrad was happy with the outcome of the evening, and Mary was quite proud of him. The only thing she did not like was the traveling part she overheard the two talking about.

"Do you have to travel a lot?" Mary asked later on while lying all cuddled up right close to him, patting his head and getting all friendly.

"Mmm" Conrad murmured; the wine took his toll on him, so Mary had no other choice but to roll over and with a slap on his butt said , "Your loss" and fell asleep too.

Early Sunday morning Conrad was awakened by a pair of small little hands tickling him.

"Come on Daddy it is Sunday, what are we going to do today?"

"Well why don't we pick up Grandma and take her for a ride out to the country; she likes that you know, the way we used to do it when Grandpa was still alive."

"Oh great!" Monica shouted. "May I have a big meringue, with ice cream and a lot of whipped cream on it?"

"Pssst Mommy is still sleeping, don't wake her up."

"Yeah right you two, who can sleep around here with the two of you making such a racket?" A big hug and kiss ended in a pillow fight among the three of them.

"Ok let's go and have breakfast I am hungry like a lion," Conrad declared.

It was not until Sunday night that Mary and Conrad finally had time to themselves to discuss the previous night's visitors and the purpose of the visit.

"Do you think you can handle this?" Mary asked.

"They promised me extensive training, and I know Haeberle, he means what he says. I think it would be a nice opportunity to grow. Who knows what it may lead to? The offer sounds good and who could refuse a money offer like that? Plus five weeks holiday, travel expenses to and from work and all the benefits, yeah I think we would make a nice living with that."

"I trust you" Mary went on to encourage him. "I know that you will be able to do it Mr. Bigshot. That last remark earned her a slap on the behind.

Tuesday night Conrad phoned Mister Haeberle, and made an appointment for the coming Friday when he would meet with all the management of the new place. He asked for a holiday for the coming Friday at his old place, then Friday at noon he met with them over lunch. They spent all afternoon negotiating with Conrad, and when he got home with a bundle of a dozen red roses, Mary knew what was up.

"We will have a very good future the three of us," Conrad explained. "Now we can even afford to really go on holiday. No more camping."

"But I like camping!" Monica piped up.

"That is not what I meant by that sweetheart," Conrad explained to her. "We still can go camping, but we also can go to Spain for two weeks or so, somewhere it is really warm you know? Like Greece, or Italy, or we can fly around the world like rich people do." It was heartwarming to hear them dreaming. After all dreaming is what keeps one going. *Without a dream in your heart you have no future, do you?*

Conrad started his new job with all the enthusiasm he could put into it. He went to France for four weeks of extensive training. Then some more training on the job plus evening classes, and after ten months it all took its toll. Mary and Monica complained that Daddy had no time for them anymore.

"It is getting better now" Conrad explained, "the training is over and done with; in two months I will have finished evening classes then I will have more time again for you two, Ok?" So they settled for it.

The job went better than Conrad expected, and after one year, the machine park had grown to four machines, and so he needed some help. Two more people came on board, Conrad brought them up to speed and the future was bright. The only headache he had was with the machine from France; the communication board would constantly burn out, then a serviceman was needed. The machine was not very efficient, but when working, it was absolutely accurate. He liked that small unit, except for the one inconvenience of the burned board.

Then the day came that would alter their lives forever. It started early in the morning; Conrad arrived at work to find the machine down again due to the burned out communication board.

"Well we will need a serviceman again, right away."

"Nope, not anymore Mister Weiss," Haeberle, his boss, explained. "You will go to France and will learn how to fix this thing right here yourself."

"Well then" Conrad said, "I shall leave Monday morning first thing; all should be settled within a couple of days."

"Very well, see you next Wednesday, have a good weekend Mister Weiss."

"Same to you, good bye." Conrad made himself available for his family on the weekend. He had a hard time explaining to his family, once more, that he would be away for a couple of days, but assured them that, when he would be back home, things would be better.

Monday, around noon, he arrived at the plant in Strassburg in France. He teamed up with a serviceman.

"I just got back from Canada you know," the guy explained to Conrad.

"Oh yeah, how was it? I always wanted to go to Canada," Conrad said, not thinking too much of it.

"Well you can have it if you want," the man explained.

"What do you mean by that?" Conrad asked.

"The Company I have been to is looking for a guy like you; they have the exact same machines that you have, but have no experienced personnel to run them. The owner gave me his phone number, in case I find someone interested."

"Well why don't you give it to me? You never know, maybe I just will give him a call," Conrad stated. He put the phone number in his jacket pocket and forgot about it. It was not until a week later, when Mary, with a not-so-happy face approached him, that he remembered. She had just put Monica to bed, and came downstairs into the living room, where Conrad was watching the news. All evening she had been very quiet, never said much during supper. It did bother Conrad to see his otherwise bubbly wife in obvious despair.

"Say, what exactly are you doing on these business trips?" she asked.

"Well you know I have to go to seminars and training, why do you ask my love?"

"Don't you give me that 'my love' treatment, you know exactly what I am talking about. You see other women don't you? Don't even bother to hide it; I have found a phone number in the jacket you wore the last time you went to France."

At that Moment it sunk into Conrad; of course, the phone number from Canada. The devil was riding Conrad at that very Moment and he decided to play the game of an unfaithful husband, just for the fun of it to see how far he could go.

"Well uh, oh that, I am not really sure what to tell you," he started by putting on a guilty look on his face.

"So you actually admit that you had an affair with another woman?" Furious Mary demanded to know. "You don't even try to hide it. Oh you, you monster, you heartless, no-good big monster! How can you do that to us?"

Conrad knew he had to stop it when he saw Mary with tears in her eyes. He could never stand to see her in tears.

"Don't worry" he wanted to start explaining.

"Don't worry, don't worry, would you listen to that! 'Don't worry' is all he has to say!" Mary interrupted.

"Now would you please stop for one minute, and listen without interrupting me?" Conrad asked.

"Shoot, but it better be good or you will wear this flowerpot over your head, you knucklehead."

"This phone number is a business number from Canada; they are looking for a Journeyman for their Traminer machine, the very same I have been trained for."

"And you expect me to believe that?" Mary asked.

"Look at the phone number" Conrad said, "what are the first three digits?"

" 519" she said after checking it out.

"Right this is the long distance number for Ontario that is where the three big lakes are… I told you about it, remember?"

"OOOPS Mary chuckled, and with a big smile, she landed in his arms, the couch almost broke apart from the impact. Her small fists hammering onto his chest,

"Don't ever do that again you dummy, next time empty your pockets first!"

"Why? I have nothing to hide sweetie, why should I empty my pockets first? Anyway, thanks for the advice." With that, the two started wrestling again as they had done so many times before, which only ended in another love scene some place other than the bedroom. This time it was the pedestal sink in the bathroom, which came loose out of the wall. Mary had a hard time keeping a straight face on Monday morning, explaining to the maintenance guy that Monica used it to do pull ups.

"So what is it you want to do with this number? Mary asked later on, resting her head in Conrad's armpit.

"I don't know I have always dreamed of going to Canada, it was a childhood dream of mine. But now, I have you and Monica, so why should we leave? We have a good life right here and now. We have everything we want, who needs more?" Conrad asked, planting a soft kiss on her neck.

"You know it must be nice to see a little bit of the world, just the three of us. This could be not only a job but also an adventure," Conrad added. The two dreamed on a little longer about the big wide world. Then Conrad, yawning, said, "Let's go to bed honey."

"Not just yet you wild man," Mary countered.

"You know as well as I do that we do actually sleep in the bed," Conrad replied with a smile. He went to look after Monica, planted a kiss on her forehead and then actually went to sleep. It was not until about two days later, when the two watched a nature show about Canada's wilderness that they started to talk about it again.

"Well do you think we should try it?" Conrad asked.

"Well why don't you give this man a call, then we take it from there?" Mary suggested.

"Good idea! Then the day after tomorrow we pack right?" He joked, having no idea of how close to the reality that statement would be.

Conrad had to wait until Saturday with the call, because of the time difference; during the day he had no way of calling, evenings he just did not have the time.

"We will give it a try Saturday and see what happens" he said. Then there it was.

"Good morning sir, this is Conrad Weiss from Switzerland. I have your business phone number from a service technician who just recently was servicing your Traminer. I am under the impression that you are looking for a trained Journeyman for this machine?"

"When can you start? The man on the other end asked laughing.

"Well" Conrad said with the little English he knew, *"I good job here, but like Canada, me want to see Rockies."*

"Ok," the man said. "I will call you back, I have someone here in the office. When is the best time to reach you Conrad?" He asked.

"I am home evenings, everyday after five o'clock," Conrad said.

"Well then I will call you back Monday ok Conrad?"

"Ok sir, thank you, good bye."

"This guy is calling me Conrad," he explained to Mary.

"It is their custom to call people by their first name I believe," Mary explained to him.

"Oh well we'll see what is going to happen, I don't think he is calling back," and once again the subject was put aside, but only until Sunday early evening. They had just finished supper, Monica was helping Mary to dry the dishes and Conrad was getting himself ready for Monday morning, when the phone rang again.

"Hello Conrad, here is Canada." Conrad quickly covered the phone with his hand to give Mary and Monica a sign to be quiet, and made them understand that it was a call from Canada by clapping his hand on his lips like the Indians do when on the warpath. They understood and immediately halted.

"Sir good evening,"

"Oh no" the man replied, "It is noon here, not too late for you Conrad I hope?"

"No sir, it is ok, we just finished supper."

"I was waiting for a call like this for quite a while, why did it take you so long to reply to my request through the serviceman?" The man asked.

"Well to be honest sir, I, I mean my wife just discovered the phone number a couple of days ago, I forgot about it sir," Conrad explained.

"Oh never mind, I need you here as soon as possible," the voice sounded desperate.

"Sir they did not build Rome in one day. That is an old saying here, meaning…"

"… Yeah, yeah I know what it means; I am familiar with some phrases in old Europe, so when can you start?"

"Sir we have not even discussed it yet, I don't believe it will be that quick."

"Tell you what Conrad, I will contact the consulate here in Toronto next week, and I call you as soon as I have more information ok?"

"Ok sir, in the meantime I will discuss the issue with my wife and our daughter, so that when you call back I will have an honest answer for you sir."

"Good bye then."

"Good bye sir."

"Well I think we should sit together with Monica, and discuss this issue," Conrad suggested. So that night Mary and Monica were sitting at the table where Conrad had placed the World Atlas for all to look at it.

"Here is Switzerland," Conrad explained. "See, in the middle of Europe, see very, very small, surrounded by mountains on all sides. Now, if I drive through it, I can make it from the east end all the way to the west end in five hours. Now look at the map, here is Ontario, this is the same distance about here. This city down by the American border, Windsor, from there it is about the same distance to Toronto," Conrad kept explaining.

205

"Wow that is big!" Monica piped up. "Are we going there?" She wanted to know.

"Maybe, maybe not" Mary said.

"Then look here, there is the Algonquin Park that is the park we have seen the other week on the nature show. They have wild animals there like bears, moose, wolf, and so on.

"Wow" Mary said, "I heard you could go camping there, and canoeing. Apparently it is so big that people have to register at the gate, so if they get lost they will come and search for you."

"What about hiking?" Monica asked; she had some more questions to delay bedtime.

"Right here, up towards the Quebec border there are some trails, I am sure we can go hiking there on a weekend, like we do here," Conrad explained to her. "So that's enough for today, Monica it is bed time, please go and get ready will you?"

"No I want to see more of that," she demanded.

"No it is too late, now go, Conrad ordered. Mary and Conrad also settled in for the night, it had been a long day.

All three discussed the issue every day; Conrad wanted to give his two girls all the knowledge he had, so they could make a decision.

"If one of us does not want to go, then we won't go," Conrad explained. "I would think this man will call back around Wednesday; even if I don't have a answer for him right away, I think he still would like us to come, otherwise he would have looked for help somewhere else."

Sure as clockwork, Wednesday at six o'clock in the evening the phone rang off the hook.

"Weiss here" Conrad answered the phone.

"Well hello there! I have good news Conrad; I have been to Toronto yesterday, on Monday I went to the Employment Center here in town, I will not have any problems getting papers for your emigration."

"Wow, wow Mister, not that fast! Look I have a family here I cannot just drop everything and leave, besides my current employer also needs a fair time to adjust. After all they have spent a lot of money on my training. I have one person here who could take over, but I believe it could take a few months before we can come. Furthermore, I would like to have a contract from you, stating that you will employ me for at least five years, stating that I have job with your company upon my arrival in Canada."

"Not a problem Conrad, I will send you everything you need."

"By the way," Conrad added, "what about housing?"

"No problem, I have a house ready for you and your family, but say, why can't you come first and the family later?"

"Sorry that is out of the question, please send me some pictures of the house so we have an idea where it is."

"Ok, will do Conrad, I shall phone you back in a couple of days, good bye for now."

"That man is desperate," Conrad said to Mary after he hung up the phone. "Wonder why."

Mary, Monica and Conrad started to look at the possibility of emigrating to Canada a little closer. Almost every night they would sit around the Atlas to discuss the issue.

"Can I have a horse over there?" Monica wanted to know.

"I cannot see why not," Mary said.

"What about Maedy?" Maedy was their family dog, Monica's pet.

"I don't know" Conrad said, "I believe that would be quite costly to take him with us." That, of course, prompted Monica to turn a sad eye.

"We'll see" Mary added quickly.

" But I make no promises yet," Conrad lamented.

"Let us make a list," Mary suggested, "see what the pros and cons are for us. There is a lot for us to do."

Conrad started to discuss the issue with a couple of his closest friends; he could see a little envy in their eyes.

"I always wanted to go there," Heinz said, "It is a big country, lots of freedom there. I heard Canadians are very laid back; they don't take stuff too seriously.

"Here in little Switzerland we are way too cramped in," Rolf explained.

"Maybe," Conrad muttered, "but why is this guy so desperate?"

"I have heard that they do not have the technology we have here in Switzerland; schooling apparently also is not on the top of the list," Rolf explained. "Just look at their politicians; what's his name?"

" …You mean Maggie Trudeau and her husband the Prime Minister?" Conrad asked.

"Apparently she has affairs all over the place."

"Looks good on them," Heinz laughed, "they are on the news almost every night."

"Let's not judge them by their politicians, we all know that they are a bunch of liars, we have a couple of them in parliament ourselves," Conrad jumped in. The three friends were at their favorite pub that evening for a beer.

"Well it's time to go home boys," Conrad said. "I have a long day ahead of me tomorrow, it is time for you guys to go too," he added.

"Ok *Daddy*," Heinz mocked Conrad. Laughing, they all went home.

For Mary, Monica, and Conrad it was now almost certain that they would jump on the opportunity to see the world, get out of their daily routine, put a little adventure into their lives. Sure, there was Sonja, Rolf's wife. She cried at the mere thought of it, at the thought that her life-long friends would leave.

"…But it is your life, you have to know what to do, I am going to miss you terribly you know…" She would say.

"At this time we are still here Sonja, we have not yet made a decision," Mary comforted her.

"Besides, we will be able to visit you guys every now and then, we are not about to cut our roots off with the place and friends with which we grew up. Also you can come and visit us, so that should take some pressure off all this," Conrad added.

"Mary I am going to put together a letter of what we are expecting, will you please help me?" Conrad asked after Sonja and Rolf had left.

"Sure love, I will. First, you will demand one million dollar pay. Just for your good looks; that should impress him," Mary smiled.

"Sounds good to me, then I am going to request another million for your workforce, I will sell you as a slave, and give Monica as a free gift, then I have two millions, you have to work and I go fishing," Conrad countered.

"Oh you heartless monster!" Mary shouted, "we'll see about that!" And she started pounding Conrad's chest again…and we already now what that leads to.

The letter got written two days later.
You the reader must now keep in mind that Monica, Mary and Conrad had no idea of the English language, other than for a couple of phrases like, 'good morning,' 'good night,' 'hello' and so on.

Letters were translated by friends or whoever was available. Telephone conversations where made with whatever few words Conrad knew, but Conrad got a dictionary, and daily they all learned a few words. Monica was quick to learn, she was a smart little girl, did not like school too much but got along with it very well. Just like her mother, she loved to be outside and play with her friends all day long down by the river, just behind the house.

From:
Mr. Conrad Weiss
Biberstrasse 19
4528 Biberist
Switzerland

Dear Mister Shiner,

  We would like to take the opportunity to thank you for considering us into your workforce. As it stands, we have agreed as a family to take on the challenge and move to Canada. However, before we can make such a life changing decision, I would like to clear up a few points, which I trust will not be too much trouble to you, to provide us with answers.
  First I would have to insist on a contract over let's say five years, where you would agree to provide me with a guaranteed job. I in return will guarantee to work for you for that period of time. In addition, I would need the sum of salary you are willing to pay. What are the standards for holiday pay, health insurance and the hours you are expecting me to work?
  How is the situation for schooling? We heard that the schools are not having the best reputation. What is the job market like, as I can see in newspapers the unemployment rate runs around 11%? Why can you not find an employee there? What is the market like for apartments? The cost of living would also be of interest to me. Average salaries and so on; please be advised that I will not

quit my job here until I have received answers to my questions. I need some kind of assurance to provide for my family, security for our child Monica, who will turn eleven in October. I trust that it is in the best interest of all parties involved that we have cleared this questions, before any further proceedings take place. I am fully aware that time seems to be a big factor I can see that and would think that you have a fair amount of outstanding work. I am willing to help you out however I can, if you need to, you may call me so we can solve occurring problems over the phone; this may help you out for the time being. You also mentioned in your last phone call that you are in the position to provide us with a house that is located in the close proximity to the work place. That of course would add convenience; could you please provide us with some pictures of the house and maybe its surroundings, so we have some idea, what we can expect?

    I realize that there are a lot of questions on my behalf, but I believe it is in the best interest of all parties involved that all is cleared up before we make such a move.

    We are looking forward to hearing from you in the near future.

Best regards,

Family
C& M Weiss

"Do you really think he is going for all your demands?" Mary asked after reading the letter.

"Well if not, then not, I am in no hurry to jeopardize our future, we have Monica to consider as well my love. Plus your back is in a condition that I have to take into consideration as well. What if it gets worse once we are older? I need to think of you two first before I make a decision which would affect all of our welfare."

"You are a good man Conrad," Mary whispered in his ear. "I have never regretted running away with you."

"Thank you my love, you are a good woman too you know. Love you, now give me some time to myself, I need to finish up a program for the machine, I need it tomorrow."

Mary settled in to watch a movie, Monica was sleeping upstairs.

Mary brought the letter to the post office the next morning, now there would be waiting to see what would happen. Mister Shiner called the same night as Mary brought the letter to the post office. Conrad was not home, he had to work late, to finish up some work.

"He sounded friendly to me," Mary explained to Conrad when he got home.

Well yeah I never said different, where is Monica?" He asked.

"She is upstairs, playing with her new dolly, why?"

"Well I need to talk to her, I just ran into Vreni our neighbor, and she wanted to know when we are going to Canada; Monica told her we are leaving soon."

"Monica can you please come down here? I need to talk to you."

"Oh hey Daddy, did not hear you coming home." With that she jumped on him, greeting him with a hug and a kiss. He sat her down at the table.

"Listen Monica, you cannot go around and tell everyone that we will move to Canada, it is too early to say so, if my boss finds out that we have plans which do not include the company I am working for, I could be in big trouble. He would be very mad to say the least." Monica promised that from then on she would keep it all to herself.

The three were a quirky little family, bursting with life. Every weekend there were family outings with Grandma, or hiking the mountain with friends. Most likely dancing Saturday night.

Conrad and Mary spent endless hours dancing to soft music on Saturday night. They danced, whether it was some festivity on a small little lake, with a improvised dance floor close to the shore, the moon mirroring on the calm water, a local band playing Waltz, Tango, Fox-trot or English Waltz, or it was somewhere in the forest with just about the same setting. There was always some reason to celebrate something and many of friends to celebrate with. Life was good to them.

Sometimes on such occasions, Conrad used to whisper in her ear how much he loved her and how happy he was; how grateful he was to the Lord, not that Conrad and Mary where regular church

215

goers, but hey had their beliefs and that God must have had something to do with the outcome of many of their adventures. Most the time the two got romantic and ended up somewhere in the bush, as European cars were too small to comfortably steam up the windows, and also driving home early was not in their minds - they were in no hurry because Monica had a sleep over at Grandma's. They ended up coming home at three or four in the morning with some friends, to have some early breakfast then finally go to bed. Life was good and they enjoyed it to the fullest.

Then the phone call came one evening.

"Conrad this is Shiner from Canada, I have received your letter. I can do a lot better than this. I will offer you partnership with the company after five years, the contract will be sent off to you within the next week or so, now I need you to work on your end to get papers ready and start to make arrangements as quick as you can. I need you here as soon as possible you hear?"

"Mister Shiner I will talk this over with my family, call me back in two days then I will give you a definitive answer."

"Why can't you move a bit faster Conrad? I need you now."

"Mister Shiner, for us it is a life changing decision and all the risks are on our side, not on yours. I am not the only one here who is making a decision. It affects all of us, therefore we will decide together."

"You're the man in the house aren't you Conrad?" The man said laughing.

"I guess so, that does not mean I make decisions all by myself. What about the pictures, from the house you have promised us?"

" I will send them as soon as possible ok?"

"Mary, could you please get Monica, so we can discuss our future? It seems this guy is more in a hurry than we are."

They decided that very same night, that yes indeed they would go for it. Now there was paper work, paper work and more paper work. Visits to the Canadian Ambassador in Bern, visits to specialized doctors, to make sure they all were in good health, then back to the consulate and so on. Time went by quickly, they were busy with getting it all together.

"I don't like the fact that he does not send us pictures of the house," Conrad explained one evening. "Every time he phones I remind him, but all he says is 'I forgot' or 'I did not have time.'"

"Oh well" Mary said, "he must have something, otherwise he would not say so." Mary tried to calm Conrad's fears then the issue got forgotten again.

The contract arrived three weeks later, and as promised, he offered partnership to Conrad after five years of service to the company, $12.00 per hour did not sound too bad either, as Mister Shiner explained that this was "top dollar" and that the average wage was around $9.00 per hour. Besides, the company would have other benefits such as health care, dental and so on.

The rent for the house was listed at $550.00, about one forth of the monthly income, so $12.00 per hour seemed not extra to Conrad, but it sounded like a good deal. After all, he got some more promises, mostly over the phone. So all three were very excited and Monica was finally allowed to tell her friends about their plans.

Now the biggest hurdle was yet to come for Conrad; he had to inform his boss Mister Haeberle. Monday morning, three months before they were to leave, Conrad made an appointment to see him in his office.

"Mister Haeberle, I have the opportunity to move to Canada, where I will take over a department of CNC controlled machines, pretty much the same way as we have here," Conrad opened the conversation. "I have been offered partnership in the company after five years of service, and I would like to jump on the offer!" Silence.

Then after a while, Mister Haeberle just nodded at first, not really believing what he just heard. Slowly he put down his pencil then looking at Conrad he said, "Mister Weiss, we have put many expenses into your training, we have built you up."

"Yes, I know you have put in a lot of effort and private hours into my training as well and I appreciate that."

"Regardless, we 'the Company' were hoping that you might retire with us; we have a long way to go and you just seem to have enough energy to keep going."

"Mister Haeberle, I am not leaving because I do not like it here, I just seem to have an opportunity to see the world, to break free and to do something different." The two argued for quite a while, and finally decided to go for a beer after work, to put some more thoughts into Conrad's plans.

The two met after work at the pub near their workplace.

"Mister Weiss," he started, "I envy you, that is a opportunity which does not come along everyday, however, I have to think of the company first. That's why I did not show too much approval at first. Now we are in private and to me it looks like a good future is awaiting you, take the chance and grab it by the horns" he said adding "I know I would." The two had a few beers and it was quite late when Conrad got home to Mary, who was in tears.

"Where the hell have you been?" She demanded to know from lopsided Conrad who walked a little like a drunken sailor.

"Oh never mind" she complained after recognizing his condition, "just go to bed now, I thought something happened to you, as you never come late without phoning first."

"That went over easy" Conrad mumbled, turned around and fell asleep as soon as his head hit the pillow.

Now things were rolling. The three were busy packing up. One day when Monica got home from school, she looked at Maedy, her dog and it was wearing a sign around his neck saying, "I am coming with you."

"Oh thank you Dad, thank you Mom!" She cried. They could not bring themselves to disappoint Monica; after all, she was leaving behind all her friends and the way she lived.

Now it was time to have one last party. All their friends were invited. Up on the mountain, it was December of 1981, it was their last get together with all the friends they had lived their lives with for so many years. They had made arrangements to have a whole restaurant to themselves, they were so many it took several barrels of beer and tons of food. The party was extensive and lasted for two full days. The floor of the restaurant was covered in beer, some of the guests blacked out. Up in the attic they had their sleeping quarters, but after a couple of hours of sleep they were back partying, ready to have some more of everything.

Then it was over, they all wished each other well for the future, promising to write to one another on a regular basis, and they all kept their promise.

Conrad was two weeks late to give notice that they would move out of the apartment, so he had to find someone to move in. Finding another tenant turned out to be no problem as the apartment was kept in shipshape by Mary. Now they needed a place to stay for their last two weeks in Switzerland, which also turned out to be no hurdle, as they could stay with a friend for that short time.

After a very last good bye to all the friends at Zurich International Airport, where they all gathered one last time for a final farewell, they boarded their plane. It was April the 24th 1982, they were to arrive in Canada at four o'clock in the afternoon, and they did. One last problem they had in Zurich was that Monica, the quirky little thing, was nowhere to be found. It took several attempts by the flight attendant to have Monica announced over the speaker system, but of course she was too busy to pay attention to it. She and her friend Nicole where occupied exploring the airport by themselves. Then suddenly and who knows why and how, the two were back with their frantic parents. At the last minute they could board the big strange looking thing called *airplane*. None of them had ever seen such a thing from the inside, they were very impressed with what they saw, and the way they were treated.

The flight attendant paid special attention to Monica and she received special treatment. Further down there was another family emigrating to Canada, they were farmers and were moving to the province of Quebec. The families exchanged a couple of thoughts and then were on their own.

"Look!" Monica shouted in excitement pointing out the window. "There is Sonja, Nicole, Heinz and Rolf, Dad's best friend!"

She was right. Also Wren, her uncle, and all the others were standing on the terrace to wave their last good byes to their friends and kin. Conrad's, Mary's and Monica's complete lives were lined up in front of them on the terrace. They took all the space they could get right up front. The three waved their passports in the small window, so they would be recognized. Then slowly the airplane taxied to the runway. To the right there was the Zurich Mountain, a small mountain, rather a hill compared to the Weissenstein, their home mountain where they grew up. Then there it was, the end to the way of life they were used to. The end of a life full of friendships, adventures, hiking, dancing on the lake at night. But it also was a new beginning, a beginning with new adventures, new friends, and maybe, just maybe they would have a lake too where Conrad and Mary could go dancing, who knew? The adventure has started.

With a powerful roar, the airplane's engines started to gain thrust. One could feel the power rushing through the big silver bird with its human cargo inside. Then the pilot let go of the brakes, and the big bird rushed down the runway and up in the air, gaining altitude, past by the last mountain of Zurich, then in the distance the Alpen range became visible. Looking down they flew over the Jura Mountain range, "their Mountain" then suddenly they were over France, westward bound.

The Author:

  To write down the last few sentences about the good-byes, was the most emotional experience I have ever had to deal with. It took me several attempts and several breaks, with tears running down my cheeks, to capture in words what likely had troubled me for so many years without really knowing what it was. It is different to emigrate from a war torn country where you have no choice but to leave, if you don't want to endanger your family and the fear of the unknown is with all of them. They all are used to certain customs, to different ideas different lifestyles. Language barrier, and culture shocks are most certain, once they arrive on their new destination.
  Stay with me to experience the "other" life of Conrad, Monica and Mary.

The Emigrant

The transformation of three lives!

At an altitude of 10 kilometers and at a speed of 900 kilometers an hour, Monica pressed her little nose on the window curiously looking down on the world rushing by way down below. One hundred and eighty people, one hundred and eighty dreams cramped into one space no bigger than a cigar, if you looked up from way down below.

    Over there that farmer with his wife and eight children, they were bound for Mirabel, in Quebec. There the farmer would get off the plane leading his family into a new future, new dreams. Why did he leave? One wonders. What did he expect from his new life there on the other side of the Atlantic, eight thousand kilometers away? He had a tiny farm in the rolling hills of Emmental, too small to support his family and no way of expanding. The farmer had to work the steep hills surrounding his small home. With a heavy steel cable, he used to secure his machine to mow the grass in the summer, up and down, up and down that damn hill, sweating under the heavy summer sun, which was beaming into the valley, the same way it did when Alf, Conrad's father, used to live there.

    How will he adapt to the suddenly wide-open spaces? How will his wife get accustomed to the suddenly changing way of life? The children I am sure will have it a lot easier, they adapt to their surroundings like flowers, they grow everywhere when nourished.

What about the young couple two rows behind Conrad and Mary? Were they going to live in Canada or were they going on an adventure? Who knew, the two did not say much as they were too involved with one another, and who cared? They all had their own thoughts, their own dreams, fears and hopes.

Conrad and Mary, sitting hand in hand in their cramped seats, holding each other's hand, were making their own plans for the future. Monica was quite busy with making new friends; already she had teamed up with one of the farmer's girls. In the midst of the isle they were playing with their dolls, and had to be reminded every now and then to keep quiet as some of the older passengers were getting rather annoyed by the two giggling and laughing.

Then after about one hour into their journey, they flew over the coast of England, leaving the old continent behind them. A continent with a history so rich it would fill more than just one library. After all, that is where Columbus, Cartier, La Salle, Padre Hennepin and all the other explorers started their way into the new world. Searching for a new world, space and possibilities to expand their Sovereign's kingdom.

King Ludwig the 14th, also called The Sun King, was in constant search of new land and riches. That name was justified, in his kingdom, as it was so big that almost the entire world was his;

the sun never really settled in his kingdom. Now about four or five hundred years later, a new breed of explorers and adventurers made their way to the new world, with different hopes, ideas and dreams. Millions before them had made the same journey and millions were to follow. Flooding the new continent with life and hopes, dreams and adventures, it was a colorful mix of life, sparkling with excitement one minute, then quiet again like a meadow full of flowers in the early morning sun. Monica, now back sitting beside Conrad and a little weary of the long journey, was looking outside when suddenly she shouted in excitement,

"Look Daddy we are there! Look at these mountains! They have still snow on them, just like our Snow Mountains back home! All is full with ice and snow, look Daddy look!" With reddened cheeks she demanded Conrad's attention.

"No honey, that is not Canada just yet," Conrad explained with a smile. "That is Iceland, it is a Northern country where there are snow and ice almost all year round. Vikings used to live up here, a wild and adventurous breed, sailing and terrorizing all the known world. That is not where we will go. But, soon we will see the coast of Canada," Conrad explained to his little girl.

"We will fly over the St. Laurent stream first, maybe you can see big icebergs coming down from way, way up north where they have come broken loose from the ice fields, just like us, drifting with the current of life. Then there will be New Foundland, Labrador, then Quebec, and then we will be in Ontario. We will have to fly at least another four hours. Now try to have a little nap princess, we have a long way to go and we would like to make a good first impression."

It was hard for Monica to settle down, too much excitement, too many new things to see and explore.

Then there it was, the first glimpse of their new, freely adopted country, the coast of New Foundland, just as Conrad predicted. Wide open spaces, so endless so big they could not see from one end to the other. Still snow on the ground, all they could see was trees, trees and more trees. Seeming an endless forest, dotted with hills, followed by mountains, more hills and more mountains, it was as if they would like to scare all these intruders away.

"Go away you foreigners, go away, we don't need humans to intrude, we have lived our lives for millions of years and we are doing well, now you are all coming and killing us!" The forest seemed to call to them. In amazement, Conrad, Mary and Monica gazed out the small tiny window, wondering what they had gotten themselves in to.

"Imagine that," Conrad started to explain, "not too long ago down there is where the Indians roamed their land, free spirited, free to go wherever they wanted to go, free to do whatever they wanted, until one day the White man came and took all this away from them. But there is still so much land down there, that we can all live in peace side by side, no matter where one is from; humans can live life with different dreams, ideas and hopes, side by side if they want to. Not all do, but that was for Conrad to find out.

It was then that Conrad remembered a conversation he had with an old friend back home before he made the decision to go to the new world.

"People over there have a different way of life," his friend explained. "They live a fast paced lifestyle. No time to relax, always after the money, they are greedy, money-hungry and stupid. They do not have time to enjoy life."

"Oh c'mon" Conrad replied, "you cannot judge these people, you have never been there" he replied.

"How can you be so short-sighted? That is exactly the problem we have here in Switzerland, we do not accept different people into our lives easily, we think too much of ourselves rather than trying to get along with everybody. We are not much different," Conrad carried on. He was always open-minded, ready to accept others the way they were, as long as they accepted him the way he was. He could be a little stubborn, yes, but sometimes that is needed if one does not want to be stepped on.

"Just look at all the 'Marios' we have, ('Marios' was the nickname for the Italians who emigrated to Switzerland) they come here and try to make a living to support their families back home, look how home-sick they are sometimes, because we don't understand them, and we don't always accept them into our society. Over in the new world they are more open-minded and accept different lifestyles easier than we do, after all, the emigrants are the backbone of the North American industry, they are used to living among different ideas, beliefs and dreams," Conrad explained to his friend.

"I am sure we will have no problem there to be accepted into their way of life, as long as we are open-minded."

With such thoughts Conrad nodded off a little bit, trying to calm down his nerves; he would not admit he was a little under pressure.

Ding-dong, the captain's deep, calm voice came on over the intercom.

"Ladies and gentlemen, we are now approaching Mirabel Airport in Quebec. Please fasten your seatbelts and stop smoking. We will be landing in five minutes, the temperature is fifteen degrees, and it is lightly overcast. Thank you for flying Swissair and have a nice day."

"Daddy now we are there right?" Monica was eager to know.

"No, not yet Monica," Conrad replied, "we are in Quebec and we still have about a one-hour flight ahead of us."

"Where is Quebec Daddy?" She wanted to know.

"Well Quebec is about five hundred kilometers east of where we are going, it is, I believe, one of the oldest Provinces. That is from where La Salle and Father Hennepin started to explore the North American continent some two hundred fifty years ago, remember, I have told you?" Monica never paid too much attention to

History so of course she did not remember. Then they were on the last leg of their journey, into their new lives, and after about fifty minutes or so the biggest city in Canada slowly entered their sight.

"Wow that is big, would you look at that?" Conrad moaned gazing out the window, drawing his two girls' attention to down below, as they approached Toronto International Airport. Slowly the plane made its approach, descending over the ocean of high-rise buildings, factories, the freeways, with cars on it looking like a big huge snake making its way through some jungle. Never had they seen such a big, bustling city; the biggest they had ever seen back home was Zurich and it had maybe two hundred thousand people. It was an exciting Moment for the three to see first-hand such a large city.

In the far distance they could see the tall CN tower, overlooking Lake Ontario, the city and its inhabitants.

"That is the tallest building in the world," Conrad explained, "they just recently finished it; one day we will go and visit it. Just a little below there are the Niagara Falls. Do you know that it took La Salle and Father Hennepin several weeks to climb the embankment of the Falls? They had to carry several tons of ship-building material from Lake Ontario to Lake Eerie, where they had built the Griffin, which they used to visit the Native Indians along the Great Lakes region to trade their furs." Conrad carried on, more to himself than to Monica, as she was not too interested.

Then there it was, the touch down. With a slight bump, the airplane touched down on the soil they would now call Home. Slowly the plane rolled down the runway then was escorted to the terminal where the passengers would disembark from the big bird that brought them safely over the Atlantic. Leaving the Swissair fleet plane was a little like a newborn baby getting its umbilical cord cut off, leaving the safety of mother's belly. All ties to their old home were now cut off for an unknown number of years.

Greeted by the friendly emigration officer, as landing immigrants they had to go through checkpoints for approval of their status. They were free to go after about one hour of signing papers, and after being checked one last time. Now they were sitting and waiting for their extensive luggage, outside the terminal.

Monica picked up a shaken but otherwise healthy Maedy. Her friend had to stay down in the luggage compartment, but now he was ready to run, and most of all Maedy had to go to the washroom then, right then! It was a long haul for her too you know. It took quite a while before they were picked up.

"I wonder whether he has forgotten us," Mary moaned.

"Oh now love, he will be here don't you worry, I have just talked to him this morning, remember?" In the meantime, sitting on their luggage in the terminal, they watched all the people rushing by.

"Mommy look! Why is this man wearing a towel on his head?"

"Be quiet Monica," Conrad reminded her, "that man is likely from India, and what he is wearing is called a turban; that is their customary headdress. People here are from all over the world, just like you Mommy and I are from Switzerland."

Then suddenly Conrad's new boss was there. A heavy-built older man with thick eyeglasses approached the three.

"Are you Conrad?" He enquired.

"Ah yes sir that's me. Good Afternoon Mister Shiner," Conrad extended him a handshake. "This is my wife Mary, and here is our daughter Monica. Nice to finally meet you sir," Conrad started the conversation. "Where do we go from here sir?"

"As I have mentioned to you Conrad we will now drive to Woodstock, this is about one and a half hour to the west of here. It is a small town of about twenty thousand people."

"Small town sir?" Conrad asked. "Our big city where we grew up had about twenty eight thousand people."

"Well you Europeans are small thinkers, here we think big, we think in different dimensions. The European brain is not developed enough to think big." It was then that the man revealed to Conrad that he was actually from the Netherlands, and that he spoke the German language rather well.

"My parents are from over there and they taught me the language," he said.

"So why did you not reveal it to me earlier sir? It would have been a lot easier."

"Well sooner or later you had to learn it anyway, so I thought why not now?"

For the first time Conrad started to develop a little bit of stomach cramps, he started to feel uneasy, just a little but not enough to make a head run with his family to catch the next plane back.

"It is going to be cramped" Mister Shiner continued to argue. "You have too much shit with you."

"Yes sir, we have many bed sheets with us as well, we did not want to sell them back home; after all we want to sleep on our own sheets." Conrad did not understand him.

"Yeah, yeah all right let's go." Mary, Monica, Conrad and Maedy, the little dog, plus big Mister Shiner all had to fit into the small pick up truck. The entire luggage had to be packed onto the small little flat bed.

"Why did he not bring a bigger car?" Conrad thought to himself. "I told him that we would arrive with a lot of luggage. Maybe it is he who has the smaller brain." Conrad did not say anything. "Well maybe he is just cranky and is having a bad day, it will be better tomorrow I am sure," Conrad reassured himself. Somehow, they managed to load the entire luggage on to the small flat bed. It was cramped all right in that small little pick up. Mary was holding Monica on her lap, while Conrad squeezed Maedy between his legs. So they went on their way down to the small little town called Woodstock.

"My wife has prepared supper, then I will unload you into a nearby Motel, you will stay there for now."

"I thought you had a place for us to stay at Mister Shiner?" Conrad gasped.

"Yes I do, but first you need to stay there, as we have to fix up the place." Conrad did not ask any further questions for then, but he sensed that something was just not the way it was promised over the phone.

"Mister Shiner," Conrad continued, "is it normal to use the first name towards people you don't know?"

"Yes it is Conrad, we all call each other by the first name."

"I am sorry sir, I don't mean to sound like a snob, but how should I address you?"

"Well, aehm, yes you may call me Adrian; seems to me that you have a problem being called Conrad."

"No sir, I am just not used to it. Superiors always called me by my last name, as in Mister Weiss; it somehow created a certain respect barrier and I have been raised that way. It is custom in Europe…."

"…Yeah, yeah I know the custom in Europe, but now you are in Canada and you better get used to it, to being called Conrad instead of Mister Weiss ok?"

"Well it is not a problem Adrian, I just need to know the rules, I have to learn what is custom here I don't want to stand out, I like to learn your way of life."

"Good then, from now on you are Conrad."

The drive down the highway was quite an adventure for the three from Europe. Unlike back home, there were no mountains, no hills as far the eye could see, nothing but one long stretch of highway.

"… Of course not, you are in another part of the country, the mountains must be just a little further up to the east and we are going to the west. I have to check this out on my first day off," Conrad thought to himself, holding Mary's hand tight. It was the first shock the three from small little Switzerland experienced. It was so completely different that they had a hard time to adapt quickly. It took them by absolute surprise. All through their lives there had been mountains in any direction, now suddenly all was flat and different.

Mrs. Shiner was a tiny quiet lady she welcomed the newcomers rather friendly but with a certain distance. Mister Shiner, "Adrian," also had a daughter about sixteen years old and a son about eighteen years old; they joined in for the meal but were rather uncomfortable with the strangers, especially after Adrian called his son a lazy bastard in front of those people. Although they did not understand what Adrian was saying, they sensed that it was likely not something to be proud of, so the two Shiner kids retired rather quickly.

Monica, shy and clutching Mary, did not say much, she ate her supper and did not move away from her parents.

"Adrian we are tired, it was a long and exciting day for us, if you don't mind we would like to retire to wherever you have made arrangements for us."

"Ok then I will drop you of at the motel, it is just a highway motel, lots of trucks, maybe a little noisy but it will have to do for now. The motel is already been sold, they will tear it down so I have gotten a special rate for a week." Conrad did not much care at the moment; they all were way too tired, too many new impressions for one day, one long journey and one hell of an adventure.

"Tomorrow it will all look different," Conrad thought to himself.

The motel Adrian had booked for the three surely had seen better days. A broken neon sign dangling down from its frame announced Saturday night dance and entertainment. It reminded Conrad and Mary of a movie they had seen a couple of years back, a so-called Spaghetti Western. "The song of Death." Conrad could not help but shiver for a minute. The hallway leading to the reception was dark, with only one light bulb trying to bring some light into the shady place. A dirty-looking and grumpy older woman was sitting behind the desk. Monica of course had to explore the place right away, and when Conrad went to look for her, she was in the bar. A lonely truck driver with long hair, dirty jeans, and cowboy boots was sitting all by himself at a table, drinking coffee out of his thermos.

"Monica, get out of here right now young lady!" Conrad ordered. In the mean time, Adrian and Mary were at the reception, Adrian filling out some papers, turning to Conrad as he came back with Monica.

"You can choose any room you like he said; there is not much going on right now."

"Well then we will take a room facing the back, away from the highway," Conrad replied.

"How long do we have to stay here?" Conrad wanted to know. "I was hoping to move into our place tomorrow, if that is possible."

"Well tomorrow is Sunday, you will have to wait till Monday for sure, then we will see, you may have to fix up the place first."

Conrad was too tired to argue with Adrian, besides he was a little scared of him by now. He could never imagine talking to any of his loved ones the way Adrian did to his family. Sure they had arguments like any other family does, but calling Monica a lazy bastard in front of other people he would never do, and talking to Mary the way this man had talked to his wife was out of the question for Conrad.

"How will this man talk to any other person, like at work?" Conrad wondered.

The three were finally able to settle into their rooms; at least the bed sheets looked somewhat clean, the room was not too dirty and there even was a television set. Now that was something for Monica to explore. While Mary started to unpack, with Conrad helping her for two minutes, (Conrad never was a good helper around the house) exhausted, Mary asked him to please let her do the unpacking.

"Look after Monica" she demanded, "I don't need the shoes on top of our bed sheets, dummy," she said.

It took a while for Monica and Conrad to understand, that the television was not actually broken, but that it was commercials, which interrupted the sitcoms the two tried to understand. As they found out rather quickly, sitcoms were the best way to learn the new language, as the dialogues were rather simple.

Finally the three were able to settle down with their first impression of their new home.

"Now we can actually live like we have seen people live in a Western movie, it feels like we are in one" Mary commented to Conrad.

"Yup" Conrad said. His adventurous side finally had taken over and he started to lighten up a bit. Monica had her own room, adjacent to Mary's and Conrad's, her own television set and all.

"But the door between the two rooms stays open" Conrad demanded; he had an uneasy feeling leaving her all by herself in that strange place.

Early in the morning, Conrad was already exploring a little bit. Monica and Mary, the two women in his life still asleep, he sneaked out of the room and outside the motel. With wonder he realized that already the big trucks were moving down the highway at top speed, and on a Sunday. Big trucks were not allowed on the road back home on a Sunday; Sunday was a day to relax and enjoy. He stretched himself, squinting his eyes in the early morning sun rising in the east.

"That is the direction of home," he thought to himself. With that he started to walk around the motel. At a short distance he could see a gravel pit, it was better yet a hill, and he decided to go with Monica and Mary later on to explore it, and maybe they could catch a glimpse of the town called Woodstock, which would be their new home from then on.

As he got back into the room the two girls also started to wake up.

"I am hungry," Monica complained.

"Yeah so am I," Mary piped up from under the blanket.

"Ok then get ready for breakfast," he shouted. "I will serve you in a minute Your Highnesses" Conrad joked.

Conrad went back out the door promising that he would be back with hot chocolate for little Monica, coffee, toast, bacon and eggs for all of them. So Conrad went back out into the hallway to find the cleaning lady he just saw a minute ago. He found her sitting at the bar, reading a paper; there was not much to do for her, she just waited for the three foreigners to leave their room so she could go and clean it up. That she hated her job was rather obvious.

"Good morning miss," Conrad approached her. "We would like to have breakfast, is that possible?" He asked politely.

"No cook," she replied. She seemed like a Mexican woman to Conrad, her English was broken like his, and she also had to search for words.

"No cook " she repeated after Conrad made the gesture of eating.

"Ok thank you miss." With that he went back to the girls.

"Where is the breakfast Daddy?" Monica demanded, "I am hungry." Conrad just looked at Mary, and then said, "Well it seems to me that Mister Shiner has forgotten to check whether or not Europeans eat too."

"Why, what is the matter?" Mary wanted to know.

"No cook," Conrad mocked the Mexican lady. "No Breakfast," he added, "we are on our own they have no cook here. So we have to find a place where we can eat. Let's get dressed, then we go over to that hill I have seen this morning. Maybe we can overlook the town and find out where we are. In the mean time I will go and get some chips and water from the vending machine I have seen down the hall."

"Yuck" Mary said, "chips and water for breakfast?"

"Just for now," Conrad replied, "we will find something I am sure." So the three went over to the big hill, overlooking Woodstock. It was a quiet day and not much going on there.

"What if we get lost?" Mary wanted to know.

"Well I have Shiner's phone number, I am going to call him, I am sure he will have some advice for us."

After a couple of tries with the phone, Conrad finally got a hold of his boss.

"Sir we don't have anything to eat here, they have no cook, what should we do?" The aggravation was quite clear and present in Conrad's voice.

"I will be there shortly after church, I will go with you and have brunch," he explained, "my treat."

"Oh thank you Adrian, so we see you in a bit."

"At least he is going to church," Conrad explained to Mary and Monica, "so he must be a good man, he will come and pick us up around noon and is inviting us to brunch. Well then let's walk around a bit and see what is there for us to explore."

All was new and strange to the three, the surrounding landscape was so strange to them that it almost scared them. The motel looked even worse in the daylight, it was dirty and falling apart. They had to wait until one o'clock in the afternoon before Shiner and his wife arrived to pick them up. Their new boss and his wife drove with them to a nearby restaurant where they had brunch together.

It was a nice setting downtown; the breakfast was rich and good. They served pancakes with maple syrup, so sweet they had never tasted before. Life started to look good again with a full tummy.

"So Adrian, would it be possible to see the house where you have planned for us to live?" Conrad asked after they finished their meal.

"It is not far from here; yes I can drive you there if you insist," Adrian said looking at his wife.

"Why don't you and Adrian go and have a look," Mary said, "Monica and I will stay here with Mrs. Shiner. Don't worry," she added, realizing Conrad had worry in his eyes.

Living the women behind at the restaurant, Conrad and Adrian went to have a look at their new home. It was a five-minute drive out of the city, on a country road, right beside a farmer's field where Adrian turned his car into a driveway.

At first, Conrad thought he wanted to introduce him to a friend or show him something new. Surely the house they had approached could not possibly be his new home. Conrad was not rich by all means, but he had a nice, clean two-story apartment back home and was used to have it clean and tidy.

It turned out that **this** was indeed the house Adrian had planned to rent to the newcomers.

"It is very conveniently located for you," Adrian explained. "Just over there in that mall is where you will work, it is within walking distance. I am renting it to you very cheap and the rent will be deducted every two weeks from your paycheck" he added.

Conrad was not able to speak, it felt as if he walked through a world of cotton, and everything seemed so unreal, Adrian's voice entering his mind from far, far away.

He needed to digest what he saw first. As he walked around the "house" there were piles of scrap steel, wood beams, garbage bags, a couple of dogs running around filthy and dirty. It was a perfect setting for a movie about slums. Weed was growing so high, Monica could play hide and seek in it.

"Let's go and check out the inside," a weary Conrad demanded.

"It is a bit smelly right now," Adrian quickly explained, "the sewer system backed up just last week, and we have to clean it out first. As it turned out, the sewer system always backed up, and it would be Shiner's joke to tell them "You guys shit too big."

"Never mind" Conrad replied, now he wanted to see it.

It was a mere trailer, set on a concrete basement, a small dark and dirty hallway leading straight in to the so called living-room, with a carpet so dirty Conrad was sure Mary would want to have it replaced. A bit down to the right there was the small washroom, able to hold no more then one person at the time, straight down at the end two small bedrooms. That was it.

"How can we fit a regular bed into this?" Conrad asked still polite and not showing too much emotion.

"Well Conrad, that here is not a European standard, all is north-American you know."

"Well yes I am aware of that" Conrad countered, "but once you have a bed in there you will not be able to turn around in it"

Conrad realized that by now Adrian was getting angry with his reaction, so he did not want to push the issue any further, not wanting to risk a bad relationship from the start with his boss.

"Well you just have to use the living-room if you want to fuck your wife," Adrian snarled. Conrad turned as if white, fresh-milled flour was in his face.

"Adrian, we are decent people, please treat us as such, and please don't use this kind of language around my family, my child in particular. We are not animals," Conrad said. Never in his life had he been treated with such disrespect. Conrad was not a *baby*, he knew some colorful expressions himself, but he would never use them in connection with his wife Mary or with Monica his little girl; he also would never use such disrespectful language towards other people, especially not people he had just met. At that very Moment, Conrad would have had no problem taking that two-by-four laying beside the stove on the kitchen floor and shoving it down Adrian's throat. Adrian realized that he pushed it too far, so he backed off a little.

By now Conrad got really quiet. On their way back it was only Adrian who was talking about the great future.

"Conrad at six o'clock tonight there is another airplane taking off from Toronto, bound for Zurich, and if you run fast enough you may catch it," the little voice in Conrad's head said. Conrad was willing to forget Adrian's remark, and wanted to turn things around. He thought it was only a slip in Adrian's dirty imagination, "stupid man-talk" he thought, so he put it aside somewhere in to the back of his mind as if into a drawer, as humans always do if they want to forget a bad experience.

Back at the restaurant Mary realized that something was not right. The two men were sitting down, Conrad with his head low.

"Listen Adrian," Conrad started, "we will take the house for now, you were right it is convenient, once we are a little more at home here we will look for another accommodation in the city. My wife needs to make new friends and so does Monica."

The three Swiss newcomers needed to learn the language and start to interact with people in their daily lives.

"Mary," he continued now looking at his wife, "the house is very dirty, a bachelor has lived there all his life and just moved out. I don't know how you are going to feel but it is really run down and dirty." Mary sensed that something more than that was bothering Conrad; she had also seen Adrian's disapproval on his face when Conrad said that he wanted to look for another accommodation. Quickly she added, "Oh it can't be that bad, Monica and I will clean it up, and I am quite sure with a little imagination we can make a home out of it."

Adrian seemed a little relived with that and ordered another round of beer, but from then on, Conrad had a hard time looking him in the eyes. Also the beer did not seem to taste too good anymore, it had left Conrad with stomach cramps, likely from all the excitement over the last couple of weeks.

"Well then I shall pick you up tomorrow morning at the motel, I need you to start working right away," Adrian finished the conversation.

"Adrian, where do we get food? We need breakfast, and what are my girls going to do all day, while I am gone? Can't we move in first, settle in? I can come by every now and then if you need me," Conrad pleaded.

I will also pick up the girls at the same time with you; they can start working on the house, all right?"

"Ok then, as long as I know where they are," Conrad said.

Seven o'clock Monday morning came Conrad and the girls were picked up by Adrian. It was the first time Mary and Monica had seen the house. Conrad did not say anything; neither did Mary, only Monica piped up.

"Is that where we are going to live?" She asked.

"Well you have to get used to it young lady," Adrian answered. "This is not Switzerland you know."

"It is going to be all right," Mary said with kind of a sad look on her face. "Don't worry, we will fix it up honey" she said to Conrad and Monica. It took her one full week to make the house ready to move in. Three containers with leftover materials, dirt, old papers and clothing from whom ever was living there were filled. Then the whole trailer had to be cleaned out, including the basement. There was a strange odor to it, Maedy the little dog would not go down there, not for her life. But Mary, Monica and a couple of neighborhood kids managed to make it somewhat of a home, though it was not even close to what they were used to. Of course they knew that things would be different, but in no way did the three ever imagine that something that small could possibly hold that much dirt.

Adrian took Conrad with him to work, it was within walking distance, and so Conrad could go and see his girls over lunch hour. The tour of the company was another small shock to Conrad's already shattered nerves.

"We will expand," Adrian explained to Conrad, "we will grow and one day we will move to Kitchener, a bigger city about fifty kilometers to the east of here. That is when I will make you my partner," he explained. The personnel was no bigger than five employees, there were three or so heavy presses, some heat-treatment equipment and one

Traminer machine. That was Conrad's machine and he was to build it up, helping the company to expand. The shop too was rather dirty and dark, as they had no windows to let the sun inside. The two men were sitting in Adrian's office, when a young lady entered.

"Good morning Jackie," Adrian greeted the young blonde lady. "This is Conrad from Switzerland, Conrad this is Jackie, my right hand. She also owns half of the house we are renting out to you."

"Miss Jackie nice to meet you," Conrad got up from his chair to greet the young lady with a handshake, which earned him a strange look from the girl, as she was not used to the custom of being greeted like that. Conrad then got introduced to the rest of the workforce.

One thing did bother Conrad; all the people seemed to have a certain fear of Adrian. They all greeted Conrad rather shyly and from a distance, then they went right back to work.

Slowly Conrad got accustomed to his new job, but rather quickly discovered that the people working with him actually did fear Adrian. He was pushy towards them, using words such as lazy fuckers, or stupid assholes, sons of bitches and so on. Most of it Conrad could not understand, but he had seen the fear in their eyes. One day he started to make conversation with one of them, as he knew Adrian was out of the office, but all he could understand was 'tyrant' and 'boss.' It was not hard for Conrad to imagine what they meant by that.

Then one day the communication board burned out again, luckily there was one at hand and Conrad was able to fix it. Within hours the machine was up and running again.

"Listen Adrian, we need to do a better clean up job on Fridays, I would recommend that every Friday we clean down the fan; in addition, the heavy press right beside the machine should be avoided, we need to move the machine away from that equipment, otherwise it will happen again and again."

"No shit mister wise guy," Adrian replied, "my son, that lazy ass, could figure that out himself.

"Well then Adrian why did you insist upon hiring me if you have such an experienced man at hand?"

"Leave that up to me all right," Adrian barked at Conrad.

"Listen Adrian, I realize that you are under a lot of pressure; I have come here to build a future together, to build a company. I am quite willing to give all I can, but I am expecting a certain amount of respect, I want to be treated with dignity. The way you talk to me does not really help me out here. Let's make one thing clear; I pay you and all the others respect, I will request the same from you and your crew. I will not be laughed at if I politely wait in front of your office until you have finished a conversation. It is custom to treat the boss you are working for with respect and he in return will treat us with respect, whether I am in Switzerland, or in

Canada does not make any difference, not to me it doesn't, do you hear?"

Conrad had talked himself into quite a storm and was not willing to back down.

"I am a human being and so are the others out there on the shop floor," he continued. "And as far as Miss Jackie goes, please keep her away from my machine, we have had enough trouble and I don't need an eighteen year old girl pushing some buttons on the command while I have my hands in the machine. I have now worked for seventeen years around machines, never had an accident and I am not intending to have one in the near future. So, that said I am now going back to work, and hopefully from now on we will have a better understanding of each other's expectations."

Adrian did not say a word; he was just sitting there, listening to Conrad's fast and mixed up speech, half English, half German. Conrad left the office shaken with nerves so strained one could play piano on them.

Conrad got home that night all shaken up.

"What is the matter?" Mary wanted to know. So Conrad made clear to her what had happened in the office.

"What have I gotten us into?" He lamented. "Look at the filth and dirt around us, the language he is using toward everybody? What is wrong with this man?" Mary tried to calm him down but it did not help much. It was a very emotional time for the two. Conrad experienced so much in such a short time, that it was necessary for him to adapt or to lose all he had. He was determined not to lose out, not to being stepped on by anyone. After all he had the full responsibility of looking after his family. That night he went to bed with quite an uneasy feeling. Finally, with Mary in his arms, he fell into a deep sleep.

One week, his first week, had gone by, Conrad worked all the hours necessary to keep things going. Adrian did not show up too much, it seemed that he kept his distance. At least for a couple of days there was no name-calling. Then Conrad had to see him again.

"Adrian what about Monica?" He asked. "She needs to go to school, have you made arrangements?" Conrad asked.

"Yes I did indeed" Adrian answered. "We have to go to the school next Tuesday, I will drive you there don't worry."

"Ok then thanks Adrian." It almost seemed that he understood the lesson Conrad had given him that afternoon. But it was only a short pause before the storm continued. After all, why should he change just because of some foreigner he had hired?

Tuesday came and they went to school with Monica. It was a private Catholic school. The first couple of months Monica would get private English lessons to help her out. Then after summer holidays she would be integrated into the regular classes. It was a heart-breaking experience for Conrad and Mary to see their little girl being driven away by a big, yellow school bus the following Monday. Conrad took a half an hour off work to see her off on her first school day. The two could not help but wipe away tears as Monica disappeared in the distance. They had a hard time waiting all day long until she would be back home again at night. Again, the experience was quite different as back home they were sitting together for lunch every day at noon.

    Mary went back into their new home to work on it and Conrad walked back to work.

    "So, is Nazi Boy bouncing back from his heart-breaking experience?" Adrian asked him with a smirk.

    "Listen Adrian, let's make one thing clear," a weary Conrad answered. "First, I was born in 1949, that was four years after World War II ended. Secondly, I am of Swiss nationality and therefore have absolutely nothing to do with the Nazi movement. So please do not start all this again."

    "Oh and what exactly is it you want to do about it? We are in 1982, in a recession, and you have nowhere to go. We have an 11% unemployment rate. Right now you will do as told won't you?"

    "All right" Conrad answered, "look Adrian, I have brought a family here, a child, and yes I am foreign here you are right, but I am quite sure that all this does not give you the right to control my life in such a way that you are close to destroying it. I am sure that even here in Canada are such laws that will prohibit you from doing what you are doing."

    "Piss on it" Adrian replied, "You have nowhere to go. You don't know anybody and you don't know where to turn for help, now get back to work."

Conrad did not want to get into any further arguments, "Serves my right" he thought instead. Now Conrad had no other choice than to adapt to the new situation, and he did that rather quickly.

One morning Jackie was about to get into the machine again while Conrad worked on it. Conrad pushed himself to the limit to stay quiet and then had to defend himself.

"Now listen Jackie," he started red faced; he had a real problem with what he figured he had to do in order to do his work.

"Get the fuck away from this machine while I am working on it. I have been hired to look after this god damned machine and if you are touching it one more time while I am working on it then there is going to be shit flying, you hear?" Conrad thundered. A red-faced Jackie left in a hurry for the office. She was not a bad person, and Conrad felt sorry for her, and that he had to use such language, but it was the only way he knew how to get respect just then. Conrad expected Adrian to come out and give him a speech, but he was not to be seen all day long. Conrad knew he was there, but he did not look for him. When he got home that night, Mary was a little on the edge but did not know how to explain it to Conrad, she did not want to stir up more problems, as she knew that Conrad had enough of his own. Of course Conrad noticed that something was not right, so after Monica went to bed the two were sitting outside to reflect on their day.

253

"What is bothering you my love?" Conrad asked sitting close to her.

"Well it is nothing really," she started, "it may be only an overreaction from me. Today while you were at work, Adrian came over with some beer. I was sunbathing in the backyard and wore only a bikini. He was sitting next to me and offered me a beer, maybe he just wanted to find out how mad you were. I think he is respecting you but does not know how to show it to you. He told me that he will go and get some potato seedlings tomorrow, and other plants and that we should grow our own vegetables right behind the house."

"Well ok then" Conrad said, "as long as he is not trying to touch you we can go along with it. I am just getting weary of all this foul language, and today I caught myself using some of those words against Miss Jackie; it does not feel right, but it seems that this is the only language they respect and understand."

The transformation of Conrad was underway!

"Saturday my love we will go downtown and look around. We have to get out of this house, so we can live our own lives without having him telling us what to do on our private time. Sunday we could go and see the Niagara Falls, what do you think?" Conrad asked. "I can take the big company truck, it is going to be fun just the three of us. Or maybe we can take the neighbors' boy with us, the one Monica always plays with. That would ensure that we come back safely, after all our language to ask for direction is not that good yet is it? What do you think Mary?

"Yes this will be a nice day also for Monica, that will get her mind off all that's going on too. I feel sorry for her, that that little thing needs to go through all this. But I am sure we will make it and soon we will see better days. One day this guy will realize that his behavior does not bring him anything."

On Thursday evening Jackie had given out the paychecks, Conrad noticed that his overtime was not paid, twelve hours where missing, plus an half an hour of his regular pay for forty-eight hours. So he got paid for only forty-seven and a half hours. Conrad took his paycheck and went to Adrian's office. He stood in front of the door and knocked on the wood frame as he always did. Adrian was sitting on his desk reading the paper.

"May I have a word with you Adrian?" Conrad asked.

"Yeah sure come in Conrad, have a seat." Conrad was relieved that he did not throw a tantrum, and placed himself in the chair in front of the desk.

"What is it you want, 'Schweinehund'?" He asked. Now that was something Adrian should have never said. "Schweinehund" is the German word for "Pigs Dog." It was used mostly during World War II by the Gestapo, Nazi Germany's secret Police. Conrad hated this word as he had seen and heard it many times during documentary films.
Schweinehund was the lowest way of putting

someone down, and Conrad was quite sure that Adrian was well aware of that fact.

"Adrian," he started, putting his anger under control, "I urge you, no, I beg you not to use such word against me. It is quite degrading and you know it. I am new here and I do not believe to deserve such treatment, and even if I had been born here I would not deserve it, so please give this some thought."

"Yeah, yeah what ever" Adrian lamented, "what is it with you? Are you a weakling? Controlled by your wife; are you not able to take a little bit of harsh treatment?"

"Listen Adrian," Conrad replied, "I have served in the Army and I was under more pressure at times than here in the work environment. However, I have never and under no circumstances heard anybody calling anyone such names. As Soldiers we were still treated with respect and at no given time were the officers allowed to use such language, it is called respect towards other humans. I don't know what it is that triggers you to use such name calling, but I have to tell you that it is very hurtful, and I beg you to stop it."

"All right wisecrack, what is it you want? I don't think you came here to give me a lesson in human behavior." Conrad gave up, he knew that Adrian would not change, but if that was the way he wanted it so be it, "...You can have it you god damn fucking bastard," Conrad thought to himself. Aloud he said, "Adrian I have noticed that I am missing twelve hours of overtime, plus half hour is missing from my regular forty eight hours, it must be a mistake."

"Oh no quite the contrary Conrad," Adrian explained. "See I will show you how you are getting paid. First this is your second week with us. Let me explain to you how things work here in Canada. First, you are on salary right?" He asked.

"Yeah that's right," Conrad agreed, "that is what the contract says anyway."

"So the first three months we pay you the hours you are working, on salary you do not get paid overtime, but you have the prospect of a partnership with me." Conrad could almost see that Adrian was right, since he did not have to punch in and out like the rest of the workforce.

"Secondly," Adrian continued, "this week you were half an hour off work to see Monica off to school, and that's why we took half an hour away. After three months of probation, this would be paid."

Conrad was not stupid he knew when someone tried to take him for a ride.

"Ok Adrian" he said instead, "I guess that is what our contract says, and I guess that is what the law is here in Canada. I am sorry to have bothered you with this, it will not happen again."

"Ok Conrad it is all right and now go back to work."

After his working hours Conrad went home to write down every single hour he had worked with date, starting time and quitting time, and every single hour thereafter. You can get into an argument even if you know you are right, but how do you prove it?

"God damn fucking bastard," he thought. *Another step forward in the transformation of a human being!*

Conrad intended to do some work on the machine on Saturday morning; he knew he would not get paid for it, but he recorded the hours anyway. It was eleven in the morning when he got back home. He noticed that Adrian's car was in the driveway.

"Oh no, not you again, can you not leave us alone at least on the weekend?" Conrad thought to himself. Monica came running across the neighbors' lawn to greet Daddy, she was playing with the neighbors' children. Kids adapt so fast.

"I am wondering how she is communicating with them," Conrad thought. As he got around the corner of the house he saw Adrian and Mary sitting on the porch, engaged in a conversation.

"Ah there you are!" Adrian said when he saw Conrad approaching them. "Where have you been?"

"I was working, finished off the last thousand parts for that NCR company in Kitchener, come Monday we can do the change over to the next batch," Conrad replied.

"Good then, come here and sit down. Mary can you go and get a beer for your man?" Adrian ordered her.

"It is all right I can get my own," Conrad quickly replied.

"What the hell is the matter with you Conrad? She is your wife why can she not get you a beer?" Adrian piped up.

"Well you know, I don't like to be served, I am very well able to get my own."

"Fuck, you're a stupid man; is this how you treat your wife?" Adrian asked him.

"It is all right honey," Mary cut in, "I will get you a beer."

"Ok now listen you two," Adrian started the conversation back up after Mary came back with a beer for Conrad. "I went to the farmers' market this morning; I have bought some potato seedlings and a lot of other vegetables that you will grow in this garden here. Mary can plow it over and then plant the seedlings next week. This woman needs to work, she cannot sit around here all the time" he continued. Conrad was taken by surprise.

"Adrian this is rather nice and thoughtful of you, but don't you think you should have asked us first? I mean this is our private life you are talking about, and I believe it should be left up to us. Besides Mary cannot possible work the garden, she has a bad back problem, and as far as going to work goes, we have a twelve years old girl my wife has to take care of. I don't want my child coming home from school and finding there is nobody home for her. It is hard enough on the child to have had such a change of life, we don't need to make it any harder for her. As far as plowing the garden goes, this is out of the question. My time is limited as you well know, but I do appreciate the fact that you went all out and bought all this stuff for us. I will plow the garden as soon as I have time, Mary then can work it a little at the time, but please next time I would appreciate if you could possibly ask me first."

"Holy shit, would you listen to that crap?" Adrian shouted while grabbing another beer. "You should be grateful to me that I have made you such an offer, you are depending on me left right and center, and I am helping you, you stupid ass. There is an unemployment rate of 11% in this fucking town, and you have nowhere to run. So just get off your high horse and do what I say."

At that Moment you could have sprayed Conrad with a water hose and he would not get wet; the water would have disintegrated before it hit Conrad, so steaming hot he was at that very Moment. But, somehow, he managed to keep his cool. One look to Mary's face told him so.

"Look Adrian, I don't know what it is with all your coursing and swearing, all I know is that I have a very hard time coping with all this name-calling and controlling behavior of yours. I really would appreciate if you could lay it off, I am not used to this way of life."

"Listen Conrad I will tell you something," Adrian picked up the conversation. "I am building up a business here, I know damn well how to handle these lazy, fucking Canadian bastards. They are stupid, stubborn, and lazy, you have to learn to control them, or you lose out."

"Adrian," Conrad interrupted the gesturing boss, "You cannot possibly think that I believe that all Canadians are stupid, lazy and stubborn; they are just like any other nation, no matter where you go in this world you always will have all kinds of people. Besides we are in a farming community here as far as I have discovered, that is not an industrialized part of the country, so you are working mostly with farmers, at minimum wages, what do you expect?" Conrad asked.

"You are too soft of a man" Adrian replied, "I need to harden you up."

"Look, I am not a business man by a far stretch, but I know my stuff and I am hard-working, in return all I am asking is to be treated with respect. When I am talking to you in the office, I don't appreciate being interrupted in the middle of a conversation by Jackie or by anybody else. I do not interrupt people when they talk to you, I do not enter your office when you are on the phone, I do not use foul language, and I am expecting the same in return. Now I have friends coming over this evening and in the afternoon we will go downtown to look for another house, as I have told you right up front, I appreciate my private life and hope you will respect it."

"YOU have friends coming over? You are only here for two weeks and you have friends?" Adrian commented.

"What is so unusual about that?" Conrad asked. "Monica met two girls going to the same class as she is, their mother is from Germany and their father from Italy so they are coming over to welcome us."

"That is not good, "Adrian gasped at the news. "You know what they are going to do to you? He asked. "They will fill your heads with some bullshit, some bright fucking ideas on how to live your life here. If I were you I would stay away from them."

" Adrian I think you are way too far into my private life by now, let's just leave it at that ok?"

"Really?" Adrian continued, "And what about this crap about you going to look for a house? I told you, you will stay here, I have rented this to you and you will definitely stay."

"We will see," a weary Conrad replied.

"Now I have some business to discuss with you." Adrian was ready for his next punch.

"May the 24th will be a long weekend, all my people will be off, and I have to fucking pay them. You on the other hand you will have to work, you are only here one month and therefore not entitled to a long weekend."

"Oh how nice, I thought I was on salary, but never mind I will work, there is so much to do that I will be able to catch up a little," Conrad agreed.

"Good then, furthermore," Adrian continued, "after the long weekend I will go on a trip to Europe, you and Jackie will look after the business, I am counting on you to keep things running smoothly you hear?

"That should not be a problem," Conrad replied.

"I will call every now and then to make sure all is in order," Adrian instructed.

"I am sure you will," a smiling Conrad countered.

Finally the boss left. Conrad headed for the shower and Mary went on to work in the kitchen; she wanted to prepare a light meal, Swiss-style to welcome the new friends they were about to meet that night.

After Conrad finished his shower the three took the big company truck they were entitled to use, and were heading to town to look for a house for them to rent. Never in his dreams Conrad would have thought that renting a house in town would alter his life in away he could never dream of.

"Well sweetheart" Conrad said while driving to town, "there is an airplane at six o'clock tonight heading back to Switzerland, if we pack now we can make it," he suggested with a smile on his face.

"Nope my love, we are going to make it, I trust you, and I know you will do fine. Just imagine going back after a few weeks, we would be the laughing stock back home, they would look at us as losers. Beside that, your old job is gone, you would have to find something new." Mary said.

"I don't think that would be too big of a problem my love, but you are right, let's not give up that easily. I guess I just have to learn to cope with this asshole."

"Shush!" Mary reminded Conrad, pointing her head to the back of the car where Monica was sitting.

"She does not need to hear such language."

"...Oops Conrad" moaned.

That Saturday they found nothing as far as renting a house goes, but they had made now contact with the town they were living in, they had seen stores, and people, how they shopped and acted; the way they dressed, their new life-style.

Monica was eager to show her parents around a bit; after all she was in town every day, she showed them where the school was again, where she played, and so on. The afternoon was quite informative for the two, now they knew where the Police station was, the courthouse, the Employment Center, the shopping mall, the fire hall.

They started to settle themselves.

"Look over there! Monica shouted, "There is McDonald's!"

"What is McDonald's?" Conrad wanted to know. "It must be where they train clowns for the circus," he explained to himself looking at the large plastic Ronald McDonald figurine outside the building.

"No that is a restaurant for fast food," Monica enlightened her Dad.

"Oh" Conrad said smiling, "I don't like my food fast, I may not catch up with it" he joked.

"Can we go there?" Monica pleaded. "All my friends go there all the time!"

"Not right now honey, we have guests tonight, you may ruin your appetite and Mommy has cooked a good supper."

"I need to find a beer store and get some wine Mary," Conrad explained. "We have nothing to drink at home for the guests tonight." With a lot of asking around they finally found a beer store; Dad got himself his first twenty-four beers case. Now he wanted some wine but was unable to find some. The guy at the beer store, noticing that Conrad was not familiar with the practice of buying alcohol in Canada, explained to him that he could only buy beer in the beer store. Wine at the liqueur store, but he would also be able to get some beer at the liqueur store, adding to Conrad's confusion.

"…So beer in the beer store, wine in the liqueur store, but also some beer at the liqueur store," he murmured to himself while getting into the car.

"What was that?" Mary wanted to know.

"What was what?" Conrad asked.

"What you just said getting in to the car."

"Oh that!" So Conrad explained to Mary all over again what he had just learned.

"And I thought that this was a free country, now you cannot even get a beer without going to a special store. All the restaurants have their curtains drawn so no one can see inside when you have a beer, hmm funny" he complained.

"Oh well" Mary said with a twinkle in her eyes, "now you just have to drink your beer at home."

It was a relaxing afternoon the three had, and after guzzling down some ice cream, they went back to their *trailer junk,* as Conrad used to call it. Mary went back into the kitchen. Monica and Conrad were to set the table then Conrad had a little time left to himself, so he went on the porch with a beer to think it all over. His future, his past, the uncertainty, and suddenly he missed his friends and his mountain terribly.

Then it was six o'clock, it was time that those people should be there by now, and after all they had made arrangements for supper to be at six. Mary got desperate in the kitchen; she could not hold the food much longer without getting it burned.

"Are you sure it was six o'clock?" Mary enquired back with Conrad.

"Yup" he said, "maybe they are being held up by something, they will be here shortly I am sure, just put the food on low."

"Yeah but the 'smashed potatoes' are getting all mushy," she lamented. She always said 'smashed potatoes.'

Finally at half an hour past six the new friends arrived; a short, quirky and tiny little German woman and a tall, heavyset Italian man with their two daughters.

"We are so sorry for being late, but we got held up by some friends of ours. Hope it is not too much of a problem." Well of course it was not, after all Mary was only cursing in the kitchen and not upfront.

Well I am Theresa; this is my husband Francesco, and our two daughters Patricia and Francesca.

"It is nice to meet you all. We know Monica already from school, so that is how we heard that there are some newcomers in town from good old Europe. I am working at City Hall in the Employment Center," Theresa explained; in fact, she was the only one talking.

"How did you folks end up in this trailer?" Theresa wanted to know.

"It is only temporary," Conrad said, "as a matter of fact we just went today into town to find another home for us. Mister Shiner is renting this one to us."

"MISTER SHINER?" Theresa shrieked. "You are working for Mister Shiner?" She had to assure herself.

"Yup" Conrad said, sensing that there was something bad just about to surface.

"I don't mean to scare your pants off Conrad, but what is your experience with Mister Shiner?"

"Well he is rough around the edges, uses a lot of foul language, and I have to defend myself all the time. Why what is the mystery behind Mister Shiner?" Conrad wanted know.

"Kids why don't you go outside a bit and play? Theresa suggested.

"Well we can all go and sit on the porch, then we can see what the children do," Conrad said.

"It is likely to be cooler out there than in here." So they went outside after dinner and made themselves comfortable on the porch.

After a while Theresa said, "I know a family here in town, the man is from Switzerland, he is working as a teacher at the Fanshaw College in London, his wife is a nurse for the Lung Association, I will contact them next week, I am sure they also would like to welcome you.

"Then outside Woodstock there is another family, the woman is from Switzerland as well, her husband is Canadian, I am sure that they also would like to welcome you. We are a very close-knit community, and since I am working at City Hall I know most of the people around here." Conrad, Mary and Monica suddenly were not all that alone anymore.

"Theresa, what is with Mister Shiner?" Conrad interrupted her cascade of words.

"Shiner? Oh yeah Shiner. Listen Conrad be careful, I know that in the last six months this guy has had eight people fired over some machine they apparently kept destroying; I know that because I work at City Hall" she responded. Mary and Conrad looked at each other with an unspoken agreement to keep quiet.

"Well I am a trained CNC programmer; I also have experience in tooling and production on his machine type. I don't think that I will have any problems as far as that goes," Conrad clarified his position.

Theresa was a bubbly little woman; with cascading words she entertained most of the evening.

"Well soon I believe we will find another house, then we will be more than glad to welcome you back for another wonderful evening."

"Oh I forgot!" Theresa continued. "We are just in the process of renovating our second house, it is a two story house and if you would like to have a look at it in about two weeks we will gladly rent it out to you. It is within walking distance from Monica's school, just two minutes away."

"Oh great then I can go home during lunch," Monica piped up.

It was an eventful evening, and when the newly made friends left, the three were not all that alone anymore.

Early the next morning the three left for Niagara Falls. Monica was the translator; after only a few weeks she had spoken the most English of them all. Slowly, unnoticed and quiet, she was slipping away getting accustomed quickly to a different society.

The Niagara Falls were quite something to see for the three. It was all so big and thundering, and full of people from all around the world. It had left them with quite an impression. On their way home Monica finally got her wish and Conrad decided to give this fast food a try.

"Well it certainly is not a home-cooked meal, it is ok on occasion, but not something we would make a habit out of," he pondered aloud. He was used to having a family meal, quiet and sitting at the table together until all were finished. He was shocked to see children running around with French fries stuffed in their mouths. For him it was too noisy a place. On the way home, Conrad and Mary started talking about their future in their new home.

"What do you think of Shiner Conrad?" Mary asked.

"Hmm he is certainly not the ideal boss, Conrad replied, "but we have to see what the outcome will be. I certainly don't like the way he talks to us, and how he wants to control our private life. I have seen a lot of fear in the people I work with. For the next few years, there is not much I will be able to do, but I hope that, one day, when he is giving me partnership, I can make a difference in the employees' lives. In no way should they have to come to work afraid to be yelled at on a daily basis," Conrad explained.

"I think that we can make a good living here, people seem to be nice and we already are starting to make new friends, if only he would stop sticking his nose into our lives… it seems to me that he does not like it when we make friends, he seemed very upset about it, and Theresa was not too fond of him either it seemed. We will see what the future holds in store for us," Conrad continued.

"Sometimes I wish we would have never come here, but to go back now would also be a financial strain; it is all gone now and we would have to start all over again. So let's try to make the best of it." Conrad added.

When the three got home that night there was a flowerpot with a note in it. It read: "Hello, I am Ruby, Bruno my husband is Swiss like you. We wanted to welcome you today but found you were not home. I will come back tomorrow to see you, good luck," signed, Ruby.

"There you go" Conrad said, handing the note to Mary. "A new friend; who says we have no luck?"

Monday morning Shiner steamed into the office.

"Conrad where the fuck were you yesterday? I wanted to see you and the neighbor told me you went to Niagara Falls, can you please explain yourself?" Adrian asked.

"Sorry sir," Conrad politely said, "but I really think that this is none of your concern, it is my private time and I don't think that I owe you an explanation for it."

"Well I really don't like it when you just take off like that; I wish you would report to me next time." Now that was something Conrad had a hard time with.

"Adrian," he replied, "I told you once and I tell you again, what I do with my time is MY business and not yours, I did not come to Canada to be told how to live my life, I wish you would lay off, please do not control me ok?"

"Next time you just let me know when you take off again or I am going to take away the company car from you."

"Nope" Conrad replied, and with that he left the office.

In the meantime Mary had a visitor at home. It was the lady who left the flowers on their doorstep the day before. She invited the three to join them for coffee in the evening, with the promise to come back frequently and to show Mary around town, so she could go shopping and explore her way through her new life. Conrad was happy to see his Mary beaming with excitement when he got home at noon for lunch.

That evening they went to visit their new friends Ruby and Bruno. Bruno was a quiet man in his late forties, he was a teacher and had lived in Canada for quite some time.

"So what made you to live in this area, I mean the trailer you live in?" He asked.

"That is only temporary" Conrad explained, "my boss is renting it out to us." Conrad was embarrassed. "…But we are looking for another house and as a matter of fact we already have an offer from a couple we met on Saturday."

"If you have trouble with anything, please let us know, we will guide you and help you out, should you need it." Bruno and Ruby explained.

Now that made the two feel a lot better, knowing that they were not all alone.

Then it was the Friday before the long weekend on May the 24th, a holiday, as Conrad understood from his co-workers, as they were all excited over an extra day off with pay. Shiner made clear to Conrad that he had to work, and that he would come to check on him, since he was all by himself. Conrad did not mind it, he had enough work piled up to keep him busy, besides, Mary and Monica would visit him as they lived just across the street.

The prospect of having a better house to rent was now closing in on them. Theresa and Francesco came to see them that Monday night.

"We are almost finished with the apartment, would you like to come and see it?" They asked.

"Sure!" Conrad, Mary and Monica shouted as one. "We can go and see it right now." The house, as promised, was all fixed up nice and tidy. It was the upper level of a two-story brick house. Out of the window they could see Monica's school. They liked it and wanted to move in right away.

"I have to fix up a rental agreement first" Theresa said, "but I will see you by the end of the week if that is all right with you?"

"Sure no problem!" A relieved Conrad and Mary said.

"I am going to wait to tell Shiner at the end of the week; I don't want to leave the trailer before we have something in writing." Conrad explained to Mary on the way home.

"Yeah I believe that would be the best. He will get the news soon enough," Conrad chuckled.

"I know he is not going to like it, but we have to get out of there and I have told him that on the first day I saw this dump."

By Friday that week, Adrian called Conrad back in the office.

"Have a seat Conrad" he started. "You know that I am going to Europe on Sunday, here are some of the drawings I need you to look over, I am expecting you to work hand in hand with Jackie, she knows all about the business, I have trained her, and she also is my right hand."

"It is all right," Conrad added, "as long as she keeps her hands away from the machines, she can do whatever she wants in the office."

"Well then as I have said before, I will call back every now and then to see how things are going," Shiner said.

"Have a nice trip and come back safe and sound" Conrad wished his boss, and with that he left for home.

It was not until Sunday, when Theresa and Francesco returned with the contract, that Conrad and Mary happily signed the papers. Conrad said, "I have to inform Jackie first thing Monday morning that we will move out by the middle of the next month; this may be short notice, but I have never signed a contract for the trailer nor did we ever make an agreement, and besides that, I have told Shiner from day one that I would look for something else."

Monday morning it was all calm and quiet in the shop, even Jackie seemed to be a bit more relaxed.

"Jackie," Conrad started to explain, "we have found a house downtown that we are going to rent, we will move out in the middle of next month, I hope that this is all right with you since you are part owner of the house."

"Yeah I can't see any problems," Jackie agreed, "I just have to let Adrian know as soon as he calls so we can make arrangements to rent it out again, which should not be a problem since your wife has fixed it up rather nicely."

Bruno and Ruby, as well as Theresa and Francesco offered to help them move. Luckily they did not have too much right then, as they had a hard time finding furniture that they liked; Woodstock was only a small town and the selection was not that large.

On Thursday, early in the morning, Adrian called from Europe; he wanted to know how things were going. He never talked to Conrad, but Jackie had the intercom on, and Conrad was sitting in the next office looking over some blueprints. Conrad could not understand the conversation, just bits and pieces. Adrian had a short conversation until Jackie told him that Conrad and Mary were about to move out. Jackie could hear him exploding with rage over in Europe.

"That fucking god damned son of a bitch, I told him that I need him to stay in that trailer, I told him not to mingle with the people from the town! Tell you what Jackie," he thundered, "you will keep his paycheck, he will not get paid until I am back from my vacation; once I'm back I have to see what I am going to do with this asshole. Furthermore, you will take the car key away from him, he does not need it anymore."

"I cannot keep his paycheck Adrian, that is illegal, and he needs the car, how else would he go shopping?" Jackie replied.

"I don't really give a shit whether he goes shopping or not," Adrian retorted. He can walk as far as I am concerned, and about the paycheck, how would he know what is legal and what is not here? I am going to teach this bastard a lesson he will never forget, just wait till I am back."

It was not until four o'clock that afternoon that Jackie, red faced, approached Conrad.

"I, hmm, I cannot give you the paycheck Conrad, Adrian told me to hold it back until he is back from his vacation. I would also need the car keys."

"Why what happened?" Conrad demanded to know. Jackie explained the situation to him.

"Tell you what, I do need the car, you know as well as I do that without a car I am pretty much lost out here, it is too far to walk downtown, we need groceries and a lot of other stuff. I keep the car keys, if you want them you have to come and get them from me if you dare. I will explain that to Mister Shiner myself when he is back," a shaken Conrad stated.

"As far as my salary goes, you can keep it, so there will be no trouble to you from him. But I am warning you; I am not as stupid as you guys may think we foreigners are. We are simply unfamiliar with a lot of things, but I know how to help myself."

Poor Jackie, there she was in the middle of two men fighting and did not know what to do.

Conrad got home that night in such a mood he could have been biting stones. He was in such a rage over all this that he now really needed a beer.

"We have to use our security money," he explained to Mary. "He cut my paycheck until he is back; what is this guy's problem with this piece of junk he calls a house? Why all this trouble?"

"We will manage" Mary tried to calm him down. "He may have just gotten out of hand because he does not know what is going on."

"My ass," Conrad replied, "he knows exactly what's going on. He wants complete control over me, or us, that's why he got so upset the other day when he found out that we have made friends. He thinks he can control us left right and center, because that way he can do whatever he wants, and we are never to find out."

It was not an easy night for Conrad to sleep; all night long he tossed and turned, his thoughts far, far away.

"What is going to happen to us?" He asked himself.

Come Saturday the three were invited to Bruno and Ruby's for supper, and to meet their three children. Conrad explained the situation to his newly made friend Bruno.

"I really don't think he can keep the paycheck back," Bruno explained, "but I will make some investigations for you. I would think you could sue him for that."

"Oh no" Conrad said, "I don't think that this would be necessary, I believe that when he comes back we can clear the situation." But Conrad was not so sure of that. Beside he did not want to get in to any trouble after that short of a stay in his host country. He never had anything to do with the Police or the courts, and here he would not even be able to, because he did not know how to go about it.

It was hard for Conrad and Mary over the two following weeks; they had to pack all up again to get ready for the move, plus the uncertainty of what's to come did not make it any easier for them. Conrad got really achy and nervous; it did not take much to get him excited anymore. But he was willing to fight for what he thought was right, he was not willing to just look away or just stand by and let it happen to him. After all he had a family to look after which he was very much committed to.

It was Monday morning when Adrian returned to work. Conrad knew that he was in the shop; he had seen his car in the parking lot. Adrian did not come out on the shop floor and Conrad was so nervous that he had to go and wash his hands every five minutes they were so sweaty, he could just feel that something was about to happen, but could not put his finger on it. Then at about ten o'clock Adrian came to see Conrad. He looked scary with his thick dark glasses; short on breath he approached Conrad.

"What the fuck are you doing asshole?" He barked at him. "You think I am offering all this to you so that you just can come over here and do whatever you like to do?" Conrad could feel that all the other employees stopped working and were looking at the two, expecting some spectacle just about to unfold. Conrad never in his live felt so small, so humiliated, and so helpless. It took all his guts to say, "Listen I don't think you can hold my paycheck back, I am working for money like everybody else, I may not be quite aware of how things work over here in Canada, but one thing I know for sure: I work and you pay. I am expecting my last two paychecks in my hands now, then we will talk about the house. Ok then?" Conrad let go and he found himself barking back at Adrian like Adrian barked at him. That earned him some respect from the coworkers, as they would never have the guts to talk back to the boss like that, they knew they would lose there jobs if they did that, but this newcomer seemed to be a little more sure of himself. Sure the guy never talked much, but it seemed it was more of a language barrier than anything else. He minded his own business, treated everybody with respect and in general was nice to people. He also had brought them some chocolate from Switzerland as a welcome gift.

The shop grew silent, nobody moved when Conrad started to bark, it was like the calm just before the storm, when all gets quiet just before the thunder starts.

"I don't think," Conrad continued in his broken English, "That you can possibly be serious bringing me over here with a contract in my pocket and a prospect of a partnership in your business, and then treat me like the fucking dirt under your shoes. Even in Canada there must be a law, which would prohibit you to do what you're doing. You are spying on my private life, you tell me what I can do and what I cannot on my own time. Adrian I am asking you one last time to please stop it."

Adrian just looked at him, he never said a word after Conrad started, but now he was white in his face then red, then finally he let it out.

"Tell you what asshole," he barked, "you are fucking fired, get the hell out of my shop and I will never see you again, you goddamned fucking bastard. GET OUT!"

It was like a bomb exploded in Conrad's head, like from far, far away... he heard the words, but it was as if he had cotton balls in his ears muffling all sound. Never in his life he got fired on a job; getting fired was the most unthinkable thing to him.

"Don't you hear me, bastard?" Adrian yelled. "Get your fucking tools and leave!" Slowly it started to dawn on Conrad that he just lost his job, a job in a country so unknown to him, so new, that he just could not believe what he just heard. He did not want to be humiliated any further in front of all the staff, so he just hung his head low in shame and left.

Like walking in his sleep, slowly Conrad made it across the parking lot with legs so heavy as if filled with lead. He did not see the fancy car parked in his driveway, nor did he see the young woman talking to Mary, who at the time worked in the garden. He just sat down on the steps leading to the porch, lowering his head into his hands and started crying. Like a little boy he was sitting there, not knowing what was going on around him. Mary and the woman came toward him but got no response when they asked what troubled him. Mary just took him in her arms to comfort him. He was completely unable to talk, tears just running down his face, a face that had seen happier times. It took a while before he could control himself, and even longer before he could talk properly.

It turned out that the young woman who was with Mary at the time was actually also from Switzerland, and she had heard that there were newcomers in town and she wanted to greet them. Her family had a very large estate out in the country, and they were very rich. After Conrad was somewhat in the position to talk, he explained what had happened earlier at the shop.

"Well I got to go now" the woman said. "If you need help here is my phone number and address, please feel free to call should you need help."

Mary and Conrad were left alone, left alone with all their worries and grief, the uncertainty of the future, and the big unknown about how this would end up for them.

Conrad let go a slew of mixed words in English and German, some of them even unknown to Mary. He worked himself into a frenzy, such that Mary thought she needed assistance with her man.

For some reason, unknown to Mary and Conrad, Shiner passed by the house several times that day; he just drove up and down the road very slowly, glancing over at the house, but never stopped, just drove up and down, and he kept that up until the day the three moved. It scared the hell out of the three; especially evenings when all was quiet, they could see him through the window, they did not know what he wanted; were they stalked? Hunted? Did he want to kill them and then bury their lifeless bodies in the basement? What kind of man was he? Was he with the Mafia they heard so much about and that they had seen in movies? It was scary enough that he watched them. Then on the day they moved out of the trailer, later on that day, they saw him following them to their new residence.

The three would have a long and winding road to recovery ahead of them. Conrad put all the blame on himself.

"I should never have opened my mouth" he complained, "I should have kept quiet and go along with it. Now what?"

A few days after they had settled into their new home they invited all their new friends.

Theresa, Francesco, Bruno, Ruby and Susan, the young woman from Switzerland, along with her husband Jack. The main topic of discussion was, of course, Mister Shiner, and what the three were now about to do with the new situation. They all promised to help them out however they could, but "....Remember," one said, "we are in a big recession, with an unemployment rate of 11%, it will not be easy to find employment that quickly, can you manage?"

"For a while anyway," Conrad said, "but I need work, and money goes fast."

"... Well, uh, that was what I wanted to talk to you about, Conrad" Theresa approached him after the others were gone.

"Mister Shiner was over at our house, last night, he found out who we are after he had seen you moving in here."

"What does this man want from me?" A startled Conrad asked.

"Well it looks like he wants to ruin your life, he came to us and said that you have very little money, he had seen it when he came to the bank with you to open an account; will you be able to pay the rent in the future?" Theresa asked.

"Don't worry" Conrad replied, "I have only taken part of my money with me, I could not possibly carry a larger sum of money, we still have some in a Swiss account, you will get your rent, on time every single month; I never was late with a payment all my life and I do not intend to change that now."

"Ok then," a relieved Theresa said, "tomorrow I will go with you to the Employment Center, I have arranged an interview for you with someone I know, I believe that you are entitled to unemployment payments."

"Well that is good news" Conrad said. "Thank you very much for your time." But it was not all that good news; Conrad only worked close to two months in Canada and therefore he was not entitled to anything, but what he found out about Mister Shiner was at least of some value, if not in money, at least in the way of information that could help Conrad. Mister Shiner was well known to the people at the Employment Center; almost every other week he was there to look for some new workers because they would either leave him or they got fired. Eight people in all over the past three months were a lot of people for a shop that size.

Theresa, informed with all those news, encouraged Conrad to sue Mister Shiner; she knew a lawyer in town who could speak German and just recently had opened his practice there in Woodstock. Theresa was a wealth of information, she knew just about everybody, and it was she who could provide Conrad with a little bit of work under the table. Conrad started to learn how to dry wall, and paint, as he fixed up an office for someone Theresa knew, or he could cut the lawn for somebody else. So there was little money coming in, and Conrad did not want to touch the Swiss account, not yet anyway; who knew what was yet to come? And things were coming.

Every morning at nine o'clock Conrad would be one of the first ones at the Employment Center; he was eager to get to work, but in that sleepy town of maybe twenty-thousand people and with an unemployment rate of 11%, the prospect of landing a job was not that great. He had seen a big factory just a little outside of town, not far to walk from where he lived, it was a lumber company, building heavy equipment to cut down big trees, but he never got past the gate, which was guarded by security.

"Listen man, you are wasting your time coming here," the guard said to Conrad one day.

"This is a Union shop and if you don't know anybody here you are wasting your time. Sorry man," a sympathetic guard informed Conrad.

Mary and Monica in the meantime tried all they could to help make ends meet. Mary baked excellent bread and Monica used to cut up a full loaf of it and went from house to house, giving out samples so Mary could bake and sell a few loaves, contributing to the meager income that Conrad had brought home from jobs he had on the black market. Conrad's two girls did whatever they could to help Daddy out, but it broke his heart to see what his girls did just to help him. He was supposed to be the provider, and he had failed them miserably.

One night late they were already in bed, Monica sound asleep, when Conrad brought the news to Mary.

"Love, I have seen the lawyer today, we will sue Mister Shiner, the lawyer is very confident that we have a case."

"Oh my god!" Mary lamented, "You want to go to court with him?"

"Yes I will, I believe that guy owes me, or us, an explanation at the very least. Besides I still did not get my two paychecks and that he owes us," Conrad explained, but poor Mary was frightened, as the two never had anything to do with a court.

"…And how exactly are we going to pay the lawyer?" Mary wanted to know.

"He is not asking for any money until the case is won, he said that he is so confident that he can wait, not wanted to make our lives any harder."

"Well that is nice of him, maybe you are right, and we should give it a try at least. Go for it big guy!" Mary encouraged him.

The two started going to English classes; it was there where they befriended a bachelor from Holland, who also had just arrived at about the same time as Conrad and Mary. He bought himself a farm in the small township of Tillsenburg, just about thirty-five kilometers south of Woodstock. He was lonely, so he got attached to his new friends rather quickly. He helped them out when he could. He worked for a small Company down in Tillsenburg, a small machine shop with not much going on.

It was a hot summer that one of 1982, Conrad had plenty of time to rummage through the town, seeking opportunities to work, but nothing happened. Slowly he had to dip into his Swiss account, just a little at the time, only what was absolutely needed to make ends meet.

One day Conrad was in town to look around for work, and when he came home he found a devastated Mary.

"You will never believe who paid us a visit today," Mary greeted him,

"Who? Shiner?" Conrad asked in despair.

"No not him, it was a man calling himself the Sheriff." Now all Conrad knew about a sheriff was what he had seen in Western movies; a whisky-guzzling and gun-slinging man, that was the picture he had of a sheriff.

"No, no, not like that," Mary explained to him smiling. "It was a regular guy with an identification that showed him as Sheriff, and he had to bring you some papers, which he is only allowed to give to you personally."

"Wonder what he wants?" Conrad asked. He did not have to wait too long for an answer; that same evening the gun-slinging , whisky-guzzling Sheriff was at the door once again.

"Sir I have to bring you a court order, Mister Shiner is suing you for two months rent, you apparently owe him. Please be in court on the date indicated in the paper."

Conrad and Mary were shaken by these news.

"How can this bastard do this to us?" Conrad moaned. "Tomorrow I have to see the lawyer again, now that is another case entirely, and I am sure he will charge us for it."

Next morning first thing Conrad walked into his lawyer's office with the letter from the Sheriff. He could not make much sense out of it; his English was improving but the legal mumbo jumbo he had a hard time with.

"That should not be a problem," the lawyer said. "You have given notice to Jackie right?" The lawyer asked.

"Yes I did." Conrad answered.

"Did she agree to let you leave the house at the date indicated?"

"Yes she did," Conrad answered again.

"Well then let's nail that guy. With the other stuff we are making progress, I think we will nail him to the floor with this too."

Slowly the money situation was getting tighter, Mary and Conrad had to dip into their Swiss account deeper and deeper as time progressed. It was not a very pleasant situation for the three.

It was the night before the first court case. Slowly Conrad made his way through the night, making sure that no one would see him; he had a large machine-gun at his side, thirty-six rounds of ammunition were loaded into the chamber. He made sure that no one could see him around the factory building where he used to work for Shiner; he assured himself by looking in all directions, making sure no one was around to see him. Then, there it was, a Police cruiser slowly made its way through the rainy night. Conrad knew that they would come, often enough he had seen them cruising around the building at night. Yes he was scared, what he was about to do was not easy for him, but he had to do it. With nerves shattering, he waited until the cruiser was gone again. He had seen the light in Adrian's office; the rest would be a piece of cake.

    Often enough he had been trained, in the Army, to do night assaults. He knew exactly what he had to do; kick in the door, aim the submachine gun right onto his chest, pull the trigger and let it go. It would be over so fast that guy would not even know what had hit him.

    Stealthily Conrad worked his way through the small factory; he had entered the building from the other side, now carefully working his way down the hall towards Shiner's office. With one hell of a kick Conrad opened the door to Shiner's office with his right foot, and at the same time aimed the rifle right into Adrian's face.

    Shiner's lower jaw dropped right to the floor in disbelief of what he saw. He certainly was not a hero; he was nothing but a fat, beer-guzzling monster.

    "Conrad what are you doing? Come on don't do this shit," he said as he was shacking, and Conrad noticed with growing pleasure that the guy he hated so much was in fear, nothing but cold damn fear, cold damn sweat running down his fat face.

    "Ok listen to me bastard," Conrad started talking.

    "You can have it easy or you can have it the hard way, it is up to you, you son of a bitch, you dirty, fat pig, you have ruined my life my wife's and our kid's life, now show me how much of a hero you are!" With that, Conrad aimed his gun lower and with a dry 'plop plop' the first two rounds of ammunition ended up in Shiner's knees, silenced by the muffler Conrad had installed. With devilish satisfaction Conrad noticed the fear and the pain in his opponent's face.

"See how easy it is?" Conrad asked. "Nobody can hear us, and piece by piece I will finish you off. I can make it with one shot and it is all over and done with, but that would be too easy for you fucking bastard, don't you think?"

Funny but all Conrad could hear was himself; he could see Shiner talking but he could not hear him. It was then that he suddenly felt a sharp pain in his chest.

"Conrad, Conrad wake up!" Mary yelled pounding her small fists on his chest.

"What is the matter with you?" A scared Mary asked. "You are shacking all over, you are sweating you must have had a bad dream?"

"Yeah I must have," Conrad nodded in agreement and at that moment he hated himself for even thinking of killing someone. With that she comforted him in her arms and slowly the two drifted back to sleep.

Monica had to give up on the small wishes a twelve-year old girl has, but she was understanding and very helpful to her parents. By now Conrad and Mary had three cases in court. On one hand, Conrad felt that he had to somehow, prove that he was well able of programming, tooling and operating Shiner's machine, because Shiner sued Conrad for not being able to have control over the machine as stipulated in Conrad's papers.

Conrad sued Shiner for not keeping to the contract, so he needed to find a job with similar applications where he could prove himself. On the other hand, Shiner sued Conrad for two months worth of rent; two different cases, but if you don't know the legal system it is scary stuff.

The next morning at eleven o'clock he had to be in court. Susan, the rich young lady from Switzerland, accompanied Mary and Conrad as a translator. She offered her help, as she knew that the two would not speak enough English to follow all court proceedings. It was a crowded courthouse, small claims court was overworked in those days.

Mary and Conrad sitting in the hallway awaiting their trial, looked on as Shiner and Miss Jackie stood a few meters away, peering and laughing at the two as if to say, "We are going to get you, asshole." Mary was devastated, her nerves tied as tight as they could be, she was so nervous that Susan had to help her walk into the courtroom.

Conrad did not feel any better. With his nerves trembling he had a hard time controlling himself, as he would have liked to walk over to the two and kick their faces in.

Such was the situation that morning in the small courthouse down there in the small town of Woodstock. You might think, "Big deal, small court claims, piece of cake," but try it with little understanding of the language, or with the prospect of your life, as you were used to it, about to be destroyed.

    The Judge was a young-looking man with a chaffy beard and messy hair; somehow Conrad liked the man from the start. He looked like a man with a good sense of what is right and what is wrong.

    Conrad got called to take the stand for questioning, with Susan by his side to translate; Conrad tried to answer any question the judge had, but his tension was running high with emotions. Sweating, and nerves as tense as they come, Conrad talked himself in to a frenzy. Susan had a hard time following him. His lawyer kept looking at him gesturing to keep a low profile, but Conrad saw his chance to finally let go of what bothered him for so long. Having to look into Shiner's laughing face was not much help either.

    The judge never interrupted him and seemed rather sympathetic to this young man with the broken language. Conrad's slew of words seemed not without a certain degree of anger as he talked about that man who lured him with his family into this strange country, foreign to them, then dropped him like a hot potato just because he wanted a house to rent and not a trailer dump.

    Then it was recess, the judge ordered Conrad not to talk with Mary during that time, as he wanted her for questioning. Then after the recess, the judge waived the questioning period for Mary, as he noticed her huge distraction, so he went right on to Shiner. Thank god he was his good old self, Mister Shiner. He started to plea for his rights of two more months of rent from Conrad.

"This son of a bitch had left the unit I was renting to him, without proper notice; this asshole does not know how to behave in another country."

"Mister Shiner," the judge interrupted him more than once, "watch your language or I will throw you out of court." But Shiner would not listen and carried on as usual. Finally the judge came to his verdict.

"Mister Shiner," he started, "Miss Jackie is part owner of what you call a house, and she agreed to let Conrad go at the time indicated by the Weiss family, therefore, you have no right to another rent payment. Next time" he added, "you may want to be a little more careful who your business partner is. But, that is beside the fact that I think that you are one hell of a lousy man; your case is dismissed. With that he turned to Conrad and Mary and wished them best of luck for their future, have a good day Mister and Mrs. Weiss." He added.

It was obvious that the two were a relieved couple. The lawyer was beaming with pride when they left the Courthouse to discuss further steps to be taken to sue this man for cheating this couple out of their livelihood.

Not much happened in the next couple of weeks, but then one evening Bruno came to see them with good news.

"Conrad I have found a job for you, I have met the businessman down in London, and he is willing to take you on. It may is not be what your trade is but at least you are working." Conrad beamed in excitement.

"When can I start?" He asked.

"Tomorrow I will drive you there," Bruno said, "you will have an interview with him personally. It is about fifty kilometers from here."

"How do I get there?" Conrad asked. "I have no car, no means of transportation, do we have to move again?" Conrad wondered aloud. "If that is what we have to do, then so be it, we will move."

"Slow down Conrad," Bruno cautioned, "first we will go and see the man then we take it from there ok?"

"Monica was not too happy about the prospect that she may have to move again, she just made new friends and she liked it at school.

"We will see tomorrow then we take it from there," Conrad said, alleviating Monica's fears.

Early the next morning Conrad was ready, dressed in his best Sunday suit complete with tie. He waited for Bruno to arrive and to drive him to this new boss.

The man turned out to be a good-natured well-mannered boss and sympathetic to Conrad's story; he was willing to hire Conrad as a machinist. Ten dollars to start with, which was not much for his battered budget, but it was a start. Conrad was all excited.

"...But how do I get to work?" He asked with a waning enthusiasm.

"We have already thought of that," his future boss answered. "I have one employee who is willing to give you a ride, he will pick you up at your house; for him it is not a big detour. What you have to pay him you may discuss with each other, I will introduce you to him, before you leave." So he did, and as it turned out it was a quite older man who would help Conrad out, and he promised to pick him up Monday morning and for a small fee he was willing to take Conrad with him to work. All he asked for was fifty bucks a week, which was a lot for Conrad, but it was better than having no job at all.

The job was not in Conrad's field as a CNC Programmer and Tooling specialist, but for the time being it would do the trick. Sooner or later something in his field would come his way; as long as he could work, things would start to look better. Conrad made new friends quickly at his new job, and the guys he worked with seemed to like this quirky quick-witted guy with the funny language. Soon he was close to being his good old self again. The guys were more than willing to help him out with the language barrier, told tons of funny jokes, and he himself started to open up again. Mary and Monica happily noticed the change in him.

Every Friday Mary would bake braid bread, about thirty loaves of it, some of which Conrad took to work to sell. The future started to look just a little brighter again, if only that up coming court case would go away. It was in the back of Conrad's mind, and he was desperately looking for a job where he could prove himself in his field.

Then one day the man who picked him up for work every day like clockwork, asked Conrad to please look around for a car of his own.

"Yes I understand," Conrad said, "but please, can you give me enough time to look for a loan so I can go and buy a car?"

"Sure" the man said. He knew Conrad's story and wanted to help as much as he could, he just liked to drive to work by himself and that Conrad understood as he himself would rather be independent.

"A loan?" The loan officer at the bank asked Conrad. "Do you have security to back up the loan? Do you own a house? Do you have money? How long have you been at your current job?" Just forget it, Conrad did not know where to turn anymore; no money, no transportation, no one willing to loan him a lousy thousand dollars so he could go to work. It was then that Conrad remembered that after all he was a citizen of Switzerland. Switzerland has a policy to help Swiss people abroad who are in need. So Conrad contacted the Swiss consulate.

"Sir this is mister Weiss; I need your help."

"How may I help you Mister Weiss?" The Consul in Toronto asked.

"Well how about loaning me some money so I can bring my family back home to Switzerland?" Conrad did not want to go back to

Switzerland, he was not about to give up, and he did not even know why he said what he did.

"Well sir we are not that quick to bring Swiss citizens back home, that is a long process Sir."

"Well I don't know why I have asked you that Mister consul, what I need is a thousand dollars so I can buy a car and go to work."

"Do you have any security Mister Weiss?" The consul asked.

"No sir I have lost all I had due to bad circumstances, but now I have a job and need a car fast."

"Ok sir," the man in Toronto said. "We have a fund for Swiss citizens in trouble in other countries around the world, we will be able to loan you let's say one thousand dollars, to be paid back at an unspecified time. We could process the money tomorrow if you can pick it up sir."

"Sir I will call you back in a few minutes to confirm that, thank you sir, thank you very much." Conrad hung up the phone; he had to call Susie to ask whether she would drive with him to Toronto. She hastily agreed, she had not much to do and was willing to go with him. In no time Conrad had the cash he had asked for, without any interest to pay. A friend at work was willing to sell him an old 1965 Dodge convertible, needed a little work but for only six-hundred and fifty bucks; it left Conrad some money to get it on the road.

Things started to look better, money was coming in and Mary and Monica did well in helping out, selling bread, which the whole neighborhood knew by now, thanks to Monica's efforts of advertising.

Then one day Willy, their friend from English school, came to visit.

"Listen Conrad" he started. "I have a job for you down in Tillsenburg where I work. These guys bought some machines and they are exactly what you are looking for." That was the happiest news Conrad had heard in a long time. He actually got a job offer coming to him, rather then he looking for it, and these were the kind of machines he was trained for; besides, one dollar and fifty cent increase in wage also did not hurt, and helped Conrad make a decision.

It was not easy for him to quit the current job as all the people were nice to him, and he liked it there, but with that he could not put butter on the bread couldn't he? So he had no choice but to quit. His German boss was not happy but was in full understanding of his situation.

That coming Monday Conrad started working down in Tillsenburg; he was very enthusiastic and put in all he could, but, only for two more months, then the small company went bankrupt. A small sign informed him and the people he worked with that the shop was closed when they arrived to work one morning. It came unexpectedly to Conrad, and it hit him hard. This time however he was entitled to unemployment insurance so at least they had something to live on.

It was then that Conrad collapsed one evening in the bathroom. A frightened Mary and Monica came racing upstairs when they heard him collapsing to the floor and knocking some stuff down with him. Conrad lay unconscious on the floor; he had lost his belief that it would ever get better. Until the money came in from the Employment Center he needed financial assistance for the first time in his life Conrad was not able to provide for his family anymore, and that hit him hard.

The man from Social Assistance Services, came over one day to hear his case. First thing he asked Conrad to do was to sell his car.

"Well" Conrad pleaded, "how exactly do I go and look for a job without a car sir?" He asked.

"Well you are right, I will take this into consideration." The man was very understanding and forgot about the old clunker in the driveway. Conrad had the hardest time being on social assistance; he was at the very bottom of society, for him it was a blow so hard that he could almost not cope with it. To make things just a little worse for the three, Susie came over shortly thereafter with not much good news.

"Listen, I have to stop socializing with you people, you just don't fit my lifestyle, you have nothing to give me or to enrich my life, so please do not contact me any longer." *Thanks Susie, that was awfully nice of you, but never mind we will manage, end of it.*

To Conrad she was not worth losing sleep over. She was only another bump in the road, as nice as it was when she helped out the odd time, which Conrad was grateful for, he did not need friends like that right then.

It was a long haul again for the three, but this time around, Conrad knew a little more how to get around, and he had his old car. Just after five weeks of social assistance, he was able to be on his own again, but the experience had left an emotional scar in him. He did not put trust into anyone coming close to him, he wanted to be left alone and sort his own problems.

It was then that Wren, his younger brother, called from Switzerland.

"Listen Conrad" he started, "I have booked holidays in Canada for four weeks, we will come and visit you how about that?" he asked.

"Well that is nice Wren, but you cannot possibly count on me with much for the holidays, you know I am unemployed; I told you earlier on, remember?"

"Yes but I am sure we can manage some how, do not worry" Wren assured Conrad.

"Well then, I will pick you up in Toronto, just hope my car does not break down. See you guys then." Wren in the meantime had gotten married.

"That is all we need right now" a weary Conrad explained to Mary. "My brother is so god damn picky I am almost certain that he will have a lot to complain about."

Sure as hell, Conrad was only too accurate with his prediction. It was a Saturday afternoon when Mary, Conrad and Monica drove to Toronto to pick up their company from Switzerland. They were excited over a family visit; after all Wren was Monica's Godfather. Carefully Conrad drove his old clunker to Toronto and parked it at the airport's parking garage, not aware of the prices there.

Wren's airplane came in late that night, two hours late to be accurate. After a lengthy hello ceremony, they finally made it to the car.

"What in the world is that?" Wren said pointing to Conrad's car.

"That? That is my car and it is working, most of the time anyway" Conrad joked. "Well then let us go, the prices here at the airport are not likely to be cheap." Conrad said as he paid. Arriving at the new home down in Woodstock, after a two-hour drive, Conrad had to go and fill up with gas, and Conrad paid. Not wanting to look cheap, Conrad and Mary did whatever they could to make the two feel welcome. Now that was a task by itself, knowing Wren's fastidiousness.

"I would like to go into the wilderness," one day Wren announced.

"Sorry my dear brother," Conrad said after another long day of searching for a job, "but I just don't have the money to go anywhere, and I believe that I have told you that."

"So what do you want us to do?" An angry Wren asked.

"Look what you do with your holidays is you problem not ours, I have told you that I just don't have the means of going on holiday, I am in the middle of a job search and to me that is way more important than your holidays."

"Well that is a nice welcome," an irate Wren answered.

"Look I am sorry but right now I don't really give a shit, I have told you and I tell you again if needed, I have no money. If you are so eager to go into the wilderness, be my guest, there is a car rental just down the road!" An angry Conrad explained.

"Car rental, what you mean car rental? Can I not have yours? You don't need it do you?"

"Wren, are you fucking blind, plain stubborn or just too god damn stupid to understand? Let me spell it out for you, I N E E D T H E C A R T O L O O K F O R A J O B, got that?" Conrad asked. It took Wren a while to 'get it' and even then, he had a hard time and could not understand why his brother was in such a rush to look for a job; after all he got unemployment money, did he not? So what was his problem?

It was a long and additionally hard four weeks with the extra two mouths to feed. Mary did bake extra bread every day, because the bread from the supermarket of course was not good enough for Mister Wren. Then finally the four weeks were over, this time Conrad did not park at the terminal, he unloaded his guests right in front of the departure terminal and waved them good-bye. *See you, bye, bye.*

He needed to extend his search for a job, so Mary made him a sandwich every morning so he could go to the bigger cities and stay there all day in search of a job. It was hard. Especially then, with Christmas just around the corner and with no money to spare for even the smallest of gifts or a Christmas tree.

The three celebrated Christmas with a tree branch, which Conrad cut off a tree; they decorated it with handmade crafts. Mary was always a talented woman with making things look nice with little or nothing. They had a small gift for Monica; it was a very sad and emotional time for them. They missed their friends back home terribly, but to go back home and just leave everything behind was just not in their minds. Conrad, joking, suggested one night, "Let's throw all the shit we have out the window, and set it on fire then go to the Consulate to move us back home." All this was not truly what they wanted to do. Besides, Conrad had some unfinished business with Shiner. He did not want to just leave and leave this guy behind laughing.

"Oh no, not with me you son of a bitch" Conrad thought.

Every now and then they got invited to Ruby and Bruno's, or Theresa and Francesco's, but they had nothing to give in return and so were left alone most of the time. Not that they were ungrateful for all the help they had received, but it just was not the kind of friendship they had back home. Sure, everybody was busy with their everyday problems, and sure they were there with suggestions and help, but what was missing was the warmth; the nice and cozy feeling one develops when with close friends.

Then one day Conrad got lucky, or so he thought. While in the big city of Kitchener, searching the help wanted section, a help add caught his attention. *"Help wanted"* he read, *"experienced CNC machinist, great opportunity for self-starter"*.

After a long search around the city, he had found the company that was looking for help. Straight in he went, looking for the Employment Officer. As it turned out he also was from Germany, as a matter of fact, half of the company's employees were from somewhere in Europe. Conrad could start his new job three days later, with a pay he never dreamed of being able to achieve: thirteen dollars to start with. It really looked good, the only thing now left to do was get the pending court case with Shiner behind him as quickly as he could. It was still high on his priority list. Now he at least could prove to the Court that he was well able to do his job, and to be an honorable member of society in his chosen country.

Quickly he drove home that afternoon to bring the good news to his family. They had not seen their Dad in such a good mood in a long, long time and it was refreshing for all of them to finally have overcome the hurdles.

Conrad started the afternoon shift, and again he was able to make new friends. Especially with that one guy who came over from Germany, just about the same time as Conrad did, but never had to suffer any job loss.

One night after their shift, that new friend invited Conrad to his home, a short distance away from where the two worked. He got his wife out of bed and they had a couple of drinks; they really liked each other, and once again it seemed that Conrad would be able to spread his wings. They talked about a hundred different things, but one thing in particular; they wanted to live on a farm so they could grow their own vegetables, maybe have a few chickens and so on. This went on for several weeks, and on Sunday Conrad would go and visit them with his two girls. After a while, the idea of the farm became a reality, as they spotted a farmhouse close by to where the two worked. Conrad was at his job now for two months and gained back some of his confidence, so renting the farm and splitting the rent was not so far off an idea and a practical one at that.

It was in Conrad's third month of employment that the adventurous couples decided that renting the farm would be good for them all. Mary and Conrad planned on raising chickens and rabbits; there was plenty of room for them to grow, and so thought Iles and Vera, their new friends. On a Friday afternoon, just at the start of his shift, Conrad went to see his boss.

"Well Mister Rothschild, I would like to move to Kitchener with my family, but first I would like to know about my future in this company. I have been here now for almost three months, and I don't want to move and then be out of a job again." Conrad had gotten very careful as far as trusting anyone went.

"Nope, you are fine, we are happy with your performance, you are never late and you are always on the job." Conrad was happy to hear the good news and could not wait to get home that Friday night to tell his beloved Mary and Monica that all was fine now and the future locked bright. Quickly a contract had been signed by the four to rent the farmhouse.

Soon it was moving day; Monica once again had to say good bye to her new friends, but on the other hand she also was looking forward to living on a farm, where her little dog, Maedy, cold run free with all the other animals.

The Farm, 100 acres large, was ideal for the four relatively 'new' comers from Europe; here they could fulfill an old dream of freedom and self-efficiency.

The farm was located on top of a hill standing all alone overlooking almost all of their newly chosen city of Kitchener. Conrad could walk to work, it was only about three or four kilometers away; this way they could save on gas and preserve the old clunker a bit.

But the new found peace and freedom would not last too long for Conrad and his family; of course, lady luck seemed to have jumped out of the airplane somewhere over the ocean when they moved to the new continent.

One day Conrad went to work only to find that all his coworkers looked at him in a strange way.

"Are you here to pick up your shoes or something?" They asked him. He sensed that something was not right when he and all others who worked on his machine where called into the office. The three guys nervously sitting in the office were waiting for their boss to arrive. None of them had any idea on what to expect; they were all fairly new on the job. One of them, a man from Yugoslavia, lamented that he wanted to go back to work and that he had no time to wait around.

Conrad had a slim idea about what was yet to come. It just was a gut feeling that told him it was not much good, but whatever was to come, he had the assurance from his boss that he did a fine job and so he thought, "What ever it is, at least I have a job, anything else is just minor problems."

After about five minutes, the supervisor and the manager called all three into the office; that was unusual, but what the hell do these new guys knew about Canadian practices anyway?

"Guys," the foreman started, "fifteen large pieces worth several thousands of dollars, produced over the last three shifts, had to be sorted and we have three parts which had to be scrapped. No one knows where these parts were made, but they were produced on your machines. We are aiming for quality, and also time is money. The three of you are all new here, so we have to assume it was one of you who made the mistake, consequently, all three of you are fired. Please go and pick up your belongings and leave the facility right away."

Conrad was stunned to hear such news. If these parts were to be scrapped by one of them, why the hell did they not try to find out who it was responsible first, and then judge?

"Oh what the hell is the matter here? I am going to see the German employment officer first thing tomorrow morning, I want to talk to him, something is just not right here, there must be some other shit involved" Conrad thought to himself. Shaken over the bad news once again, Conrad had a hard time driving home and tell his Mary that he was out of a job, so for a while he drove around in his car to relax a bit first. This was the second time in his short employment history here in the new land that he had been fired. Never was he fired back home in all his working time, he just could not understand what was going on. After a while his nerves calmed down and he was able to drive home and bring the news to his beloved family.

Mary was sitting at the kitchen table preparing some food for Conrad when he came home late from his afternoon shift, and Monica was running around with her dog. Mary new that something was terribly wrong, Conrad should not have been home at that time. The two just locked eyes; Mary understood completely when Conrad was sitting down at the table with tears running down his cheeks.

"Again?" She just asked.

"Yep" was all he was able to say. Then after a while, he started to complain, more to himself than to anyone in particular.

"Why the hell can't we find some peace here? Why is everything we touch going wrong, no matter what we do? We just don't seem to be able to succeed here," he lamented. "Where is god when you need him? Did He forget we are here and not in Switzerland anymore? He must have lost track of us…" Conrad went on and on, he was completely devastated.

The court case with Shiner still on his mind did not make things easier for him either.

"Tomorrow I will go and see this guy once again," he explained to Mary. "Something is just not right here, something is against me here, I can feel it."

Early the next morning, it was nine o'clock exactly and he was at the front desk to ask for Mister Rothschild, the friendly German guy. He was let in right away. Once in his office his head was low once again; Conrad could not hold his head up too often lately, he was a changed man. He sat down as Mister Rothschild asked him, "So Conrad, what is it I can help you with?"

"Well sir, I just feel that this was uncalled for; a little while ago you assured me that I am doing a fine job and that I had nothing to lose moving to Kitchener. Next thing I know I am out of a job, what is going on?"

"Listen Conrad, every now and then the owner shows up here, and when he is in a bad mood someone has to go, no matter who it is, and I am telling you this in confidence, do you hear?" Conrad just nodded.

"Are these parts really bad?" Conrad wanted to know.

"Well we are able to fix them, it was not that big of a deal, you were just in the wrong place at the wrong time."

"Well that is comforting to know!" Conrad interrupted, knowing damn well that there was nothing that he could do to prove that the whole thing was just plain wrong.

"Listen Conrad, I feel sorry for all this, I have talked to a friend last night about you, I knew you would come back. He has a small shop in Waterloo and is willing to hire you, it is only a small shop, he will not pay much, but at least you have a job right?"

"Yeah, right," Conrad nodded, "thank you Mister Rothschild," and with the address in his pocket Conrad left the office in search of his new boss. Conrad was pretty much at the end of his rope, his nerves were shattered; by now he was not able to do much anymore, he would start to cry whenever he was alone, he felt devastated and alone in the whole wide world. He had two girls to look after, whom he loved immensely. A wreck he was, down and out on the ground, not understanding what was going on around him. He had lost trust in anything that was seemingly good, he just would not let anyone come near him anymore. But he did not give up, because he knew that after every fall one must get up again, life cannot go down forever, there must be a hill somewhere, even for Conrad. Lady luck was too busy somewhere else, but sooner, or later she eventually would show up. She just had to, there was no question about it, but how do you know, when the luck turns in your favor?

The new boss turned out not too bad but the job he had given Conrad was rather just a way to help-out. He was to clean out a warehouse in the midst of February, without any heat in the building, the pipes frozen and with ice on them; it was hard to work, heavy clothing and thick gloves did not make the job easier.

"We cannot really afford to heat the building," Conrad was told. "First we have to make it workable." So he did whatever he could just to keep working. Bitterness had come upon him, but he kept going. From his lawyer down in Woodstock, Conrad had gotten the news that the first hearing in court was just a couple of months away, just to make Conrad a little more uncomfortable.

One Morning, the new boss came to see lonely Conrad and how he was doing.

"Listen Conrad, I can give you a job in the factory, one of the guys just quit; can you solder brass metal?" He asked. Conrad had no idea what brass or soldering was and was shaken over the news. If someone would have explained to him what it was, or Conrad would have had the nerves to ask he might have said yes, but this way all he could do was shake his head, "Don't know sir!"

"Well anyway, come on over, I may find something else for you."

Conrad the next day went to see his boss at the factory, and after a few minutes of discussion, he was to operate a CNC machine. One now would think that this was just what Conrad needed! But at that time he would much rather slip in to a hole that would mercifully swallow him up. No longer was he confident in his ability to do anything right.

About two days into his new job a drill in the machine broke off, and when Conrad was about to fix it he just lost it. He closed his toolbox with tears in his eyes fearing that he would get fired over this, and silently he left the building. For three hours he drove around in the stormy winter weather, without knowing where to go. He had a nervous breakdown; when he got home that night, Mary had a hard time calming him down.

"Come on Conrad" she pleaded, "go and feed the rabbits and the chickens," she went on, hoping that this would help him to cope with the problem.

"… Then when you are finished we will call your boss I am sure he will be understanding."

"Yeah sure," Conrad murmured, "who will understand me know?" He asked, but he did go into the barn to feed the rabbits and the chickens. By now they had thirty-five rabbits, twenty chickens for eggs, and fifteen chickens for meat. It was hard work to keep all that going after work but it helped. At least that way they had food on the table no matter what.

Every night the rabbits needed fresh straw for their nest, the chicken den needed to be cleaned out and so on; this helped Conrad to cope with a lot of his problems.

The next morning as promised, he called his boss to apologize.

"Listen, sir, I just lost my nerve yesterday over that broken drill, I have no explanation for it, I just called to say I am sorry."

"Well that does not help me much," the boss complained, "I have lost four hours of production before we found out that you were gone, please come over here to pick up your paycheck."

The following few days, Conrad wandered about the farm; he no longer had any ambition to do anything else, endless hours he would spend with his rabbits and chickens. He no longer had the inclination to deal with Humans; there with his animals at least he could not get hurt anymore. He had lost complete confidence in himself and people. Down and under he was.

Mary was devastated to see her once so happy and lively Conrad in such a state of despair. Then one day, not too long after he had lost his last job because of his nerves, Lady Luck knocked on his door, in the form of an Insurance Salesman. But how do you know it is lady luck? How do you define lady luck when you have lost all trust and ambition? Well she is just approaching you and you will not recognize her, unless you let her help you.

"I am sorry sir," Conrad told the salesman, "but I have absolutely not one penny to spare for any insurance, I am out of a job and have a court case pending with my first boss, and it just does not look any better for the future right now."

The young and friendly salesman was not about to give up; he went home that night without making a sale, because he understood Conrad's position completely and he did not want to put pressure on this man who obviously was on his last leg. However, two days later the friendly salesman knocked on Conrad's door again.

"You just don't give up do you?" Conrad said.

"Well sir I did not come to sell you anything, but I believe I have good news for you."

"Did I win some kind of a contest?" Conrad asked.

"Not really, but I would like you to listen to what I have to say; could you please let me in? It is damn cold out here."

"Oh sure, I am sorry" Conrad said, stepping aside to let the young man into the house. The two were sitting down as Mary brewed some coffee. Monica was in her room doing her homework.

"So shoot!" Conrad started the conversation. "What is so good about your news?"

"I have a friend, he is working in a machine shop just a short distance from here. His boss is looking for a man with CNC programming ability. It is only a small shop downtown, about twenty-five guys, but as far as I know they are a heck of a crew, my friend really likes it there, the boss is a little of an alcoholic but seems to treat his people right," the salesman explained. Conrad was not too enthused; he did not trust himself to do any job right anymore, but after Mary's plea to give it a try at least one more time, he gave in. Conrad promised the salesman that in three months, should things have improved, he would indeed buy some insurance from him and from no one else.

With mixed feelings, Conrad went the next day to see this machine shop. It was obvious that this man was an alcoholic, Conrad could see it on his face, how swollen it was, his clothes were dirty and it smelled of stale beer in the office.

"Sometimes I sleep here," the man explained to Conrad when he noticed his startled look.

"There is so much to do that I just don't have the time to go home." The truth was that he did not want to go home to his family, because his wife gave him a hard time about his drinking habits.

"Go out on the shop floor and have a look around," he suggested to Conrad. "Talk to the guys and if you like what you see come back to see me."

Conrad by himself, willing to give it at least a try, went to look around and to see the small shop. He talked to the guys on the shop floor, they were all very friendly and seemed to like Conrad.

"You just have to overlook his drinking habits," one of them explained to Conrad, "otherwise he is ok, and sometimes on Fridays he buys beer for all of us. We have a good relationship among us and things are not looking too bad.

"Over there in the corner is the machine he just purchased, but we have nobody to program it," the guys explained to Conrad. It was a twelve-station CNC Turret lathe from Japan, Conrad recognized the computer system, it was the same as he had seen back home in Switzerland. He started to trust those guys, as they seemed to be really a bunch of good friends. They even had a few good laughs together and slowly Conrad opened himself up, so he decided to give a try. After about one hour on the shop floor Conrad went back in to the boss' office to tell him that he was willing to tackle the machine.

"Sir before you hire me, there is something I have to explain to you about me," Conrad started.

"Shoot" the boss said. So Conrad explained to him the journey he had had so far, he explained his situation and that he was very nervous about the upcoming court case with Shiner.

"That is a bunch of bullshit," the new boss said, opening a fresh beer. "We will take care of you Conrad, it seems that you need a change in life don't you?" Conrad almost chocked, he could feel tears rushing to his eyes, he could feel that life was about to take a turn for the better.

"I will give you all the time you need to get back on track. You can start tomorrow, I do not expect you to run production I want you to get familiar with the machine first. I will pay you fifteen bucks to start, we don't really have work for the machine until late next month, that's when it will all start, I believe that by then you will be ready, I will give you some scrap material which you can use to get back in to the programming."

Conrad could not believe it! So much luck in so little time, he had a hard time understanding that this was for real, not just a dream he had, but he was quick to promise to start the next day.

A happy and smiling Conrad eagerly brought the good news to his Mary and Monica after he left the company; this looked too good to be true, but it was!

Quickly Conrad became one with the machine and its technology, and in no time they were in production. His buddies at work were a happy bunch and slowly Conrad changed a little. Renewed trust and a better outlook toward life lead him to be a little closer to what he once was, and sometimes he even had a little song on his lips. Singing a song about adoring the mountains, or the freedom, which laid within them.

Spring was just around the corner and there was plenty of work to be done at the farm. A big garden needed to be plowed, but with not much money yet, to rent equipment, Conrad took on the task of working it all by hand, after all the demanding and long hours he had at work. Mary and Monica helped however they could, but now they had a good outlook on the future.

Then one day the lawyer from Woodstock called.

"Conrad I need you down here at once, how soon can you come? He asked a startled Conrad.

"Well I cannot really afford to take a day off, but can you see me in the evening?"

"Yeah sure, why don't you come down here tomorrow? I think I have good news for you" the lawyer said. And so it was that Conrad, Mary and Monica went to see him the following night.

"Listen Conrad," the lawyer started the conversation. "Next week there will be the first hearing in court, but Shiner offered an out of court settlement." One could hear the release falling off Conrad's chest; could it really be over after all they went through? Did that son of a bitch finally give in?

Conrad was not too eager to go to court; too little did he understand the language, the rules and the law. All he wanted was peace, quiet and finally a better future for Mary, Monica and for himself.

"What is it this guy wants exactly?" Conrad asked the lawyer.

"Well he agreed to pay you for all the air fare for you and your family; he agreed to pay you the outstanding two weeks he owes you, and he agrees to pay for all costs you had."

Wow, that was a change; Conrad did not ask further questions, he was happy to finally get rid of that nightmare, and relieved, he signed the papers and with that it was over.

Not looking back one minute, he pondered how over the past three years he endured so much in this strange country he had chosen, and how he went on to a better future, at least for a little while until one day fate struck once again.

It was one hot summer afternoon; Conrad was at work when he got a phone call from his neighbor who rented the farm with him.

"You have to come home right away," the woman pleaded with Conrad.

"I had to call the ambulance, they will be here in a few minutes to take Mary to the hospital; I have found her unconscious behind the barn."

Without waiting on further explanation, Conrad rushed off from work. Eyes filled with tears he drove home as if the devil himself was after him. He could see the ambulance already by the farmhouse.

"When, when is all this ending?" He pleaded with God, with God and the whole world.

"Is all this never coming to and end? What have I done to deserve this?" He asked himself over and over.

"What happened to Mary?" He yelled as he jumped out of the car, engine still running. They were just finished placing his Mary in the ambulance on a stretcher.

"Sir please follow us, we will bring her to the Emergency at St. Mary's Hospital, we can tell you more there." Off they went, with sirens and an angry, lost, and desperate Conrad in pursuit. What could possibly have happened to her? Question over question raced through his mind, as it turned out, Mary had collapsed in the midst of her daily chores on the farm, she just collapsed. The last couple of years she was always the stronghold in Conrad's life, always looking out for him, always giving him strength to keep going, nurturing him when they seemed without a future. Always there, always strong and with a positive outlook on life, now they seemingly were on the road to recovery, and she just collapsed.

It took Mary two weeks in the hospital to somewhat recover. Although she was a nervous wreck once she was able to get back home, and it was now up to Conrad to nurture his Mary. It was a long and painful road for all three; it was not easy on Monica either to see her Mother suffer that way.

After a while, Conrad had no choice but to admit Mary once again to the hospital; Mary suffered from a form of anxiety. Several times a day she had to phone Conrad at work to reassure herself that all was right. Luckily Conrad's new boss had full understanding of the situation and he could work his lost hours in the evening.

Almost every night Conrad took Monica to see Mary at the hospital, but now they had moved Mary to the psychiatric section of the hospital, and pumped her full of pills. It was heart wrenching for Conrad to see his once so lively Mary just sitting there, no longer aware of what was going on around her.

Monica had a hard time as well seeing her mother that way. After a while Conrad decided to take her out of there before it would be too late. He had the promise from their friends at the farmhouse that they would look after for her during the day, and Conrad's boss assured him that what ever was needed to be done Conrad could do; he would fully support them. His new friends at work also would pitch in and help-out if needed.

With so much goodness suddenly going on around the three, it was easy for them to hit the road of recovery. One could see the three starting to bloom once again, and the love for life once again returning, but the farm was just too much of a task with all this going on. Conrad was unable to work all the hours at the office, plus the work on the farm. Monica also was on the road to young adulthood, and needed a change in life in her favor. So the three decided once again to make a change in their lives and leave the farm behind.

Moving to the city was just making so much more sense. There was no need for another car; Monica now would be able to take the bus to school; Mary could go shopping whenever she needed, and Conrad, should the car break down, would also be able to take the bus to work.

For the next five years, all went well for the three from this tiny country in the midst of Europe. Conrad was not willing to let anything come between them anymore, he just would fight or do whatever he needed to do to survive, whatever that may be. One small problem however remained. As good as a boss he was, his boss' drinking habit was not really promoting the growth of the business. Conrad and his friends could see how the business slowly went downhill. They all were more than aware that such a good thing would soon end. This time Conrad was prepared; he had plenty of time to look for another job, he now lived in the city and things were just easier to tackle from there than from the farm out in the country.

He head heard of a young company with a fast growing rate with an owner who also was from the old continent. Friends told Conrad to try his luck there, but Conrad hesitated for quite a while, because first he liked his boss for obvious reasons, second he did not want to go into an uncertain future again, and thirdly it seemed unfair to him to quit the job that had helped him so much. Then one day fate took Conrad's decision into her own hands. It was as if Lady Luck would take Conrad by the hand and say, "Don't worry I look out for you this time, I am right beside you, trust me I will make a decision for you." Therefore, so it was.

One day Conrad came home from work, and Mary awaited him with the good news. She had gotten a phone call from this fast growing company he had heard so much about. Someone had found his lost resume by sheer coincidence and called him. On Saturday at noon, Conrad was to have an interview with the owner himself. He, Conrad, was quite nervous now; after all it was a change about to take place again, and Conrad did not like changes too much anymore. As it turned out, he would be hired right away, or at least within two weeks, as Conrad did not want to just drop his current job as he was quite grateful to his present boss, and he did not know how to the tell him that he had the prospect of a better future. Then on Monday morning, this too would sort it self out without

Conrad's doing. As the boys started working on that Monday morning, they all got called into the office. Their boss was awaiting them with bad news; his business went into receivership, he had one week to finish his ongoing work, and then the doors would be closed indefinitely. The crew was expecting something like that for quite a while but no one would just quit and leave, they were all pretty loyal to their boss, and nobody liked the situation. It was plain good old luck for Conrad that he was where he was, at the right time, in the right place.

It turned out to be a very fast growing and very demanding job Conrad had to tackle with all his other new friends. It was well worth the effort, for years to come he and his coworkers would work endless hours and nobody wanted to stay back, it was a fast-paced environment with many changes on a daily basis. Conrad liked it and this time he was lucky, and he was not willing to let go again. Quite a few managers were changing places, but Conrad was holding on, doing whatever was necessary to succeed. He gave up his private life for quite many years, ten, twelve, sixteen hours daily had become routine. Seven days a week and quite often Conrad went into work to check out that all was ok with his machines.

Then something went wrong with one of the specialty machines. The machine park was not able to produce enough parts on time, and a weekend shift was needed to produce the missing parts. Conrad agreed to fix the troubled park. Luck continued to be on his side, and soon they were able to do it without the extra shift. Conrad became a group leader, but it was a hard time for him and the people who worked with him. In order to succeed, Conrad needed to push equipment and equipment operators to the limit, so he demanded all he could from his crew and himself. He would not let go, he knew what it meant to be on the list, and he was more than just scared to lose it all again, always having the past few years in the back of his mind.

Then one day a new supervisor started. Jim was not a bad guy but had a drinking problem, which prompted Conrad to be on alert again. After a while for some reason, Jim thought that Conrad's equipment could run smoother.

"Listen Conrad I will assign you to a different machine park; Bob, my friend, will take over your equipment."

"No way Jim," Conrad said. "You know damn well that I have worked hard with this equipment for the past ten years, and I am not willing to just give it up again. Besides, he has only been with us for a little over six months and has no previous experience, so what would he possibly improve?" Conrad asked.

"Never mind, tomorrow you are going to take care of the other equipment as discussed, end of it."

"Here we go again," Conrad thought to himself. *"But not with me you son of a bitch!"*

Conrad had no other choice but to work on his newly assigned machine park. Not happy with his new assignment, but with no other choice he had to carry on. Once again, there seemed to be a change in his life heading his way, but lady luck remained on his side. After a week Conrad was ordered back to his old job; the new man was not up to speed with the assignment and production started to fall behind again. One would think that this was a bad enough experience for the foreman; would he now give up? No way, he just gave it a rest for a while, just long enough to get back on track with the order.

Then once again the supervisor repeated his game with Conrad. No matter how much Conrad pleaded with his supervisor to let him work the job he loved and was used to, he was transferred again to a job he hated.

"That is enough of that," Conrad thought to himself. "I am going to quit. I worked hard and for many years for all this, just like all the others did in their department, I don't think I deserve this kind of treatment. I don't think that I have to fight for all this, I want to work in peace and I have earned it." Conrad had enough of it all and quietly he looked around for another job once again, but always hoping that al would work out for the better.

All his coworkers where right on Conrad's side agreeing that this kind of treatment by the foreman was not acceptable, but what could they do? They all need to work and they all needed a job to go to in the morning, every morning.

After a relatively short search, Conrad found himself another promising job somewhere else and with kind of a sad feeling, he brought in his resignation. Luckily, the General Manager did not see it that way. Immediately he called for a meeting to sort the problems out. He was not the kind of manager who would just let people quit, especially not the ones who were on the job for such a long time. Conrad's problem finally got looked after, sorted out and put aside. Conrad still works for the same company and is grateful for all he has, grateful to Lady Luck, and all the people who made a difference in his and Mary's life.

What is there more to say than thank you, thank you Lady Luck, thank you to all the people who believed in me, thank you all the people who still believe in me and thank you to all who went out of their way to make a difference in our lives!

Monica now is happily married to a wonderful, hard-working man. Their greatest gift to Conrad and Mary are two wonderful Grandchildren. If you look carefully around you, you can see Mary and Conrad still dancing the odd time, arm in arm swaying to the music they love so much and which reminds them of a time when they were a little crazy with a lots of friends.

They have gotten a little more settled now, a little more round in front and anywhere else, but they still have each other, and no matter what, they always will.

Just recently the two celebrated their thirty-fourth wedding anniversary; quietly and by themselves the two swayed to the music once again reassuring each other that whatever the future may hold in store, they would always have each other. They would love it very much to celebrate with tons of friends or just a little small family circle, but life is just too busy to celebrate, each person in his or her own little world, with not much time to enjoy life. Conrad has gotten a little more quiet and keeps rather to himself or just with his Mary, life goes on.

No matter whether you decide to immigrate to another country, or you move around in your own, leaving friends and family behind. Sometimes it looks like there is no way out and it is just downhill from where you are, remember, after every downhill there is an uphill, you just have to trust your self and the people around you.

The End

Thank you for purchasing my book. I hope that you have enjoyed our story.

If you wish to contact me, or you would like to share your own story, you may do so by email me; makura@golden.net please make sure to use the word "Book" in the subject line. Or visit us online at http://canadaimmigrant.freewebspace.com to see more pictures of our home- town and our early times.

ISBN 141202005-0

9 781412 020053